CHINA-US

ISSUE 6

JOURNAL OF

HUMANITIES

Books Beyond Boundaries

ROYAL COLLINS

China-US Journal of Humanities (Issue 6)

china-usjournalofhumanities.com

First published in 2022 by Royal Collins Publishing Group Inc.
Groupe Publication Royal Collins Inc.
BKM Royalcollins Publishers Private Limited

Headquarters: 550-555 boul. René-Lévesque O Montréal
(Québec) H2Z1B1 Canada

India office: 805 Hemkunt House, 8th Floor, Rajendra Place,
New Delhi 110 008

ISBN: 978-1-4878-0920-1

To find out more about our publications,
please visit www.royalcollins.com.

HIGHLIGHTS

INDEX

1 China Studies in America in the Post-Cold War Era: From a Theoretical Shift to Self-reflective Dialogue

Gengsong Gao, University of Richmond

ABSTRACT

This article examines the strengths and weaknesses of theoretically-informed China studies in the United States in the post-Cold War era, and proposes a self-reflective dialogue as a tentative solution to the problem currently facing the discipline. This article is composed of three sections. Through a critical review of Lydia Liu's influential postcolonial and poststructuralist study of the canonical Chinese writer Lu Xun, the first section discusses the strengths and weaknesses of theoretically-informed China studies. The second section examines two contrastive criticisms of poststructuralist China studies. China-centered scholars find poststructuralist China studies to be not Chinese enough, as it ignores the relatively historical and cultural stability and the empirical complexity of China, while poststructuralist-informed scholars viewed it as not theoretical enough to make contributions to disciplinary innovations. The third section proposes a self-reflective dialogical model to address the problems with the current debate over China studies. Such a self-reflective dialogical model calls on China-centered and poststructuralist-informed China scholars to reflect critically upon their own basic assumptions and problematics in the light of the others', to form a more inclusive and more dialectical theoretical framework. This self-reflective dialogical model demonstrates that accurate descriptions of China and theoretical contributions are not mutually exclusive, but could be mutually enriching and enhancing.

KEYWORDS
America's China studies post-Cold War, theories

INTRODUCTION

Prior to World War II, Europe was the center of China studies in the West. However, as America became the superpower after World War II, it substantially enhanced its foreign-area studies in order to understand foreign countries better, advance America's influence across the world, and effectively respond to threats from the Soviet Union and China in the context of the emerging Cold War. With enormous financial and institutional support from private foundations and government institutions, China studies achieved rapid development in American universities starting in the early 1950s.

However, influenced by the Cold War mentality, China studies in America in the 1950s mostly followed the "totalitarian model" that "focused on the ideology, structures, key personalities and activities of the so-called 'Party police state, and assumed that the Chinese Communist party was able to exert a monolithic control over all aspects of Chinese society'" (Jeffreys, 28). With the rise of the Civil Rights Movement and various progressive anti-imperialist, anti-war, and feminist social movements, American academia took a leftist turn in the 1960s. Meanwhile, the escalation of conflict between China and the Soviet Union since the late 1950s made America's China scholars realize that China was not a puppet of the totalitarian communist Soviet Union but an independent country. In the 1960s, China's domestic anti-capitalist, anti-bureaucrat movements gained momentum, and the Proletariat Cultural Revolution that claimed to wipe out "capitalist roaders" broke out. These seemingly leftist political movements and campaigns drew American left-wing scholars' attention and appreciation. Some left-leaning American graduate students and junior faculty members established the Committee of Concerned Asian Scholars (CCAS) in1968, denouncing the American Association of Asian Studies for its complicity with the American government's expansionist Asian policy. The CCAS's "Founding Statement" proclaimed that "it seeks to develop a humane and knowledgeable understanding of Asian societies and their efforts to maintain integrity and to confront such problems as poverty, oppression, and imperialism."[1] For these left-leaning China scholars, China was not an evil totalitarian country but "held out hope for a utopian egalitarian alternative to a corrupt bourgeois American society" (Zito, 3). However, no matter whether it depicted China as a totalitarian and backward country or idealized it as a socialist utopia in which authentic egalitarian and participatory politics was realized, China studies in America during the Cold War were obviously shaped by the binary opposition of self versus other. When American China scholars understood their own country as a beacon of light and the shining exemplar of the free world, they treated China as the premodern totalitarian other. By contrast, when viewing the United States as an imperialist, hegemonic, and capitalistic evil power, they thought of China as a progressive and genuinely democratic socialist country as opposed to the corrupt Western powers. However, no matter how far America's Cold War China studies deviated from the Chinese realities, most China scholars' self-designated goal remained the same. As the late eminent China scholar Ezra Vogel observed: "almost all of us take the accurate description of China as the criteria for judging our works" (123). However, the pursuit of truthful China knowledge as the primary purpose of the American China studies community has changed, as various fashionable theories (in particular, poststructuralist and postcolonial theories) have been applied to the discipline since the 1980s. This theoretical shift has produced insights and incurred criticisms. This article examines the strengths and weaknesses of this theoretical shift, and proposes a "self-reflective dialogue" as a tentative solution to the problems facing theoretically-informed China studies.

FIRST SECTION: POSTSTRUCTURALIST AND POSTCOLONIAL STUDIES OF LU XUN

Since the 1980s, a plethora of theories have been introduced to China studies. The highest pursuit of Chinese scholars is no longer just to provide empirical knowledge about China, but also to make original theoretical contributions to their disciplines through their own work. Although China studies prior to the 1980s also applied various theories from the social sciences, the aim was mainly to describe and interpret Chinese history and reality more effectively, rather than to provide theoretical innovation. Furthermore, the research was primarily published in regional studies journals, and academic exchanges occurred primarily among regional research experts rather than with colleagues in other social sciences and humanities fields. Therefore, according to Vogel, China studies experts of the post-World War II generation were all "marginalized social scientists" (124). The theoretical shift in China studies since the 1980s was caused by a variety of factors. First, the overall trend towards theorization in the circle of Western humanities and social sciences has been intensified. Since the end of the 1960s, various new Western theories, such as poststructuralism, deconstructionism, postcolonialism, feminism, new historicism, and cultural studies, and various complex quantitative analysis theories have emerged, and have gradually spread to various research areas. Meanwhile, the academic evaluation system changes in accordance with the rise of theoretical study, which is manifested in the encouragement of regional researchers to publish their research in more theoretical and disciplinary academic journals and books with a greater impact factor. Second, the main issues related to Chinese history, politics, economy, and culture have already been studied, and thus, the field of China studies itself needs to learn from new theoretical concepts, methods, and ideas to broaden the existing research paths. Third, since the 1980s, many Chinese students have gone to universities in the United States, and have thus joined American teams of China studies scholars. Unlike American scholars, these Chinese students do not need to spend a great deal of time learning the Chinese language and acquiring basic knowledge about China. They are more interested in new Western theories and methods they cannot learn in China. The mastery and application of Western theories can not only broaden their knowledge and views but can also allow them to gain a foothold quickly in American academic circles (Walder, 331–333).

This theoretical and disciplinary shift has raised many new research questions and ideas in China studies, and has lessened the isolation of China studies in Western academia, allowing more non-China specialists to understand the discipline while bringing China studies closer to Western theoretical issues and disciplinary debates. Under the influence of this theorization and disciplinary shift, the common mode of China studies is to use one or more Western theories and concepts to raise basic research questions and frameworks, and then verify or partially correct them with Chinese texts, experience, and history. However, the basic problematics and assumptions of Western theories have not been questioned or altered. Here, using the postcolonialist and poststructuralist interpretation of Lu Xun's *The True Story of Ah Q* by Chinese American scholar Lydia H. Liu as an example, this section analyzes the advantages and disadvantages of postmodern theorization of China studies.

Prior to Lydia H. Liu's study, Lu Xun's *The True Story of Ah Q* was always interpreted according to realist models. It is considered a true depiction of the Chinese national character, and what is under debate is only whether this national character represents the nature of all Chinese people or the characteristics of only lower-class people. Based on postcolonial theory, Liu questions this traditional realist interpretation. According to postcolonialism, the Western discourse on oriental societies is an ideological construction that serves imperialist aggression and expansion rather than providing a true description (Liu, 146). Based on this postcolonialist presupposition, Liu attempts to deconstruct the traditional realist interpretative model. Through historical examination of the text, Liu argues that all of Lu Xun's criticism of China's national character comes from descriptions by Western missionaries, especially in *Chinese Characteristics*, a book by American missionary Arthur Smith. However, when analyzing *The True Story of Ah Q*, Liu finds that Lu Xun did not simply repeat the discourse of Western missionaries, but instead drew from the satirical styles of the Russian writer Nikolai Gogol and the Polish writer Henryk Sienkiewicz. The focus of Liu's interpretation shifted from the traditional mode of determining what type of Chinese person is represented by the literary figure Ah Q to examining how the author constructs a superior textual position to maintain a distance from other characters of the story, which allows him to criticize and mock them (Liu, 70).

Undoubtedly, by emphasizing the connection between Lu Xun's literary texts and foreign texts, i.e. their intertextuality, Liu's postcolonialist interpretation enables studies of Lu Xun to have a truly global and cross-cultural perspective. In the past, literary critics tended to think that Lu Xun vividly portrayed China's real society and characters simply through his literary genius, and intentionally or unconsciously ignored or downplayed the influence of foreign theories and literature, especially that of Western missionaries, on Lu Xun. Influenced by literary realism, previous critics have focused on how Lu Xun's literary works are connected to China's reality, and thus have more or less ignored the issues pertinent to Lu Xun's literary work itself, e.g. textuality, rhetoricity, and narrative point of view. By drawing on terms of narratology, e.g. "parodic stylization," "heteroglossia," "extradiegetic elements," and "diegetic elements," Liu accurately describes how the narrator of Lu Xun's story constructs a textual process of fictional narrative subjectivity. Lastly, by analyzing Lu Xun and other Chinese writers and intellectuals (e.g. Shen Congwen, Lao She, and Xiao Hong), Liu not only confirms the validity of postcolonialism in the analysis of texts by Chinese writers and intellectuals, but also addresses the deficiencies of postcolonial theory. For example, Liu argues that although Said's postcolonial theory proposes four stages of the dissemination of Western theories throughout the world, it does not discuss in detail by whom and through what means and specific routes these theories are spread (Liu, 20–21). Liu advocates for translingual studies because she wants to address the shortcomings of Said's theory through her studies of the specific historical and textual processes in which Western theories on national character, individualism, and literary theories are accepted and transformed by Chinese writers and intellectuals.

Liu is not content with simply applying Western theories; she strives to improve and revise them through China studies. Her academic courage and critical thinking are worthy of recognition. However, Liu's critical thinking is still not complete. The biggest problem in her work is that she only criticizes the partial discourse of postcolonial theory, without further questioning the fundamental theoretical presupposition of postcolonial theory regarding the separation of Western discourse and Eastern reality. It is precisely because this poststructuralist presupposition is not challenged that Liu assumes that the negative descriptions of China in the West are all "myths" and "false representations" that serve imperialist aggression (Liu, 47), and completely ignores some of the reasonable parts of these descriptions. When discussing Lu Xun's literary works, due to the overemphasis on their rhetoricity, she completely overlooks the connection between Lu Xun's works and Chinese reality. As the American sinologist Theodore Huters has previously noted, before missionaries entered China, Chinese diplomats and intellectuals who had been in contact with the West in the middle of the 19th century had already witnessed the problems of Chinese people as described by Western missionaries at the time, for example, that they lacked social ethics, sophisticated thinking, and time concepts (Huters, 576). In other words, Western missionaries had criticized the negative qualities of the Chinese population, and these criticisms were not necessarily a fiction that vilified Chinese people, but may have contained some reasonable elements that were in line with reality. Second, when analyzing the text of Lu Xun's *The True Story of Ah Q*, Liu maintains that the story created a new intellectual narrative subject that transformed Western criticisms of China into criticism of lower-class Chinese by Chinese intellectuals (Liu, 76). Although Liu indicates that Lu Xun is innovative in his use of rhetorical methods and narrative point of view, she does not analyze his substantive criticism of the discourse of Western missionaries. Lu Xun's attitude toward the lower classes of Chinese people, i.e. "anguished at their misfortunes but enraged by their unwillingness to fight," does reveal a certain intellectual superiority, and the acquisition of this superiority may indeed have been influenced by Western education and works. However, this does not mean that Lu Xun uncritically accepted Western missionaries' criticism of China. Citing Lu Xun's text, Dongfeng Tao, a Chinese critic, shows that despite holding Smith's work in high regard, Lu Xun pointed out that "it also contains many errors" (Tao, 20). Moreover, in terms of the text of the story, the narrator created by Lu Xun is indeed full of mockery of the lower-class character of Ah Q. However, after carefully reading the text, we can see that Lu Xun's narrator not only criticizes the closemindedness and backwardness of Ah Q and the lower-class people of the Wei Village, but also bitterly mocks the local intellectual elites and westernized figures represented by "Mr. Chao" and "Imitation Foreign Devil." The agency that Liu's analysis teases out is mostly restricted to the formal and narrative aspects, and fails to grasp the substantial complexity and flexibility of the narratorial subjectivity that Lu Xun creates in Ah Q. A close reading of the novella shows that the narrator is not Ah Q's opposite, not signaling a condescending Chinese intellectual position that only decries their own tradition and the stupidity of their illiterate countrymen, but representing a highly individuated, reflective, flexible, ironical, critical, skeptical, and capacious subjectivity that is able to simultaneously criticize, learn from, and identify with the lower social classes. There is no such thing as "a vast chasm" between the intellectual narrator and social underdog character Ah Q, as Liu claims.

At the very beginning, the narrator deliberates on the limits of conventional Chinese and Western biographical genres that are exclusively devoted to emperors, courtiers, and cultural elites. He finds it difficult to locate a proper genre from both the existing Chinese and Western elitist genres, such as "official biographies, autobiographies, unauthorized biographies, legends, supplementary biographies, family histories, sketches," to name and tell his story about a social underdog like Ah Q. As the narrator says, "unfortunately none of these suited my purpose" (91). Bringing this difficulty to the fore indicates that the narrator does not see the existing language as adequate and transparent, but casts critical reflection upon the established discursive system dominated by both the Chinese and Western upper social class. However, this doubt about the existing discursive system does not lead the narrator to the poststructuralist wholesale rejection of language's reference to truth and reality. After sardonically elaborating on the difficulty of fitting Ah Q into extant elitist biographical genres, the narrator turns to the traditional Chinese low-brow language and genre:

> In short, this is really a "life," but since I write in vulgar vein using the language of hucksters
> and peddlers, I dare not presume to give it so high-sounding a title. So from the stock phrase
> of the novelists, who are not reckoned among the Three Cults and Nine Schools. "Enough
> of this digression, and back to the true story!" I will take the last two words as my title. (92)

The traditional Chinese novelist was associated less with writing for the upper social class than with speaking about and for the masses. The novel was a genre for entertaining laborers, small business owners, and other members of the lower social class. Traditional Chinese literati despised the spoken language of the hucksters and peddlers as too vulgar and too trivial for the writing and transmission of any worthy principles and moral messages. The narrator's resort to a "true story" – the language and genre of the lowbrow storyteller – to name and tell his own story implies his mockery and rejection of the falsity and pretension of traditional literati's written genre and language. Liu is right in pointing out that Lu Xun's fiction seeks to "redefine the role of the literary elite." However, this redefining and creation of a new narratorial subjectivity is not constructed through setting up a divide between educated intellectuals and illiterate masses as Liu argues, but through the former's critical reflections upon and learning from the latter. Moreover, the constructed narratorial subjectivity does not merely serve to criticize Chinese tradition but also to draw upon the ignored and scorned Chinese oral and folk tradition to disclose and oppose the hypocrisy, hegemony, and alienation of intellectuals' writing-centered discursive system from the masses' speech-centered lives and experiences.

As shown in the analysis above, by borrowing from postcolonial and poststructuralist theory, Liu's study uncovers the previously neglected connection between Chinese literary work and Western missionary texts, and accurately describes and analyzes the rhetorical approach and narrative perspective of Lu Xun's literary works using narratological terms. Her process of textually constructing the narrative subject has effectively compensated for the shortcomings of previous studies of stories that focus only on analyzing the characters. The "translingual practice" advocated by Liu under the influence of postcolonial and narratological theory serves to bridge the gaps in Western theories by examining the specific process by which Western discourse, theories, and literary works are disseminated and received in China. However, because Liu's questioning and revising of Western theories are only partial, she does not take a step further to rethink the fundamental theoretical premise of the separation of discourse and reality in poststructuralist and postcolonial theory. This causes her to fail to fully grasp the complexity of Chinese history and literary texts.

Liu's postcolonial and poststructuralist study of Chinese literature and intellectual history is not an isolated case. Rather, it represents a common mode in China studies after the increasingly theorizing trend that has emerged since the 1980s: the description and analysis of Chinese texts, history, and reality using borrowed Western presuppositions and concepts to inspire and explore new problems and new ideas in China studies and the bridging of certain gaps in Western theories with the study of a specific area of China studies. This research model has indeed yielded much outstanding work in China studies, but the biggest problem with this paradigm is that the core issues and academic concerns of China studies are all established by the West, and the basic theoretical assumptions and premises of this approach have not been effectively questioned and corrected. As a result, the complexity and diversity of Chinese text, history, and experience have not been effectively analyzed.

SECTION TWO: TWO CONTRASTIVE CRITICISMS OF THEORETICALLY-INFORMED CHINA STUDIES

A host of fashionable postmodernist theories have been introduced to China studies since the 1980s, such as poststructuralism, deconstructionism, postcolonialism, psychoanalysis, and new historicism. While these theories include "a diverse and often contradictory group of ideas on the specious basis of what preceded them in a chronology of Parsian thought," they share a common theoretical presupposition: as Rey Chow described it, "the one unmistakable accomplishment of 'theory' understood in this restricted sense is what one might call 'fundamental problematization of referentiality'" (Chow, xiii). In the past, language was considered as a transparent tool that can truly reference reality. However, in light of postmodernism, language is not an externally referential reality but a self-referential reality; the so-called facts expressed through language are not real facts but a construction of discourse that is closely related to a certain oppressive power. Based on this poststructuralist theoretical assumption, many theoretical achievements have been made in China since the 1980s that have overturned the previous knowledge of Chinese history, society, literature, and culture. For example, in *Cherishing Men from Afar: Qing Guest Ritual and the Macartney Embassy of 1793*, the American historian James L. Hevia proposes that the notion that Macartney's visit to China was viewed through the bigotry and ignorance of the Chinese feudal dynasty towards the modern world is just a discursive construction of Western countries that purports to provide some legitimacy for the West's invasion of China and implies a certain Western colonialism and hegemony. Hevia argues that what the Macartney mission's visit reflected was not the ridicule and injustice that open, modern Western nations received from a closed and backward premodern Eastern country, but an encounter between two expanding empires, i.e. the pluralistic Manchu empire and the pluralistic British Empire (Hevia, 2–29). For another example, in *National Past-Times: Narrative, Representation and Power in Modern China,* the American anthropologist Ann Anagnost investigates China's problems with overpopulation and low population quality. However, what Anagnost discusses is not whether China was truly overpopulated, or whether China's population quality was actually low, but how the discourse on China's overpopulation and low population quality was constructed by the state and was used by it to achieve oppressive social control (Anagnost, 117–137). In yet another example, in *Worrying about China: The Language of Chinese Critical Inquiry,* the Australian scholar Gloria Davies examines debates among contemporary Chinese intellectuals. She does not focus on which school of Chinese intellectuals made the diagnoses and proposed solutions that were most in line with China's reality; rather, she focuses on the language of their debate and their rhetorical skills, and criticizes the Chinese intellectuals' sentiment in "being concerned about the nation and the people," including the backwards realist view of language that believes academic discourse can be referential to reality (Davies, 11–12). China studies under the influence of postmodernist theories have a common feature, i.e. they question and deconstruct the basic assumptions previously used in China studies, e.g. China, Chineseness, nation, state, people, and women, and believe that in China studies previously, the understanding of these basic concepts was monolithic and essentialist. In the introduction to her edited volume *Modern Chinese Literary and Cultural Studies in the Age of Theory,* Rey Chow emphasizes that to study China further, it is necessary to regard "China" as "a provisional open signifier" (Chow, 18), to erase the stable concept of "China," and to realize the concept's mobility. The field of Sinophone Studies, which has become a recent fad in the USA, has emerged under the influence of this postmodernist theoretical paradigm. These disciplines all aim to deconstruct China studies that have previously focused on Mainland China and the Han Chinese, and believe that the China studies of the past are full of great-power chauvinism and Han ethnocentrism and ignore minorities and overseas Chinese groups.[2]

This kind of poststructuralist deconstruction of "Chineseness" and de-sinification has aroused criticism from some scholars of China studies. Referencing the Chinese historian Zhaoguang Ge, Zhang Longxi argues that the concept of China has indeed undergone some changes throughout history, but this does not influence the historical fact that since the Song Dynasty, China has been a relatively stable modern nation-state with the Han Chinese as its core (Zhang, 193–206). In other words, the concept of "China" is not just a discursive construction but an objective historical fact that has existed since ancient times. Mingdong Gu, a Chinese American literary scholar, collectively refers to various practices that cater to Western theories, categories, and concepts at the expense of the authenticity and complexity of Chinese history, experience, and texts as "sinologism." He further clarifies that although both sinologism and Said's Orientalism, which he criticizes, are distortions of China and the Orient, they are different. Orientalism mainly serves Western colonialism, and has direct and obvious political goals, while sinologism mainly exists in academic research and is a deep epistemological and methodological fallacy without direct political motives (Gu, 5–8).

This criticism of China studies involving Western de-sinification and theorization is reflected not only in the humanities but also in the social sciences. Kevin O'Brien, a senior professor of political science, notes that currently, all Chinese political studies focus on a specific, subdivided field, and combine in-depth studies of these subdivided fields with theoretical topics that are frequently discussed in the political sciences (e.g. state-society relations, democratization and transformation, and grassroots governance), to use China's experience and practice in these subdivided fields to improve and complement related Western theories. Such over-subdivisions and theorizations in Chinese political studies have rarely integrated the fields of Chinese politics horizontally to provide a generalized consideration and analysis of Chinese politics as a whole, and as a result, "China" is slowly disappearing from Chinese political studies. What O'Brien wants is not to negate the subdivided and theorized China studies but to emphasize that with the rise of China, the demand of the outside world for knowledge about Chinese politics as a whole is surging. In order to ensure that Chinese political studies do not become disconnected from public demand, we should correct the problems of over-subdivision and theorization in studies of Chinese politics, and increase the focus on integrative studies that can integrate these subdivided fields and holistically enhance the understanding of Chinese politics. O'Brien emphasizes that in retrospect, in past decades, "All kinds of social theories have come and gone, but China will last forever" (O'Brien, 541). China studies scholars should not sacrifice the description, analysis, and understanding of the long-existing China as a whole to cater to the prevailing theories.

Very interestingly, in addition to criticism based on China's actual experience and historical facts, postmodernist China studies have also aroused criticism from more radical poststructuralist scholars in the same camp. For example, Australian scholars Elaine Jeffreys and Gloria Davies both claim that although poststructuralist China studies advocate the deconstruction of essentialist concepts of China, Chineseness, and the Chinese nation, in their research practices, postmodernist theories are only used to describe and explain the differences between China and the West, which have produced more knowledge about China but have not contributed much to the development of disciplines and the production of theoretical knowledge (Jeffreys, 35). Therefore, Jeffreys believes that although China studies conducted since the Cold War have applied many Western theories, they have essentially repeated work that conducted under the Cold War ideology. In other words, China studies remain at the level of producing knowledge about China, meeting imperialist and capitalist countries' needs for empirical knowledge about China (Jeffreys, 29–30). Davies argues that China studies have failed to become theoretical and global in the way that India's subaltern studies have. India's subaltern studies originally aimed to study lower-class society and people, but a subdivision of this field later gradually evolved into a highly theoretical interdisciplinary field that studies the lower-class societies and people of the whole world. According to Davies, the failure of China studies to go beyond subdivided fields of regional study and become theoretical and global still lies in the problem of understanding the fundamental concept of "China." The reason that India's subaltern studies have developed into a new interdisciplinary theory is that the concept of the "subaltern" is no longer a geopolitical term but an abstract theoretical concept. In contrast, China studies have been unable to gain theoretical status because in China studies, "China" is still a geopolitical concept, and within this concept, various studies of China still adhere to a narrow regionality and nationality that cannot be expanded to other countries and regions outside China, thereby failing to rise to the theoretical level of general interest (Davies, 17–18).

In short, China studies in the West since the 1980s have been profoundly influenced by fashionable Western theories, and have created many new issues, ideas, and achievements while receiving criticism from two opposing directions. According to the China-centered scholars who emphasize that scholarship should comply with Chinese historical, social, and textual realities, theorized China studies cater to Western theories at the expense of the complexity of the Chinese experience, making them insufficiently Chinese. However, according to poststructuralist-informed scholars who emphasize theoretical innovation and disciplinary contribution, the current theorized China studies are still under the influence of the Cold War ideology, and do nothing but generate knowledge about China; they make little contribution to the cross-regional theoretical field, and thus are not theoretical enough.

SECTION THREE: THE FUTURE OF CHINA STUDIES – TOWARDS A SELF-REFLECTIVE DIALOGUE

Faced with criticism from two opposing directions, how should China studies develop? The Chinese American historian Zongzhi Huang argues:

> The most influential problematics of China studies in the US is more influenced by the US's own problems than by China's actual problems and shaped more by the US political and ideological environment than by China's own problems. It reflects mainly politics, ideology, and theory about the US rather than China itself. To really decentralize the West and centralize China, we must base our problematics on the actual problems of China rather than the theoretical constructions of the West (175).

The China-centered China studies that Huang advocates aim not to reject Western theories and abandon theoretical innovation, but to critically adopt Western theories based on China's actual conditions; to develop concepts, categories, and systems that are suitable for describing, analyzing, and interpreting Chinese history and reality based on the critical application of Western theories; and to create the best blueprint for China's future development. According to Huang, hundreds of years of China studies in the West have been profoundly controlled by the dualistic model of "China vs. the West," in which China has always been regarded as the "other" in contrast to the West, albeit sometimes negative and sometimes positive. However, the actual situation in modern China is the "outcome of the coexistence of the past and the present as well as the mutual penetration of China and the West and thus must not be either one or the other" (Huang, 175). Huang has a clear understanding of the shortcomings of China studies in the West, and the reality of Chinese society, but the problem is that when he criticizes the dualistic thinking of China studies in the West, he inadvertently falls into another kind of dualistic thinking that pits West-centered China studies against China-centered China studies. As pointed out at the beginning of this article, Western scholars of China studies during the Cold War era were certainly subject to the dualistic ideologies of "East and West," "tradition and modernity," "authoritarianism and liberalism," "socialism and capitalism," and other such dichotomies, but there are still many China studies scholars whose subjective intent, as Vogel put it, is an "accurate description of China" – a goal that coincides with the notion emphasized by Huang that research results should be in line with China's objective, realistic, empirical path. Huang criticizes the fact that China studies in the USA are more influenced by America's own problems and environment than by China's, and therefore, "they actually reflect more about the US's politics, ideology, and theory than China's." However, Huang was educated in the USA, and his celebrated research on China's population and its legal system was conducted in an American academic environment. How, then, can he jump out of the dualistic-thinking box that most of his China studies peers in America occupy? We agree with Huang's basic assertion that China studies in the USA are more influenced by the American political and social environment and reflect the US's problematics, theories, and ideas more than China's reality. Certainly, there are differences in ideology, knowledge background, and academic objectives between China studies conducted by Chinese scholars and those conducted by Western scholars, but these differences should not be absolutized or exaggerated. If not for the academic pursuit of describing and interpreting Chinese history and reality as objectively and truthfully as possible in American China studies, it would be difficult for Huang to engage in studies that can objectively reflect Chinese history and reality. Huang's notion that "modern China must be the outcome of the coexistence of the past and the present and the mutual penetration of China and the West" is actually true for modern China studies. Today, China's description, analysis, research, and understanding of itself are profoundly shaped and influenced by the West.

To advance China studies further, we propose a self-reflexive dialogical model. To realize China studies with self-reflective dialogue, we must first recognize that the existing China-centered or empirically-oriented China studies and the West-centered or poststructuralist-informed China studies have already mutually penetrated, i.e. "we are in you, and you are in us." Any China studies based on an exclusive standpoint and dualistic thinking are undesirable. For example, China-centered scholars are mostly born and raised in China, and sometimes matter-of-factly regard their own Chinese identity and personal experience of China as a privileged knowledge and understanding of China, and naturally believe that they are superior to foreigners who lack Chinese language training and a long lived experience in China. When foreigners draw conclusions that are not in line with the personal experience and feelings of native Chinese scholars, they conclude that the foreigners have an erroneous external perspective. Obviously, China is such an extremely complex and large country that even the native Chinese can only have a very limited experience and perception of it. An individual's adoption of his or her own local, personal experience without reflection as a criterion against which to judge others' studies lacks rigor. A rich life experience in China may bring insights to researchers, but when used without critical thinking, it can create blind spots in cognition and the closed-mindedness of self-perception, giving rise to a "native blindness" similar to that reported in anthropology (quoted in Goh, *Decentring and Diversifying Southeast Asian Studies*, 6). It is well established that the understanding of personal experience is affected by a certain cognitive framework and power relations, and today, the cognitive framework of Chinese people and the power relations of the society in which they live are profoundly influenced and shaped by the West. In other words, it is hard to say that even the so-called China-centered China studies or the self-perceptions of ordinary Chinese people constitute a purely Chinese internal perspective. Without deep self-reflection on the cognitive framework and power relations underlying personal experience and the understanding acquired from both Chinese and Western perspectives, an individual's personal experience in China may become an obstacle rather than an asset to his/her own China studies. China-centered scholars often believe that the highest goal of such studies is to diagnose China's problems and provide solutions. Therefore, this research path has a narrow nationalist approach, and this nationalism itself is an object that needs to be deconstructed. On the other hand, Western poststructuralist-informed China studies that are preoccupied with theoretical innovation are adept at applying Western theories, but they are often inclined to conduct the type of China studies that rejects empiricism-oriented research. In fact, this Western poststructuralist trend towards downplaying or deconstructing the established categories concerning area studies and emphasizing theoretical contributions is reflected not only in China studies but also in other non-Western regional and national studies. For instance, a couple of native Southeast Asian scholars have noted the similar poststructuralist interrogation of reified categories of nation, region, race, and culture in Southeast Asian studies in the West. This tide of poststructuralist denationalization does effectively expose the mobility and constructedness of the previously taken-for-granted concepts, and criticizes the racial nationalism and cultural essentialism and their neglect and oppression of the racial and cultural minorities within the nation-state. Yet, as Arif Dirlik observes, if taken to extremes, the radical poststructuralist approach to nation-state and local culture may be "counterproductive to a better comprehension of the world around us" and may "serve the interest of (Western) powers when deployed against the weak and powerless (nation-state) to undermine their cultural claims against oppressive Western powers" (163–166). In other words, the poststructuralist-informed scholars' deconstruction of reified political, racial, and cultural categories that seeks to subvert the hierarchical and the hegemonic may end up reproducing and reinforcing what they oppose.

We very much endorse the notion suggested by the Southeast Asian scholar Goh Beng-Lan that native scholars of Asia studies and their Western counterparts should "listen to each other, respect each other, and learn from each other" and "develop theoretical perspectives which can consider the simultaneity and interaction of the global and the local, the inside and outside, the old and new, the center and the periphery, the stable and the unstable, rather than seek to replace one by the other" (Goh, 9–14). But we must add that this kind of dialogue and mutual learning should not be shallow but deep. It should not just be an ornament on the research in which each party learns from the other's individual experience and ideas; instead, each side should question one another, remind each other of their respective blind spots, and complement each other on the use of one another's meta-theoretical hypotheses and academic concerns. As mentioned above, the meta-theoretical presupposition of China studies under the influence of Western postmodernism is the separation of discourse from reality. It is precisely on the basis of this presupposition that postmodernist China studies have attempted to subvert previous basic concepts of nation, state, and people and have emphasized that these concepts are fictions of discourse rather than objective realities. We must admit that these postmodernist studies do reveal the artificially constructed components of the basic concepts of "China," "the Chinese nation," and "Chinese people." However, these seemingly critical poststructuralist studies have drawn many conclusions that are not in line with Chinese reality or with real theoretical innovation, because they have uncritically accepted the meta-theoretical presupposition of the complete separation of discourse and reality. If poststructuralist China studies can use the presupposition of the connection between discourse and reality in the Chinese intellectual tradition to reflect on the drawbacks of the presupposition of the complete separation of discourse and reality and can ultimately apply a more dialectical and complex discourse-reality relationship to the study of Chinese history and texts, then they are more likely to produce insights that are both consistent with China's reality and conducive to theoretical innovations. Gloria Davies, the Australian scholar of China studies, has noticed the difference between the local Chinese language view and the Western poststructuralist language view. However, she does not fully respect and absorb the rationality of the former. Instead, she takes a Western poststructuralist stand for granted, and treats Chinese intellectuals' view of linking discourse with reality as backward and outdated, thereby failing to develop her own theory of the history of Chinese ideas.

For Chinese and Western China studies, it is not easy to truly realize a self-reflective dialogue in China studies for the purposes of developing China and theoretical innovation, because this kind of deep, equitable, and constructive academic dialogue requires changing not only the researcher's personal thinking and research methods, but also reflecting on the entire academic system and knowledge production system. In his book *China and Orientalism,* the Hong Kong-based cultural critic Daniel Vukovich notes that Western production of knowledge on China also follows the Marxist logic of capitalist commodity production. According to Marx, for commodities to be exchanged, circulated, and consumed smoothly in the market, it is necessary to transform the various complex and diverse types of concrete labor required to produce different commodities into an abstract form of labor that can be measured in terms of time, allowing different use values of the commodities to be transformed into quantifiable abstract exchange values and making it possible for commodities to be exchanged and circulated smoothly in a globalized market. The production of knowledge about China also follows this capitalist commodity production logic. That is to say, to allow the smooth exchange and circulation of knowledge about China throughout the world, it is necessary to transform China's specific reality and history into some abstract theoretical and disciplinary knowledge, and what is sacrificed in this transformation process is the complexity and diversity of Chinese history and reality, experience, and text (Vukovich, 142–145). Vukovich's analysis, which presents an analogy between the production of knowledge about China and commodity production is very insightful. It allows us to see the logic of the capitalist commodity economy behind knowledge production, and to recognize that to change knowledge production, we must not rely solely on changes in individual researchers' thoughts and methods, but also on the reform of macro-economic structures and institutions, and such changes cannot be accomplished overnight. But we do not have to be pessimistic. As we have seen, many overseas scholars of China studies, including Daniel Vukovich, Longxi Zhang, Mingdong Gu, and Phillip Huang, who operate within the capitalist market economy and economic commodity system, have also made academic achievements in unveiling the complexity of Chinese textual and historical realities. In other words, even though capitalist economic logic and institutions permeate all aspects of academic production, they are not monolithic. In the current circumstances, it is impossible to completely change the penetration of capitalist commodity production into China's knowledge production, but it is still possible to achieve breakthroughs and changes. However, this requires different schools of China studies to learn from and communicate with each other while constantly reflecting on their respective theoretical presuppositions, assuming a vigilant and critical attitude towards the power relations and economic structure behind the research, and forming a more inclusive, dialectical, and critical theoretical framework. In this way, future China studies can not only accurately describe and analyze China, but can also make appropriate contributions to theoretical development.

ENDNOTES

[1] See the official website of the Committee of Concerned Asian Scholars' journal Critical Asian Studies, http://bcasnet.org/about-us/bcas-founding-statement.html. Accessed 20 September 2018.

[2] For an introduction to Sinophone studies, see Shu-mei Shih's *Sinophone Studies: A Critical Reader, New York: Columbia University Press,* 2013, pp. 1–16.

REFERENCES

Anagnost, Ann. (1997). *National Past-Times: Narrative, Representation and Power in Modern China.* Durham: Duke University Press.

Chow, Rey. (1998). *Ethics after Idealism: Theory, Culture, Ethnicity, Reading.* Bloomington: Indiana University Press.

Chow, Rey, ed. (2000). *Modern Chinese Literary and Cultural Studies in the Age of Theory.* Durham: Duke University Press.

"Critical Asian Studies." http://bcasnet.org/about-us/bcas-founding-statement.html. Accessed 20 September 2018.

Davies, Gloria. (2007). *Worrying about China: The Language of Chinese Critical Inquiry.* Cambridge, Mass.: Harvard University Press.

———. "Theory, Professionalism and Chinese Studies." *Modern Chinese Literature and Culture* 12.1 (2000): 1–42.

Dirlik, Arif. "Asia Pacific Studies in an Age of Global Modernity." *Inter-Asia Cultural Studies* 6.2 (2005): 158–170.

Goh, Beng-Lan, ed. (2011). *Decentring and Diversifying Southeast Asian Studies.* Singapore: Institute of Southeast Asian Studies.

Gu, Mingdong. (2013). *Sinologism: An Alternative to Orientalism and Postcolonialism.* Routledge: London.

Hevia, James L. (1995). *Cherishing Men from Afar: Qing Guest Ritual and the Macartney Embassy of 1793.* Durham: Duke University Press.

Huang, Zongzhi. "Women de wenti yishi: dui mei guo de zhongguo yanjiu de fansi" 我们的问题意识: 对美国的中国研究的反思 (Our Problematics: Reflections on America's China Studies), *Kaifang shidai* 开放时代 (Open Times) 1 (2016): 155–183.

Huters, Theodore. "Translingual Practice: Literature, National Culture, and Translated Modernity: China, 1900–1937." Review. *Harvard Journal of Asiatic Studies*, 1998: 2, 568–580.

Jeffreys, Elaine. (2004). *China, Sex and Prostitution.* London: Routledge.

Liu, Lydia H. (1995). *Translingual Practice: Literature, National Culture, and Translated Modernity: China, 1900–1937.* Stanford: Stanford University Press.

Lu, Xun. *Selected Works of Lu Xun.* (1980). Translated by Xianyi Yang and Gladys Yang, Beijing: Foreign Language Press.

O' Brien, Kevin J. "Studying Chinese Politics in an Age of Specialization." *Journal of Contemporary China* 20.71 (2011): 535–541.

Tao, Dongfeng, 陶东风. (2012). *Wenxue lilun yu gonggong yanshuo* 文学理论与公共言说 (Literary Theory and Public Discourse). Beijing: Zhongguo shehui kexue chubanshe.

Shih, Shu-mei, ed. (2013). *Sinophone Studies: A Critical Reader* [M]. New York: Columbia University Press.

Vogel, Ezra 傅高义. (2004). "Dangdai zhongguo yanjiu zai beimei" 当代中国研究在北美 (Contemporary China Studies in North America). Zhou Xiaohong 周晓虹, Ed. *Zhongguo shehui yu zhongguo yanjiu* 中国社会与中国研究 (Chinese Society and China Studies). Beijing: Shehuikexue chuban she.

Vukovich, Daniel. *China and Orientalism: Western Knowledge Production and the PRC.* London: Routledge, 2013.

Walder, Andrew G. (2004). "Transformation of Contemporary China Studies, 1977–2002" in *The Politics of Knowledge: Area Studies and the Disciplines.* David Szanton, ed. Berkeley: University of California Press.

Zhang, Longxi. "Re-conceptualizing China in Our China: From a Chinese Perspective." *European Review* 23.2 (2015): 193–209.

Zito, A. and Barlow, T. E., eds. (1994). *Body, Subject and Power in China*, Chicago: University of Chicago Press.

AUTHOR'S BIO

GENGSONG GAO received his PhD in comparative literature from the University of South Carolina. He is currently an assistant professor and coordinator of the Chinese program at the University of Richmond. He specializes in contemporary Chinese literature, intellectual discourse, and second language acquisition.

2 How Does His Story Become Others' Stories, and How Does the Historical Turn "Histrionic"?: The Evolution of the Story of Jing Ke

Xinda Lian, Denison University

ABSTRACT

This paper examines how the story of Jing Ke is used to serve different purposes through an examination of its evolution from its origin in ancient historical texts, through its theatric reproductions over time, all the way to contemporary cinematic versions. The reception of this time-honored narrative tradition in both China and in the West reflects concerns about the morals and ethics of revenge, views on the interdependence between historiography and literary narrative, and thoughts on the binary relationship between conflicting powers in China's cultural tradition.

KEYWORDS

Revenge as requital, Truth in Chinese historical and literary narrative, Binary of powers

Imagine a story like this. The incident it records – an attempt on the life of China's first emperor, who later started the construction of the now famous Great Wall – took place in 227 BCE. It had entered several historical records by around 100 BCE, providing subject matter for at least two theatrical works in the early 17th century, then another one in the mid-20th century, and inspired numerous cinematic and theatrical productions in the late 1990's and at the turn of the 21st century.

This is the story of Jing Ke 荆轲 (?–227 BCE).

According to historical records, the events surrounding the unsuccessful assassination unfolded in the final years of the Warring States Period (475–221 BCE), when the State of Qin, the most powerful of the seven remaining vassal states of the former Zhou royal house (1066–256 BCE), was poised to annex its rivals one by one.

The ambition of the King of Qin made enemies of all his neighbors, but his most bitter foe was Prince Dan of the State of Yan. The relationship between the two dated back to the days when the latter was a hostage in the State of Zhao[1] and befriended the former, who was born in Zhao and spent his difficult youth there. Later, when Dan was sent to Qin as a hostage, his childhood friend, now the King of Qin, treated him badly. Deeply humiliated, Dan escaped home from Qin and began to plot his revenge. As Qin's threat to its neighbors grew, Dan's thoughts of revenge intensified. To make the situation even more tense, the Qin general Fan Wuqi 樊於期 (?–227 BCE) offended the Qin king, defected to Yan, and became Prince Dan's guest. The king was enraged, and offered a large reward for Fan's head. Knowing the dire consequences of his hostile gestures toward the powerful Qin, Dan asked his tutor for advice. The tutor referred him to a Master Tian

Guang 田光 (?–227 BCE), to whom the prince confided his plan: something was to be done to the King of Qin to save the state of Yan, and a brave man was needed to do the job. Tian Guang recommended Jing Ke. The prince thereupon asked Tian to introduce him to Jing Ke, and cautioned him not to leak the secret.

After passing Dan's words to Jing Ke, Tian said, "A man of honor does not arouse distrust in others. It is obvious that when the prince told me not to leak his secret, he did not trust me. I want you to go see him and tell him that I am already dead, and the secret will be tightly kept." With this, he slit his own throat.

Greatly moved by Tian's sense of honor, and persuaded by Prince Dan's earnest request, Jing Ke agreed to carry out the mission: to go to the court of Qin, surprise the king with some weapon, and force him to return all the land he had seized from the other states – or, if this failed, kill him.

To guarantee Jing Ke's help, the prince honored him with high titles, paid him respectful visits every day, and provided him with all kinds of luxuries. In the meantime, the Qin army swept its way through and advanced to the southern border of Yan. In a panic, Prince Dan pressured Jing Ke to take action. Jing Ke asked for two things, which he said were necessary to gain access to the king: a map of a fertile region of Yan, which the king had long coveted, and the head of Fan Wuqi. While the map was easy to arrange, the life of General Fan was something Dan would not relinquish. So Jing Ke went to Fan himself. After listening to Jing Ke's explanation, Fan gave him what he wanted without hesitation.

With so many things at stake, and two lives already sacrificed for the mission, it was time for Jing Ke to go. The prince and those who knew about the plot came in white mourning dress to see him off. On the bank of the Yi River, his bosom friend Gao Jianli plucked his lute, and all those present shed tears when they heard Jing Ke sing his parting song:

> *The wind cries. The Yi River is cold.*
> *The brave man, once gone, will never return.*

On arriving in Qin, Jing Ke presented the king with the map and Fan Wuqi's head, and was allowed to approach the throne. As the king unfolded the scroll of map, a dagger appeared. Jing Ke leaped up, grabbed the dagger in one hand, and seized the king in the other. Before the dagger could reach its target, however, the king broke away and ran around a large pillar to shun the attack. Finally, he was able to use his sword to bring Jing Ke down. Before the palace guards finished him off, Jing Ke laughed at the king and cursed him, saying that he had failed to kill him not because he could not do so, but because he was only trying to force a promise from him to take back to Prince Dan.

After recovering from the shock, the king retaliated, and saw to it that the state of Yan was conquered, Prince Dan slain, and all his associates hunted down. Gao Jianli 高渐离 (fl. 227 BCE), Jing Ke's best friend and a well-known lute player, managed to run away, and went into hiding. But before too long, his love for lute playing gave him away. Too fond of his music to kill him, the king spared his life, had him blinded, and let him play the lute at court. As time went by, the king relaxed his vigilance and allowed him to come closer. Gao stuffed the inside of his lute with lead and, when summoned again by the king, struck at him with the instrument. He missed and got himself executed. The king was so terrified by this second assault that he never dared to allow the former followers of the feudal lords to get close to him.

Jing Ke's story was first recorded in the *Intrigues of the Warring States* (*Zhanguo ce* 战国策). It was only after Sima Qian 司马迁 (145 BCE–?) retold the story in his *Records of the Historian* (*Shiji* 史记), ranking Jing among the great kings, nobles, military strategists, politicians, and thinkers, that this assassin of obscure origin secured his place in the collective memory of the Chinese nation.

Jing Ke had to wait for more than 1800 years for a playwright to place him on stage. Finally in 1629, a four-act play entitled *Cold is the Yi River* (*Yishui han* 易水寒) was published under the name of Ye Xianzu 叶宪祖 (1566–1641). Before it reaches its end, the play seems to follow Sima Qian's version of the story. Scenes and dialogues are created in such a way as to allow the specifics and details from the original version to fit in. In more than one place Ye takes lines directly from

Sima Qian and pastes them verbatim to the dialogues in the play, sometimes even at the expense of its narrative logic and the smooth layout of the storyline. Ye's apparent respect for the original version of the story, however, only makes the totally unexpected ending of his play more puzzling. Instead of dying a heroic death, Ye's Jing Ke succeeds in forcing the king to give up all the land he seized and pledge to make peace with his neighbors. This miracle is then followed by yet another. Jing Ke turns out to be a Daoist immortal who came to the mundane world temporarily to perform the heroic deed. Now that the mission has been accomplished, a fellow Daoist immortal descends from Heaven to wake him up from his human involvement and accompany him back to the celestial kingdom.

These incredible happy endings seem to weaken the aesthetic beauty resulting from the tragic death of the protagonist in the original story. The sentimental musing on the regrettable failure of Jing Ke's mission was the focus of many poetic works. The following verses by Tao Yuanming 陶渊明 (365–427) speak not just for the poet himself:

> *Alas, he was not good at swordsmanship*
> *And therefore his fantastic plan did not succeed.* (Gong, 331)

Ye was not unaware of the powerful artistic effect of the tragic ending in the original story (Wang Gulu, 223), but he opted for the happy ending for a good reason. If historical justice was denied to the brave man, then it is imperative for dramatic justice to be done.

Revenge is a complicated issue in the Chinese socio-cultural tradition. Confucianism preached the idea of forgiveness and yielding, and it would therefore seem unlikely that it would promote the idea of revenge. Since revenge always involved people's obligation to the five human relationships (father-son, elder brother-younger brother, husband-wife, lord-minister, and friend-friend), which were the "concrete manifestations" of the Confucian idea of "cohumanity" (Tu, 18), it proved to be an unavoidable topic in the Confucian classics. For instance, in a recent study of *The Spring and Autumn Annals* and the three interpretive traditions attached to it, Michael Nylan observes that revenge is an "important topic" in the texts, through the discussion of which can be seen the divergences in moral judgment between different exegetic traditions (261). Even Confucius himself is said to find the topic unavoidable, according to comments attributed to him in a passage in the *Book of Rites* (*Liji* 礼记):

> Zi Xia once asked Confucius, "What should one do to avenge one's parents?" The Master said, "You [give up all luxuries in life and] sleep on a straw bed and pillow on your weapon. You do not take office, and do not live under the same sky with your enemy. When seeing him in the market, you go after him then and there, without coming back for a weapon. "How about avenging one's brothers?" "You do not live in the same country with your enemy. Nevertheless, when you are on a mission for your lord and come across your enemy on the way, you do not engage him." "How about avenging one's parental cousins?" "You do not take the lead. If your cousins can do it themselves, you just follow them with a weapon." (*Liji*, 3:40)

The Master makes it clear that one cannot talk about the appropriateness of revenge in general terms. To determine whether an act of revenge is justifiable and how one should carry it out, one needs to ask a series of specific questions, such as, what injury has been committed, and by whom; who is wronged, and to what degree; how close one is to the person involved, and how the revenge will hinder one from performing other duties. The bottom line is that the degree of urgency of an act of revenge and the way in which it is carried out should be proportional to the avenger's duty to the person to be avenged according to the state and family hierarchy.[2] Revenge is thus a game of "matching" in more than one sense of the word.

The Chinese term for revenge is *baochou* 报仇 (讎), literally meaning "to repay vengeance." The original meaning of *bao* (the first character in the compound) is "to mete out punishment that fits the crime," hence "to return" and, perhaps more important, "to match." *Chou* (the second character in the compound) can mean anything from "answer," "response," "match," "equal," and "enemy," to "requital" and "vengeance" (Hu and Fang, 21–22). A *chou* enemy, therefore, is an "opposite match," a "reverse," and the *chou* vengeance means requital in kind and in proportion. Notice how the social content of revenge discussed above is also implied here. Interestingly, this tit-for-tat "matching" nature of *baochou* is vividly reflected in the traditional form of the ideograph for *chou* 讎, which shows two birds 佳 on opposite sides of language 言: a pair of opponents locked in language, matching their words against each other.

The same persistence in matching and paying off is seen in another Chinese term *bao'en* 报恩 (repaying a favor) or *baode* 报德 (repaying virtue), which also means requital in kind, but the pay-off made here is for kindnesses and favors received, not for wrongs done. The two terms *baochou* and *bao'en* thus form an interesting pair, illustrating the two sides of the principle of requital. It is no coincidence that in the only passage in the *Analects* in which the issue of requital is discussed, Confucius would deem that these two sides of the issue should not be separated from each other:

> Someone asked, "What do you think about repaying grudge with virtue?" Confucius replied, "Then what do you repay virtue with? Repay grudge with uprightness; repay virtue with virtue. (*Analects*, 14:36)

Confucius was reluctant to say that one should repay evil with evil. He did not, however, embrace the doctrine of repaying evil with good, either. For him, not responding to wrongdoings in an upright – or impartial – manner was no less erroneous than not rewarding good deeds. What is noteworthy here is the suggestion that there is a right match for everything. If you use good will, which should be the match for virtue, to repay a grudge, not only do you squander it and thus have nothing left to repay virtue, but – more seriously – you also upset the equilibrium of the whole value system. Knowing how to repay a grudge will enable one to repay virtue properly, and *vice versa*.

Confucius' firm belief in the proper interchange in the interpersonal relationship is reflected in his well-known principle of "reciprocity" (*shu* 恕). "Do not do to others what you do not want to be done to yourself" (*Analects*, 15:23). What is left unsaid here, however, should not be ignored: ". . . otherwise, other people might do that to you." The rationale for requital is implied. There is no denying that Confucius only emphasized one side of the principle of reciprocity – the "duty" side – and deliberately refrained from talking about the "rights" side.[3] It is also evident that the "rights" a virtuous person deserved was also within the scope of his attention.

Ye's *Yi River* reflects his understanding of this symbiotic relationship between repaying a grudge and repaying virtue. The play focuses on one thing: requital. In the climactic scene, when he subdues the king and makes him promise not to bully his neighbors anymore, not only does Jing Ke wipe away the humiliation and disgrace Prince Dan suffered, but also avenges his comrades who laid down their lives for their common cause. Whereas the historian Sima Qian sets his eyes on the tragic beauty in Jing Ke's failure, the dramatist Ye Xianzu realizes that nothing can satisfy his audience but the total success of Jing Ke's mission. The king is humiliated, Prince Dan gets his revenge, and better yet, the hero who carries out the revenge does not die in the hands of the king's guards. The happy ending of Ye's play seems to be the only solution.

Although Ye's theatrical treatment of the ending of Jing Ke's story disappointed many people, including those who praise the play in general,[4] it received enthusiastic praise from his friend Qi Biaojia 祁彪佳 (fl. 1602–1645), a literary critic of the time. Qi says,

> Carrying only a dagger with him, Master Jing entered the unpredictable powerful state of Qin. Even though his attempt ended in failure and he lost his life, his deeds were still thrilling enough to go down in history.

Now Tongbai 桐柏 (Ye's stylized name) brings the dead hero back to life and changes his failure into success. Master Jing has got someone who understands him indeed! (Huang and Feng, 538–539)

Ye's empathic understanding of Jing Ke can be explained by his personal experience. The father of his son-in-law Huang Zongxi 黄宗羲 (1610–1695, an eminent philosopher) was murdered by the wicked eunuch Wei Zhongxian 魏忠贤 (1568–1627) and his lackeys in 1626. After the eunuch died, several of his followers who were responsible for the murder were put on trial. When Huang appeared in court to confront his father's murderers, he attacked and injured one of them with a weapon. This dramatic act of revenge became the sensation of the day (Xu Dingbao, 276–277). The parallel between Jing Ke and Huang Zongxi could not have escaped Huang's father-in-law.

"Repaying vengeance," or *baochou*, is only one side of the picture. One misses the main point of the *Yi River* if one overlooks the issue of "repaying kindness," or *bao'en*. At the end of the play, the Daoist immortal summarizes the moral implication of Jing Ke's action. "You might not know this, Master Jing," says the immortal, "You were bound to do service to Prince Dan, simply because you owed him some special favor from previous lives" (Shen, 20b). Ye does not find it improper to put the Buddhist ideas of karma and retribution in the mouth of a Daoist god, for he knows this is the best way to allow his audience to understand what happens on stage in terms of requital. By helping Prince Dan settle an old score with the King of Qin, Jing Ke repays his debt of gratitude to the prince. In fact, this is the organizing theme that runs through the whole play. In the parting scene on the bank of the Yi River, from which the play gets its title, Jing Ke sings his heart's intent before embarking on his journey to the Qin court, which is meant to be a journey of no return:

Let me just lend you this body of mine
So that both [my] gratitude and [your] grudge can be paid off. (Shen, 12a)

The play does not specify the "special favor" Jing Ke owes the prince "from previous lives," but it does elaborate on the favor he receives in this life: the prince "knows" him and recognizes him as a superior person. In the opening statement at the beginning of the play in which Jing Ke introduces himself to the audience, he sighs:

A man should have someone who knows him, and need not worry about the common herd in the world. . . . I often wish to demonstrate my unusual quality. Right now, indulging in drinking and gambling, I just mix myself with the ordinary folks temporarily. (Shen, 1a)

In his study of Sima Qian's *Record*, modern scholar Li Changzhi observes that the historical character Jing Ke, like other assassins depicted in the text, is a very lonely man, and is more than willing to dedicate himself to anyone who truly knows him (99). Li is only talking about Sima Qian's Jing Ke. The Jing Ke we see in the *Yi River* is even more so. This is a man who believes that he is so unusual that he stands alone in this world. At present, however, he can only mix with the commonplace, wasting his life. The dilemma he faces is that precisely because he is extraordinary, it is impossible for the ordinary to recognize him. As he says half-jokingly that he has cultivated the "skill of butchering dragons" (Guo Qingfan, Vol. 4, 1046). When his friend Gao Jianli asks why he does not find a buyer for this special skill, he replies in metaphorical language that precious white jade should not be given away easily and without good reason, implying that his special feat is saved for the grandest cause only.

Jing Ke's unusual quality is exactly what Prince Dan needs, for he has a "dragon" to slaughter. To avenge his personal wrongs and to prevent the King of Qin from taking over his country, he needs the help from someone of Jing Ke's caliber. At first, when the prince sends Tian Guang to recruit him, Jing Ke is not persuaded. It is only after Tian assures him that there is not a second hero like him in the whole state, and that compared with him, all the other candidates look like "dogs and chickens with trivial skills," that Jing Ke gives his consent. After all, he wants nothing but appreciation from those who truly know him. Later, in a royal banquet in his honor, Prince Dan showers him with still greater honor and claims that his valor and virtue place him even above the three great worthies known for their remarkable service to the state of Yan in the past. Deeply moved, Jing Ke begins to feel "uneasy" at heart (Shen, 7b). A subtle change takes place in the dynamics behind the relationship between the two characters. In the first place, it is the prince who needs Jing Ke. The latter is the one who is going to risk his life for the former. After the prince demonstrates his recognition of Jing Ke's value, however, Jing becomes the one indebted. He owes the realization of his "unusual quality" to the prince, and is willing to return this favor with his life. As his friend Gao Jianli says, "A worthy man will give his life to the one who knows him" (Shen, 4a).

Around the time Ye Xianzu put out *Yi River*, his contemporary Mao Wei 茅维 (fl. 1590) wrote *The Lute at the Court of Qin* (*Qin ting zhu* 秦廷筑). The play was probably meant to be a correction to Ye's revision of history.[5] The main character of Mao's play is not Jing Ke, but his friend Gao Jianli. In the play, just as Sima Qian's version of the story goes, after Jing Ke dies his heroic death, Gao tries to wreak revenge. According to James Liu, for those who are unsatisfied with the happy ending of the *Yi River*, *The Lute* is "historically more accurate and artistically more satisfying" (170). The play is not merely a theatrical version of Sima Qian's story. It demonstrates some psychological depth. For instance, at the end of the play, the king wonders how his enemy Prince Dan managed to win the hearts of those brave and altruistic assassins, to whom the king cannot but show respect and admiration. This thought-provoking ending lends the play a dimension beyond revenge.

Although the storyline of the Gao Jianli episode is relatively simple compared with that of Jing Ke, Gao's revenge is perhaps more focused and intense, and has its own special appeal. Some five hundred years after Mao, Guo Moruo 郭沫若 (1892–1978), one of the most prominent leftist writers during the first half of the 20th century, also directed his attention to Jing Ke's loyal friend, and wrote the full-scale modern drama *Gao Jianli* (1942). Guo's intention, however, was not just to retell history. As he himself admitted, the King of Qin in the play was an allusion to Chiang Kai-shek 蒋介石 (1887–1975), the leader of the Nationalist Party (129). The old story is thus unapologetically burdened with the weight of what Frederic Jameson terms "national allegory" (69). The moral and ethical concerns in traditional Chinese thought touched off by the sensitive issue of revenge is now further complicated by new worries resulting from the political struggle and the Communist revolution in 20th-century China. The old rule still holds true. The manner with which an avenger carries out his task should match the magnitude of his moral duty. No wonder that the conflict between good and evil in the play is not only represented by the contrast between a cruel king and a loyal friend but also – more significantly – by the contrast between a crude and lewd tyrant and an accomplished artist with a noble heart and refined taste (one cannot but be tempted to ponder the possible link between the author himself and the hero he created). The title character's revenge can even be justified on intellectual and cultural grounds.

With the complexity of the characters involved and the high-stakes plot of the story, the dramatic potential of the Jing Ke narrative proves to be nearly limitless. Beginning in the last decade of the second millennium there suddenly came a new interest in the tragic hero from the ancient past. In 2011, Mo Yan staged his 10-act play *Women de Jing Ke* 我们的荆轲 (*Our Jing Ke*). The title of the play reveals its intent, that is, to bring the heroic figure down from his pedestal and make him one of us. As the author stated in an interview, it would be meaningless to re-represent an "overused" character like Jing Ke or to interpret his deeds in the traditional way unless this historical figure is "remolded" and the "motive" behind his action reexamined (Zhang Tongdao, 116). The choices for a modern writer to achieve this seem not many, and what Mo does is to "deconstruct." Under his microscope, the sole drive for Jing Ke to let himself be used as a hired killer is simply to become famous (Mo, 7–96). Considering the cultural milieu in the 2010s China, when it was fashionable to turn a cynical eye to established values of any shades, one can say that Mo's effort served to add some noise to a new cliché by discrediting an "overused" story.

Liu Cixin, the famous sci-fi writer, also tried to make use of the Jing Ke narrative in a short story *Circle* (*Yuan* 圆), but from a different angle. Using the concluding scene in the original *Shiji* record as his point of departure, Liu allows the assassin to spare the life of the king and thus gain the latter's trust. Jing Ke is still an assassin and has a mission to accomplish, but his loyalty lies first with science, or to be exact, mathematics. Although he does eventually help Prince Dan get his revenge, he has an axe of his own to grind. By persuading the king to let him use the formidable Qin army to form an echelon of three million soldiers, he creates an ideal array data structure to play with in his search for the "language of Heaven," which he claims might reveal the secret of immortality the king yearns for. Had he succeeded, the convenient toy we call a "computer" today would have been invented in the year 224 BCE (Liu Cixin, 417–431).

To examine the evolution of Jing Ke's story just up to this point is already to recall T. S. Eliot's rumination on the living organism of a literary "tradition." For the existing order of a tradition to "persist after the supervention of novelty," says Eliot, the order itself must develop and change. "[T]he *whole* existing order must be, if ever so slightly, altered; and so the relations, proportions, values of each work of art toward the whole are readjusted; and this is conformity between the old and the new" (Eliot, 5). If we take the Jing Ke story as the case study of a "mini-tradition," we can see that after the "supervention" of the new productions about Jing Ke, the whole existing order of the story is altered. The emphasis of the thematic purport, the moral implication, even the personal traits of the protagonist in each story towards the whole tradition are readjusted. New meanings are added to the "Jing Ke tradition" with the participation of each new member, so much so that when one looks back to the "original" Jing Ke, one would find certain "novel" qualities about him that were not there originally.

This "conformity between the old and the new" in the stories about Jing Ke, however, is even more complicated than the one Eliot so ingeniously lays out in his theoretical module. The Jing Ke narrative does not only involve literary creation. It starts as "history."

When Derk Bodde published his translation of the Jing Ke story in 1940 (the first in English), it appeared to him as a piece of authentic history. "Ching K'o's [Jing Ke] biography," observes Bodde, "fortunately for the reader, is almost entirely free from the textual and historical difficulties" seen in many of its counterparts in the *Shiji* (39). Bodde's assurance in the authenticity of the episode even leads him to a lengthy investigation into the history of the use of iron sword in China, evidenced in the weapon the King of Qin used to repel Jing Ke's assault (45–49). Half century later, when Stephen Durrant was also captivated by the stories of Jing Ke and other famous assassins recorded in "one of the most literarily significant chapters" in the *Shiji*, this professor of Chinese literature believed that, "[w]hen all is said and done," Sima Qian is "a literary genius who writes his story as much as history" (143). Obviously, Durrant detected elements other than "history" in the ancient text. By adding a modifier to a Chinese term used to define the function of history, he calls Sima Qian's *Record of the Historian* a "cloudy mirror," and uses it as the title of his book on the subject.[6]

Just as they look at the authenticity of the story somewhat differently, Bodde and Durrant do not see eye to eye in their judgment of Jing Ke as a historical figure. Suspending the caution of a historian, Bodde expresses enthusiastic admiration for Jing Ke's personality. "Though skilled with the sword and a lover of wine, he was at the same time a man who liked to read books, was faithful to his friends, and esteemed by those who knew him." Bodde also calls readers' attention to the "fact" – obviously on the basis of Sima Qian's rather life-like representation of the character from an omniscient point of view – that, contrary to what one would presume an assassin to be, Jing Ke was also "a reasonable and conciliatory man, ready in small matters to avoid all trouble, even though by so doing he might seem to play the coward." "To be a true hero he must at the same time possess culture, strength of character, a gentle calm, and evenness of temper." He even goes so far as to imply that Jing Ke exemplifies an ideal person with true "great valor," a noble personal quality Mencius discusses in detail (*Mencius*, 2A:2) (39, note 1). In comparison, Durrant's assessment of Jing Ke is much more reserved. "The very inclusion of such a chapter ["Biographies of the Assassins"] in *Records of the Historian* is something of an un-Confucian act. After all, the several men immortalized there, 'whose names are passed down to later generations' and whom Sima Qian credits for 'not disregarding the dictates of their conscience,' were men of violence who threatened or killed political authorities" (105).

It is also worth noting that Bodde, a historian, would literally label Jing Ke as a "patriot," while acknowledging that the King of Qin's later "creation of a unified empire did, in some ways, represent an advance over the groups of warring feudal states it replaced." "In any case, it is unlikely that Ching K'o's [Jing Ke] attempt, even if successful, could long have halted the course of history" (38). Durrant, who is more fascinated with the literary significance of the Jing Ke episode, concerns himself with the chapter's moral implication, taking into consideration the potential historical consequences of the assassination attempt. The unique nature of this story almost causes these two sinologists to cross the boundary between history and literature, and between reason and emotion, in their responses to its hero.

This comes as no surprise. The interdependence between history and fiction is a much-debated topic in the study of traditional Chinese literature outside China. "Since both history and fiction are engaged in the mimesis of action, it is often difficult to draw the line neatly between the two" (Plaks, 312). Today, outside China, Sima Qian's *Record of the Historian* stands as "the single most important source for the history of pre-Ch'in (Qin) China" (Nienhauser, xxvii). This does not prevent the biography of Jing Ke to sit squarely in almost all anthologies of Chinese *literature* in English.[7] The rationale for this interrelation between historical writing and "literary" narrative can be found in Andrew Plaks' explanation. "In both the historical and the fictional branches of the Chinese tradition, the final justification for the enterprise of narrative may be said to lie in the *transmission* of known facts" (312). "The necessary assumption of such transmission," continues Plaks, "is that every given narrative is in some sense a faithful representation of what did, or what typically does, happen in human experience – that is, that the facts in question are true" (313).

Bodde can make a confident statement that "[w]e today, looking back over those troubled times with the cool detachment of the historian, can see the Ch'in [Qin] conquest of China, with its abolition of feudalism, as necessary steps in China's progress towards later glorious maturity." At the same time, he can also say without qualm that "we of the modern world . . . cannot but read of the deaths of those men [Jing Ke and his comrades] with sorrowing compassion" (38). Here Bodde speaks of two different facts, and both facts are *true*.

The word "fact," in this context, is not equivalent to "truth." For one thing, is the scene on the bank of the Yi River, where Jing Ke bids farewell to Prince Dan (one of the most touching scenes in Chinese history/literature) a solid fact that can be backed up by participants or eyewitnesses of the event? Yet, as Plaks says, in the Chinese context, the "underpinning of narrative transmission, despite the obvious untruths of hyperbole, supernatural detail, or ideological distortion," is still that "what is recorded is ultimately true – either true to fact or true to life" (313).

Plaks' observation, especially the dashed emphasis at the end of the statement above, is insightful, and gets to the core of the issue. Those privileged few in ancient China, who knew how to, and cared to, narrate by putting pen to paper (or bamboo strips, or silk), were not obsessed with what did happen, but paid more attention to what typically does, or should, happen. The function of the Chinese writing system can be a useful analogy here. Chinese characters are not a writing system to record sound, but a representation system that helps to create a "virtual reality," a copy of *the* reality.[8] Likewise, Chinese narrative does not follow at the heels of what really happens, but also takes as its mission to establish a "virtual reality" of a higher order, which is not necessarily "true to fact," but certainly "true to life." The discussion of this topic is reminiscent of Aristotle's famous remarks that "poetry is a more philosophical and a higher thing than history." The reason is that literature is about the "universal," or "how a person of a certain type will on occasion speak or act, according to the law of probability or necessity," which is different from the "particular," or "what has happened," but only accidentally and very probably will not happen again (Butcher, 35).

It is relevant to notice that, when Plaks tries to elicit specifically the "aesthetic system" sustaining the "deft psychological realism in character delineation," which is "true to life," the first example that comes to his mind is Sima Qian's portrayal of Jing Ke. Setting aside the issue of authenticity, Plaks focuses his attention on the deliberate "impression of *inconsistency*: wavering, backtracking, side switching, mood-changing, in the portrayal of the heroes of the narrative tradition," and finds a typical example in Jing Ke's "sudden switch from procrastination to self-sacrifice." What Plaks marvels at most is the representational art that "leaves considerable room for ambivalence, or even contradiction." "Far from being a critical fault," he says, "this sort of flexibility, or fluidity, in character portrayal stands as a clear index of the greatness of a given work" (341). He is not talking about literature; he is talking about historiography.

When practitioners of Chinese cinema turned to the country's rich history for subject matter in the 1990s and around the turn of the 21st century, they also discovered Jing Ke. Three big-budget movies based on the story were produced within six years. More than any "reteller" of the story did in previous times, these movie makers tried to read varied ethical and political meanings and even philosophies into it. When one subjects this group of reproductions in the Jing Ke narrative to scrutiny, one faces a very different kind of "truth."

In *The Emperor and the Assassin* (*Jing Ke Ci Qin Wang*) (1998) by Chen Kaige, the role of the avenger is played not by Jing Ke, but by the King of Qin. Every time he recalls the days when his family were kept as political hostages in Zhao, the fire of revenge burns in his heart. When someone reminds him that this bitter vengeance goes against his ambition to become a benevolent king who brings peace to the people of a unified China, his answer is, "The case with the state of Zhao is different!" Personal hatred blurs his outlook. The movie does not forget to also point out emphatically that, while the king fulfills one side of his pledge to requital, i.e. *baochou*, he fails the other side, *baoen*. Many kind-hearted people in Zhao helped him in his childhood. Now instead of repaying their kindness with gratitude, he returns good with evil. It is here that Jing Ke's function as the "scourge of Heaven" becomes clear.

In Zhou Xiaowen's *The Emperor's Shadow* (*Qin Song*, literally "Ode to the Qin Empire") (1996), although Jing Ke still goes to Qin to make an attempt on the king's life, his story is only a minor episode, used as a footnote to history. The center stage is now taken by the lute-player Gao Jianli and the King of Qin. The two sworn enemies in the original story now start as sworn brothers in the movie. They were breast-fed by the same women – Gao's mother – in their infancy, and suffered hardship together as they grew up in a foreign country. The two were separated later by different destinies and by their pursuit of different goals in life. When they meet again, one is the king of the powerful state of Qin, victorious on his way to becoming the first emperor of a unified China, while the other is his captive. The king wants his childhood friend – the best lute player on earth – to become his court composer and write the imperial anthem for his future empire. He needs the help of Gao's music "to fight for hearts and minds" of his subjects. The problem is that he has to win Gao's heart and mind first. The king might condescendingly consider Gao an old friend from his childhood, but Gao, having seen his country trampled by the king, has every reason to call him a blood enemy.

The two are thus bound by both love and hate. The king and the musician form a pair of *chou*. They are adversaries in the sense that they are "adverse matches" to each other. The symbolic meaning of the relationship between them cannot pass unnoticed. Even when they were small babies, their milk-mother already noticed that they were a pair of binary opposites, with one like a wolf cub and the other as meek as a lamb. The stamina and stubbornness of the lamb can overcome the ferocity of the wolf. The king claims that Gao is his "eternal shadow." Maybe Gao can do the same to him: this shadow is something the king can never shake off. It haunts him, controlling his moods and actions. The king conquers, whereas the musician captivates. Even the king's spoiled daughter easily falls prey to his charm. The love-hate relationship between the two is thus a "match" between bitter adversaries, between two sets of diametrically different values. The ending of the movie does not lack its symbolic meaning. Gao smashes his lute against the towering, statue-like figure of the king during the ceremony that marks the beginning of the Qin Dynasty. His assault looks so futile; it does not even affect the king's ritual performance. As the ritual music rises and permeates the altar in the next scene, the king is totally humbled and cannot hold back his tears, at least partly because he is overpowered by his love and hate towards his shadow and adversary. For that moment, the musician gets his revenge. It is interesting to note that the movie uses the more general name for the string instrument *qin* 琴 – instead of *zhu* in the original story – to refer to Gao's lute. The audience is thus allowed to pick up the pun on the power of Gao's *qin* music and the military might of the *Qin* empire, and encouraged to read the Chinese title of the movie *Qin song* as "Ode to the Lute" 琴颂 rather than "Ode to the Qin Empire" 秦颂. The matching game will never end.

In his 2002 movie *Hero* (*Yingxiong* 英雄), Zhang Yimou gives the Jing Ke tradition a subtle twist. The revenge story is changed into a *kungfu* saga. There is no Jing Ke or Gao Jianli in the movie, but careful audiences will have no difficulty detecting them in the shadows of the best-known assassin in Chinese history and his comrades. A group of knights errant, or *xia*, band together to get the King. Two of them almost succeed, but both spare his life at the last moment. The reason? When seeing the king in person, they suddenly realize that this is the only hero able to unify China and bring peace to the land. Compared with the pain suffered by the people because of the endless wars between rival states, the bitterness of their personal hatred pales. They decide to sink their personal feuds for the common good of "all under heaven" (*tianxia* 天下). They are true heroes. The message carries a Confucian ring. Individual interest should yield to the common good of society.

The images and sounds of the three movies affect domestic and foreign audiences alike, but they leave very different impressions on foreign audiences, who go to a theater without the benefit of knowledge about Chinese history, about the popular culture generated by the legend of Jing Ke, about martial arts and *xia* 侠 plus the moral values they stand for, and – more importantly – without an understanding of the ethos of the general populace in China at the time, or the national sentiment, so to speak, that affected the reception of these movies in China. Globalization changed a lot of things in this rejuvenated country, but not everything was altered.

Of the three cinematic productions in question here, *Hero* is the one that has attracted most attention outside China.[9] One major focal point of this movie that aroused heated debates centers on its political implications.[10] If we examine the whole gamut of ambivalent responses, we can see that the majority of the praise goes to the "aesthetics, commercial/art aspects and relationship to the martial arts film tradition" (Larson, 2010, 153), whereas the harshest criticism is aimed at the movie's political implications.

Even a quick glimpse of the comments about the political implications of the cinematic versions shows that the most controversial issues are the approval, either explicit or implicit, of national unity and the alleged support for authoritarianism. Comments of this type in harsh language are not difficult to find on film review websites and Amateur blogs, but comments like the following – not a criticism, but a rather positive comment sparked by Chen Kaige's treatment of the King of Qin – is quite eye-catching, as it appears in an academic journal: "The varied historical urges toward cultural, linguistic, political, or aesthetic unification in China emerge, then, as obsessions with resolving the illegitimacy of an empire that will cannot – will not – know itself" (Porter, 31). Reading this, one cannot but recall Derk Bodde's comment on the same topic almost seventy years ago, quoted earlier in this paper.

The King of Qin seems to be the same source from which different interpreters tease out the troubling political implications. It is taken for granted that the king is exactly *that* king in real history. Maybe there is a problem here. Pointing his finger at this problem, Jia-xuan Zhang proposes that we "view the king as an allegorical symbol of monarchy rather than as the actual historical tyrant" (48), and takes the movie as a conflict between the two forces, represented by the king and the assassins. The upshot of this allegorical reading coincides with a historical-psychological reading of the story by Yuri Pines. Pines believes that the scene of the powerful king "barely escap[ing] the assassin's dagger, running pathetically around the column of his audience hall, and being unable to utilize all his might to repel a man of humble origins armed with nothing but a dagger" is emblematic of the confrontation between the power of the king on one side, and the power of "the lower segment of the *shi* 士 stratum, the 'plain-clothed 布衣 *shi*" on the other (24).

The shape of this binary relationship becomes even clearer when we look at another binary model Wendy Larson proposes, namely a "binary of cultural versus political/military power" (277). The confrontation between the emperor and his assassin, together with other cinematic reincarnations of Jing Ke, is "not just a struggle between two people but a meeting of two worlds, each carrying its own logic" (278). The careful choice of the word "meeting" here is reminiscent of the reciprocal nature of the "requital." The "meeting" is contentious, yet still a dialogue. "By staging a conflict between a pure, direct, and undeniably violent form of political power in the Qin king and his warriors, and the culturally rich, evocative, ethereal *xia*, the film puts into contention two kinds of power that are supposed to be closely entwined and mutually supportive . . ." (278).

This "cultural" approach to the conflicts represented in the Jing Ke story rejects the rigid historical interpretation. It is allegorical, yet with real world relevance; "universal" enough to rise above political, even geopolitical, ideology in the study of history/literature. Such an approach will fare better with time, and is in spirit more in line with the loyalty to truth, exemplified in Sima Qian's *Record*, and in its first English translator's candor, and in the loyalty to a cause Jing Ke the assassin holds so high and demonstrates in his personal "history," the Greek origin of which – *istoreo* – means "knowing by inquiry."

ENDNOTES

1   During the Warring States period, royal family of one state would send its sons to other allied states as "hostages" to guarantee good relations between the states.

2   Rosemont's comment on the "particularism" of Confucian morality is relevant here: "Confucian morality is particularistic, in that it insists that at all times we do what is appropriate, depending on whom we are interacting with, and when" (193).

3   Here I borrow the terms "duty" and "rights" from T'ang Chün-I's and Tu Wei-ming's readings of "reciprocity." Tang Chün-I asserts that "reciprocity" is actually "practicing the morality of doing one's duty to others but not asking them to do their duties, reciprocally" (193), which Tu Wei-ming summarizes as the "duty consciousness" of Confucianism, as opposed to the "rights-consciousness" (26–27).

4   For example, while admitting that the ending of the play is a regrettable "fault," Wang Chaohong insists that it should not prevent us from appreciating the achievement of the play in general (p. 83). Japanese critic Aoki Masaru also regrets the missing of the "lingering tone" at its end, but still considers the play the best of Ye's works (Aoki, 223).

5   Xu Zifang believes that Mao Wei deliberately makes his version of the story different from that of Ye Xianzu. Xu's theory, though very viable, is yet to be supported by the proof that Mao Wei's play was written after Ye's *Yi River* (Xu Zifang, 450).

6   "Founded as much by the heat of personal anxiety as by the cold facts of the past," says Durrant, "Sima Qian's mirror is a distorted and cloudy one" (147).

7   Derk Bodde's translation is included in Victor H. Mair (ed). *The Columbia Anthology of Traditional Chinese Literature*. New York: Columbia University Press, 1994. pp. 671–683. A different translation by Burton Watson is included first in Cyril Birch (ed). *Anthology of Chinese Literature: From Early Times to the Fourteenth Century*. New York: Grove Weidenfeld, 1965. 106–118, and then in John Minford and Joseph S.M. Lau, (eds.). *Classical Chinese literature: An Anthology of Translations*. Vol. I, *From Antiquity to the Tang Dynasty*. New York: Columbia University Press, 2000. 331–341. The only major anthology of Chinese literature in the English language that does not include Jing Ke is Stephen Owen's *An Anthology of Chinese Literature, Beginnings to 1911*. New York and London: W. W. Norton & company, 1996. But, maybe not by accident, the episode Owen chooses to include is the story of another assassin Nie Zheng 聂政 (pp. 152–154) from the same *Shiji* chapter where Jing Ke is recorded.

8   For a brief discussion of this issue, see Xinda Lian 连心达, "Xushi wenhuaxue yanjiu zhong de Zhongguo xueshu jingshen" 叙事文化学研究中的中国学术精神 (Towards A Thematology with Chinese Characteristics), *Journal of Nankai University* 南开大学学报, 2020.3 (May 2020): 133.

9   Strong interest in *Hero* refuses to subside. As a result, a collection of serious research papers on the movie, *Global Chinese Cinema*, edited by Gary D. Rawnsley and Ming-yeh T. Rawnsley (London and New York: Rutledge, 2010), was published several years after the movie's release. Most of the topics dealt with in this volume do not sound unfamiliar, such as national unity, cultural identity, traditional moral standards, especially those with strong contemporary implications. The volume also includes discussions on the new developments in Chinese society, especially those resulting from the "globalization" of Chinese film production.

10   Identifying the two main points of the conflict and the debate in response to Zhang Yimou's *Hero*, Wendy Larson points out that "[r]oughly speaking, the themes that critics identify are *Hero*'s political implications, film techniques and aesthetics, commercial/art aspects and relationship to the martial arts film tradition" (Larson, 2010, 153).

REFERENCES

Aoki, Masaru 青木正儿 (1958). *Zhongguo jinshi xijushi* 中国近世戏剧史 (History of Early Modern Chinese Drama), Vol. 1, Translated by Wang Gulu 王古鲁. Beijing: Zuojia chubanshe.

Bodde, Derk (trans. & discuss) (1940). *Statesman, Patriot, and General in Ancient China: Three Shih Chi Biographies of the Ch'in Dynasty (255–206 B. C.).* New Haven: American Oriental Society, 1940. 23–52.

Butcher, Samuel Henry (1907). *Aristotle's Theory of Poetry and Fine Art, with a Critical Text and Translation of the Poetics.* London: Macmillan.

Durrant, Stephen W. (1995). *The Cloudy Mirror: Tension and Conflict in the Writings of Sima Qian.* Albany: State University of New York Press.

Eliot, T. S. (1932). "Tradition and Individual Talent." In *Selected Essays.* New York: Harcourt, Brace & World, Inc. pp. 3–11.

Gernet, Jacques (1982). *A History of Chinese Civilization,* translated by J. R. Foster and Charles Hartman. Cambridge and New York: Cambridge University Press.

Gong Bin 龚斌 (1996). *Tao Yuanming ji jiao jian* 陶渊明集校笺 (Complete Works of Tao Yuanming Collated and Annotated). Shanghai: Shanghai guji chubanshe.

Guo Moruo (1986). "Guanyu zhu" 关于筑 (About the *Zhu* Instrument). In *Guo Moruo Quanji, wenxue pian* 郭沫若全集 文学篇 (Complete Works of Guo Moruo, Literature Section), Vol. 7. Beijing: Renmin wenxue chubanshe.

———. (1986). "Jiao hou ji zhi er" 校后集之二 (Notes Made after Revising, II). In *Guo Moruo Quanji, Wenxue pian.*

Guo Qingfan 郭庆藩 (1961) (ed.). *Zhuangzi jishi* 庄子集释 (Collected Annotations and Comments on the *Zhuangzi*), Vol. 4. Beijing: Zhonghua shuju.

Hu Qiguang 胡奇光 and Fang Huanhai 方环海 (1999). *Erya yi zhu* 尔雅译注 (Annotated Translation of the *Erya*). Shanghai: Shanghai guji chubanshe.

Huang Zhusan 黄竹三 and Feng Junjie 冯俊杰 (eds.) (1998). *Liushi zhong qu ping zhu* 六十种曲评注 (Sixty Annotated *Qu* Plays), Vol. 12. Changchung: Jiling renmin chubanshe.

Jameson, Fredric (1986). "Third-World Literature in the Era of Multinational Capitalism." In *Social Text.* Issue 15. Fall 1986.

Larson, Wendy (2010). "North American Reception of Zhang Yimou's *Hero.*" In Gary D. Rawnsley and Ming-yeh T. Rawnsley (eds.), *Global Chinese Cinema.* London and New York: Routledge, pp. 152–168.

———. (2017). *Zhang Yimou: Globalization and the Subject of Culture.* Amherst, New York: Cambria Press.

Li, Changzhi 李长之 (1984). *Sima Qian zhi renge yu fengge* 司马迁之人格与风格 (The Character and Style of Sima Qian). Beijing: Sanlian shudian.

Liu, Cixin 刘慈欣 (2015). "Yuan" 圆 (Circle). In *Meng zhi hai: Liu Cixin kehuan duanpian xiaoshuoji II* 梦之海：刘慈欣科幻短篇小说集II (Sea of Dreams: Liu Cixin's Sci-fi Stories, Vol. 2). Chengdu: Sichuan keji chubanshe. pp. 417–431.

Liu, James J. Y. (1967). *The Chinese Knight-Errant.* Chicago: The University of Chicago Press.

Mo, Yan 莫言 (2012). *Women de Jing Ke* 我们的荆轲 (Our Jing Ke). Beijing: Xin shijie chubanshe. pp. 7–96.

Nienhauser, William Jr. (ed.) (1994). "A Note on Chronology." In *The Grand Scribe's Records,* Vol. 1. Bloomington & Indianapolis: Indiana University Press, 1994.

Nylan, Michael (2001). *The Five "Confucian" Classics.* New Haven & London: Yale University Press;

Pines, Yuri (2008). "A Hero Terrorist: Adoration of Jing Ke Revisited." *Asia Major.* Third Series. Vol. 21, No. 2. 2008, pp. 1–34.

Plaks, Andrew (1977). "Towards a Critical Theory of Chinese narrative." In Andrew Plaks (ed.), *Chinese narrative: Critical and Theoretical Essays.* Princeton: Princeton University Press. pp. 309–352.

Porter, Deborah (2008). "Character Assassination?: Empire Building and Cultural Pathology in Chen Kaige's *The Emperor and the Assassin.*" *Film & History: An Interdisciplinary Journal of Film and Television Studies.* Vol. 38, No. 2. Fall 2008, pp. 21–31.

Rosemont, Henry Jr. (2000). "On Confucian Civility." In Leroy S. Rouner (ed.), *Civility.* South Bend: University of Notre Dame Press.

Shao, Zengqi 邵曾祺 (1983). *Zhongguo gudian beiju xiju lunji* 中国古典悲剧喜剧论集 (Collected Essays on Chinese Classical Tragedies and Comedies). Shanghai: Shanghai wenyi chubanshe.

Shen, Tai 沈泰 (ed.) (1958). *Sheng Ming zaju* 盛明杂剧 (The Zaju Plays of High Ming), Vol. 2. Beijing: Zhongguo xuju zhubanshe.

T'ang, Chün-I (1967). "The Development of Ideas of Spiritual Value in Chinese Philosophy." In Charles A. Moore (ed.), *The Chinese Mind.* Honolulu: East-West Center Press. pp. 188–212.

Tu, Wei-ming (1979). *Humanity and Self-Cultivation: Essays in Confucian Thought.* Berkeley: Asian Humanities Press.

Wang, Chaohong 汪超宏 (1995). "Ye Xianzu juzuo de xianshi jingshen" 叶宪祖剧作的现实精神 (Realism in Ye Xianzu's Dramatic Works). *Huazhong ligong daxue xuebao* 华中理工大学学报 (Journal of Central China Technology University). Issue 25. March 1995, pp. 79–84.

Wu, Guang 吴光 (1990). *Huang Zongxi zhuzuo huikao* 黄宗羲著作汇考 (Textual Criticism of Huang Zongxi's Works. Taipei: Taiwan xuesheng shuju.

Xu, Dingbao 徐定宝 (1995). *Huang Zongxi nianpu* 黄宗羲年谱 (Chronological Biography of Huang Zongxi). Shanghai: Huadong shida chubanshe.

Xu, Zifang 徐子方 (1998). *Ming zaju yanjiu* 明杂剧研究 (A Study of the Ming *Zaju* Plays). Taipei: Wenjin chubanshe.

Zhang, Tongdao 张同道 (2019). "Mo Yan: Meigeren de neixin shenchu dou you yige Jing Ke" 每个人的内心深处都有一个荆轲 (Everyone Has a Jing Ke Deep Down in His Heart). *Zhongguo wenyi pinglun*《中国文艺评论》(China Literature and Art Criticism. March 2019. pp. 114–122.

Zhang, Jia-xuan (2005). "*Hero*." *Film Quarterly*. Vol. 58, No. 4. Summer 2005, pp. 47–52.

AUTHOR'S BIO

XINDA LIAN is Professor of Chinese Language and Literature at Denison University. He received his MA and PhD from the University of Michigan. His research interests include Song Dynasty poetry, Song Dynasty literati culture, and the stylistic analysis of the *Zhuangzi* text. He is the author of *The Wild and Arrogant: Expression of Self in Xin Qiji's Song Lyrics* as well as a variety of articles and book chapters on Song Dynasty literature and the study of the *Zhuangzi*.

3 The Remaking of Chinese Myths: Maxine Hong Kingston's Appropriation of Her Chinese Sources in *The Woman Warrior*

Liang Shi, Miami University at Ohio

ABSTRACT

Maxine Hong Kingston's *The Woman Warrior* has attracted an enormous amount of critical attention. Much of the criticism has focused, not surprisingly, on the author's treatment of Chinese source materials and the authenticity of her cultural references in the work. This article tries to look beyond the textual signifiers of *The Woman Warrior* to discuss how Kingston's treatment of Chinese sources is shaped by American cultural-ideological discourses. Before the publication of *The Woman Warrior*, Kingston obtained her knowledge of China from a variety of secondary sources and her work registers her personal critical responses derived straight from her Western background. In representing Chinese people and culture, Kingston borrows, consciously or unconsciously, from the Western literary tradition with which she is well acquainted. Through the analysis of the story of the "no name woman," the Chinese attitude toward women and sex, and the story of Fa Mulan, the article explores the intricacy of the cross- cultural intertwining that underpins Kingston's *The Woman Warrior*.

KEYWORDS

Asian American literature, cross-cultural studies, Maxine Hong Kingston, *The Woman Warrior*, feminist literature

Written by one of the most acclaimed Chinese American writers, *The Woman Warrior* by Maxine Hong Kingston has attracted an enormous amount of critical attention. Helena Grice claims that "[t]he appearance of *The Woman Warrior* on the literary landscape in 1976 caused nothing less than a revolution in Asian American literary studies" (Grice 2006, 5). In her work published in 1999, Sau-ling Cynthia Wong calls *The Woman Warrior* "one of the most widely circulated and frequently taught literary texts by a living American author" (Wong 1999, 3). Citing Wong and other sources, Julia Lee reaffirms the lasting popularity and status of Kingston and her works in her 2018 book (Lee 2018, pp. 16–17). Anthony Fonseca goes as far as to say that Kingston is "the most influential Asian American writer of the twentieth century," and *The Woman Warrior* is "the yardstick against which Asian American writers are measured" (Fonseca 2005, 164).

Much of the criticism has focused, not surprisingly, on Kingston's treatment of Chinese source materials in *The Woman Warrior*. As Helena Grice points out, this critical acclamation "precipitated a vicious and ongoing controversy in Asian American letters over the authenticity, or fakery, of Kingston's cultural references (Grice 2006, 2). While some critics – Frank Chin, for instance – find fault with Kingston for distorting and misrepresenting Chinese culture, the majority of voices agree with Kingston herself that her works do not aim at Chinese authenticity, but rather give a unique and powerful expression of the experience of Chinese immigrants. With the acknowledgment of the Americanness of Kingston's work, however, the consensus ends, and critics contend with one another in their interpretations of these works. *The Woman Warrior, China Men*, and *Tripmaster Monkey* have been subjected to various readings including feminist, autobiographic, ethnographic, confessional, postmodernist, psychoanalytical, and cross-cultural.[1]

The remaking of Chinese myths in Kingston's work is often seen as a deliberate artistic move to explore and express the Chinese American experience. This move has been discussed, for example, in terms of "intercultural communication" by Sämi Ludwig and "the art of parody" by Yan Gao, as suggested by the title of their respective works.[2] Most of these studies focus on interpreting the complex signifying structures of Kingston's works. This article will try to look beyond the textual signifiers of *The Woman Warrior* to discuss how Kingston's treatment of Chinese sources is shaped by American cultural-ideological discourses. By showing the Western influence behind Kingston's representation of Chinese culture in *The Woman Warrior*, I do not in the least intend to suggest the value of the book is mitigated because of this. This cross-cultural study is not based on the belief that there is a correlation between literary quality and cultural authenticity.

Kingston's knowledge of China comes from a variety of sources, and is of a mixed nature. Although Chinese by heritage, she first set foot in China in 1982, after the publication of *The Woman Warrior*. Her immediate experience of Chinese culture before then had been confined to her family and Chinatown. One main source of information for her work is the stories told by her mother and other immigrants. There is an essential difference between the knowledge obtained from personal experience and that from stories that are representations of experience. Furthermore, Kingston does not merely retell her mother's stories about China. Her work registers her personal critical responses to those stories, and these responses are derived straight from her Western background.

There exists a huge body of work about China by Western writers, which constitutes a Western discourse of China. As Edward Said points out in his *Orientalism*, Western representation of the Orient is rooted in and controlled by Western ideologies and values. It is less about the Orient than a reflection of the West itself. What is true of the concept of Orientalism as a whole is also applicable to the Western image of China in particular. Graduating from Berkeley with a master's degree, Kingston is well educated in Western tradition. She received excellent training in philosophy, history, and especially literature. She is, therefore, well acquainted with the Western representation of China, which has found its way into many parts of her work. Julia Lee observes, "Kingston certainly invokes Chinese myths and histories in her writing frequently ... But it seems safe to say that Kingston's explicit literary influences have been from the world of Anglo-American letters" (Lee 2018, 13).

Kingston's education equipped her with a remarkably rich Western narrative convention. By employing this convention in treating her subject matter, she inevitably let it shape her materials and determine, to a great extent, the outcome of her work. The following examples are aimed at showing how Western discourse of China and Western literary tradition come into play in Kingston's representation of Chinese culture in *The Woman Warrior*.

'No Name Woman' is a story of a Chinese woman who is not tolerated in society because she has a baby out of wedlock. Through the story, Kingston presents a most powerful critique of Chinese culture in the aspect of the oppression of women. While the criticism itself is totally justified, what is interesting here is the way in which it is made.

Kingston heard the story from her mother, who told Kingston that she has an aunt who is not to be mentioned or remembered because she is considered a disgrace to the family. That is why the aunt does not have a name. Kingston felt the urge to uncover the life of this "no name woman" – a symbol of the fate of all Chinese women, and since the story she heard from her mother was too simple, she had to fill the gaps with invented details from her imagination. There is a scene that describes how the villagers raided the house of the aunt's family the day she gave birth to the baby.

The attack took place at night. The whole village was out, coming from all directions. The villagers destroyed the crops, threw eggs at the house, slaughtered livestock, broke down the door, smashed furniture, surrounded her family members and cursed them, and took away their food, clothes, and other possessions.

For readers familiar with Chinese literature, several details will appear quite alien. First of all, a scene of this nature is usually set during the day. Since adultery is regarded as a serious and unforgivable wrongdoing in traditional Chinese society, people do not have to wait for the night to come out and attack the offenders. They need not hide their identities, since there is no risk of them being punished by law. Furthermore, the acts of the villagers – killing domestic animals, destroying crops, and throwing eggs – are not familiar images to Chinese readers. Finally, there is the description of some villagers wearing white masks during the raid. Besides being an unnecessary precaution for the occasion, the color of their masks is somewhat unusual. In Chinese literature, there are, to be sure, examples of mask wearing, often by knights-errant or robbers. The color of the masks is normally black rather than white, because they serve to hide not only the characters' faces but also their movements.

The image of a gang of attackers wearing white masks is quite familiar, however, in Western literature and modern media. What immediately comes to mind is a classic scene of Ku Klux Klan members dressed all in white, raiding a black family's home. If we replace the lanterns in the Chinese villagers' hands with torches, the similarity between the two scenes becomes even more striking.

The above example shows that in representing Chinese people and culture, Kingston borrows, consciously or unconsciously, from the Western literary tradition with which she is well acquainted. Considering Kingston's source of knowledge and literary training, as discussed previously, it is not surprising that there is a lot of resemblance in the images of China between *The Woman Warrior* and other Western literary works. The scene in which the "crazy" woman is stoned by the villagers does not have its origin in Chinese literature, yet for Western readers, it is a well-known convention of punishment for women who commit adultery. In another place, Kingston mentions the story about her grandfather who was "crazy ever since the little Jap bayoneted him in the head." "He used to put his naked penis on the dinner table, laughing." (Kingston 1976, 10–11). Such an image is unknown in Chinese literature, and is quite alien to Chinese readers' sensibilities, although it may not strike American readers as foreign or strange.

In addition to specific details and images in Kingston's stories, the influence of Western discourse can be seen on a higher level in subject matter and narrative tactics. Among other things, China has long been an exotic country to many Americans. The idea that Chinese people eat mice, snakes, dogs, and monkeys is widespread in America. Besides the fact that these stereotypes show that the Chinese have peculiar eating habits and tastes, they sometimes indicate different attitudes that the Chinese have toward animals, and even the cruelty in such customs. A story Kingston's mother tells at the dinner table is that when Chinese people have money, they have a monkey feast. People sit around a table with a monkey chained in the hole in the middle. They will kill the animal by cutting and taking off the lid of its skull, and eat its brain alive, laughing at monkey's screams and the faces it makes (Kingston 1976, 91–92). If this custom exists at all, it is very rare, because the practice of eating a monkey live is just as alien to Chinese readers as to Americans. From the literary point of view, there is nothing wrong in selecting this subject matter. Kingston herself has made it clear that her works are intended to be neither ethnically authentic nor factually true. There is no denying, nevertheless, that this story appeals to an interest in the exotic China. It also serves as part of the powerful critique of Chinese culture that Kingston constructs in her book. Like the rest of the critique, this story reflects a view affected by the Western discourse about China. The scene under consideration clearly violates American sensibility towards animals then and now. Whether the author intends it or not, American readers cannot help but feel the cruelty of the situation, which confirms the conventional message conveyed in the tales that the Chinese eat dogs, mice, and snakes.

Of the many aspects about Chinese society, its treatment of women draws particularly severe criticism in the West. The injustice done to Chinese women as symbolized by the notorious practice of foot-binding rightfully stirs indignation and horror in Western readers. There is a well-established discourse in Western literature about China when it comes to describing the inequality and oppression suffered by women. Not surprisingly, such critique constitutes a major voice in *The Woman Warrior*.

The author makes her interest clear in the first paragraph, where she provides an account of her aunt committing suicide and the male members of the family refusing to acknowledge that she had ever been born (Kingston 1976, 3). The aunt's sin is that she had an adulterous relationship and conceived an illegitimate child. With the raid staged on the day she gives birth, the aunt brings disgrace to the whole family and death to herself and the baby, whereas the male adulterer is never identified and gets away unpunished. To emphasize the gender inequality in dealing with adulterers in China, Kingston imagines that the man involved with her aunt could be one of the masked raiders (Kingston 1976, 6).

Polygamy is another aspect of traditional Chinese society that draws frequent attention in the West. Like foot-binding, it is considered a disgrace that Chinese men could have several wives who were forced to compete with each other for their husband's favor. Kingston is well aware of the Western criticism of Chinese polygamy, and lends her voice to the critique. "Whenever my parents said 'home,'" writes Kingston in *The Woman Warrior*, "they suspended America. They suspended enjoyment, but I did not want to go to China. In China my parents would sell my sisters and me. My father would marry two or three more wives, who would spatter cooking oil on our bare toes and lie that we were crying for naughtiness" (Kingston 1976, 99). It is not clear if this is a statement from Kingston as a little girl or Kingston as a Chinese American writer. What is certain is that the fear of, and the outcry against, the great injustice derived from Chinese polygamy is not the result of Kingston's upbringing at home. Her critique of polygamy could only develop outside her family environment, where she was exposed to American culture and values. Her realization of the injustice, and the moral outrage thereof, originated from this exposure.

Quoting Susanne Mayer, June Ock Yum, Francis Hsu, and Kingston herself, Sämi Ludwig points out the traces of American individualism in the way the unnamed aunt's story is narrated. Ludwig finds that the account proceeds from the outside to the inside. Kingston first mentions Chinese social conditions to suggest that the aunt, who did not have the right to choose her man, was coerced into the adultery. Kingston then describes the aunt from the inside, revealing her aspiration for independence. Kingston writes, "She often worked at herself in the mirror . . . At the mirror my aunt combed individuality into her bob" (Kingston 1976, 9). For Ludwig, this "use of the MIRROR indicates that the no name aunt tries to be self-sufficient, to rely only on herself for the image of herself, and, moreover, to shape that image actively" (Ludwig 1996, 64). The aunt's individualism lies in the fact that she does not conform to the socially accepted pattern for a woman to have a sexual relationship with a man (Ludwig 1996, 63–4).

The subject of sex is a taboo in China, while it is talked about more freely and openly in America. Chinese people's unwillingness to mention sex sometimes suggests, to some Western readers, a degree of ignorance, close-mindedness, hypocrisy, and backwardness. It is in this light that the stigma surrounding sex in Chinese culture is brought up in *The Woman Warrior*. When Kingston was a little girl, she noticed that in her family and the Chinese community "No one talked sex, ever "(Kingston 1976, 7). Later on, after her mother told her not to mention the unnamed aunt's name, Kingston relates, "I have believed that sex was unspeakable and words so strong and fathers so frail that 'aunt' would do my father mysterious harm" (Kingston 1976, 15).

Ludwig argues that the attitude toward sex described in these passages is inconsistent with the traditional Chinese view. To support his point, he cites Francis Hsu's comparative study of pornography, which insists that "few Chinese would have any qualms about privately viewing the frankest pictures together with their husbands, wives, sweethearts or prostitutes. To the average American, with his puritan background, such behavior would at least result in a guilty conscience, if not the fear and the probability of social ostracism" (Ludwig 1996, 65). Ludwig does not mean to suggest that Kingston misrepresents Chinese culture. Instead he understands the meaning of sex in Kingston's book not as confined to physical intimacy but also as "a metaphor of the general issue of ATTRACTION." Ludwig, therefore, concludes that "To Maxine, the example of the aunt seems to be the best way to explain the nature of sex, not primarily because of the physical rape but because of the dimension of cognitive desire involved in the aunt's encounter with Otherness, the most powerful image of which is the OTHER SEX" (Ludwig 1996, 65–6).

The role and status of sex in traditional Chinese culture is a very complicated subject, and as far as Hsu's and Ludwig's discussions are concerned, there are at least four points to be noted:

1) The Chinese open-mindedness toward sex is recorded mainly in traditional fiction and does not exist in other genres of literature, such as poetry, history, and essays.

2) In comparison with the other genres, fiction developed much later in China, and was regarded as a marginal form of writing all the way up to the end of the pre-modern period. It is well documented that the majority of the elite literati class along with the authorities considered fiction inferior to poetry, history, and essays. They accused fiction of promoting pornography, among many other things (Shi 2002, chaps. 5 & 6).

3) Confucianism was the dominant ideological and cultural discourse in traditional China, and its suppression of sexual relationships constituted an important aspect of that discourse. The view that Hsu and Ludwig present is derived from a Daoist perspective that considers sex a natural behavior. Being incompatible with Confucianism on this issue, in pre-modern China this strand of Daoism did not have official support, and was a suppressed voice.

4) After the end of the Qing Dynasty, the Chinese attitude toward sex found in tradition fiction was not carried over into the modern period. The way sexual relationships are treated in modern China is by and large in line with Confucianism as described by Kingston, namely, that sex is unspeakable.

In light of these facts, Kingston's representation of the Chinese attitude toward sex is not, as Ludwig suggests in his book, inconsistent with Chinese tradition. Kingston's American sensibility does not lie in her account of China's reality but in her criticism of the Chinese view. The reluctance to talk about sex in public has prevailed in modern China up to the present day, long after Confucianist values were rejected. The majority of the Chinese population are still shy from saying the word "sex" in public. Kingston's criticism reflects an awareness that connects the Chinese silence on the subject of sex with the patriarchal effort to suppress women's sex – a view framed within the paradigm of Western feminism.

In Kingston's complex work, women are not presented as just victims, but warriors as well. Like Ludwig, Yan Gao sees the spirit of American individualism in Kingston's narrative of the "No Name Woman." After noting that "Kingston's perspective runs flatly counter to her mother's point of view as well as to the Chinese cultural norm," Yan Gao describes the origin of the aunt's adultery as "both her love of beauty and her own desire." She proceeds to argue that what Kingston does is no less than proposing "a new model of heroic woman" defined by American individualism. "It would have taken," says Yan Gao, "tremendous courage for a young woman in an old Chinese village in the early twentieth century to revolt against convention and community. No Name Woman, in this view, is a rebel, a personified challenge to her village whose attention to her looks is totally alien to its moral culture" (Gao 1996, 29). If Yan Gao is right, the aunt's heroism, then, is the result of Kingston's reinventing the meaning of her mother's story. As the reader, we only hear her mother's stories from the author, and through retelling, Kingston modifies and appropriates these stories before she presents them to us.

Sidonie Smith points to the same cultural appropriation when she remarks, "Yet while Kingston repeats her mother's words, she does so with a critical difference. Unlike her mother, she engenders a story for her aunt, fleshing out the narrative and incorporating the subjectivity previously denied that woman. Individualizing her mother's cautionary and impersonal tale, she transforms in the process both her aunt's text and her aunt's body from a maxim (a mere vessel to hold patriarchal signifiers) into a 'life.' Moreover, she ensures that she herself becomes more than a mere vessel preserving her mother's maxims, however deeply they may be embedded in her consciousness" (Smith 1987, 155). It is the process Smith describes that adds a new cultural meaning in the image of No Name Woman, turning her from being a mere victim of gender injustice into a heroine as well.

While the theme of establishing women as warriors runs throughout *The Woman Warrior*, Kingston turns its narrative into a celebration of Chinese heroines with the story of Fa Mulan. Traditionally Fa Mulan's heroism is defined in terms of the Confucianist virtue of filial piety. It is her determination to spare her aged father from the trial and danger of war more than her military feats that is emphasized in Chinese culture. Instead of being seen as an act of transgression, Fa Mulan's cross-dressing is interpreted as self-sacrifice of feminine comfort to take on the hardship of the male world.

Kingston redefined Fa Mulan entirely. Not only did she drastically rewrite the storyline by adding a great deal of details drawn from other classical tales, but she also projected many new qualities into Fa Mulan. Kingston allows her warrior to go through a series of experiences, and in doing so Fa Mulan is able to play all the roles traditionally assigned to male heroes, fulfilling men's obligations toward both family and country. Moreover, Fa Mulan has the privilege of being loved by her parents and husband. Kingston makes it clear in her work that there is no parental and conjugal love toward female members of Chinese society. It is significant, therefore, for Kingston to let Fa Mulan have this love.

By enjoying all the male privileges, Kingston's woman warrior erases the gender difference and subverts the conventional power structure. Many critics have pointed out that it is hard to separate Fa Mulan from Kingston. The woman warrior functions as the narrator's persona. Smith sees that Kingston's identification with Fa Mulan "enables her to escape confinement in conventional female scripts and to enter the realm of heroic masculine pursuits – of education, adventure, public accomplishment, and fame" (Smith 1987, 157). Smith continues to observe that "[i]ronically, however, Kingston's mythical autobiography betrays the ontological bases on which that love, power, and compliance with perfect filiality rest" (Smith 1987, 157). Underlying Fa Mulan's image is Kingston's postmodernist consciousness that keeps deconstructing the traditional values until the traditional Chinese woman warrior becomes a modern Western heroine.

ENDNOTES

[1] For a summary of these views, see Sämi Ludwig, *Concrete Language: Intercultural Communication in Maxine Hong Kingston's The Woman Warrior and Ishmael Reed's Mumbo Jumbo*, Chapter 3.1; Yan Gao, *The Art of Parody: Maxine Hong Kingston's Use of Chinese Sources*, Introduction.

[2] See note 1.

REFERENCES

Fonseca, J. Anthony. (2005). "Maxine Hong Kingston," in *Dictionary of Literary Biography: Asian American Writers*, ed. Deborah L. Madsen. Farmington Hills: Thompson Gale, pp. 163–180.

Gao, Yan. (1996). *The Art of Parody: Maxine Hong Kingston's Use of Chinese Sources*. New York: Peter Lang.

Grice, Helena. (2006). *Maxine Hong Kingston*. New York: Manchester University Press.

Kingston, Maxine Hong. (1990). *Tripmaster Monkey: His Fake Book*. New York: Vintage International.

Kingston, Maxine Hong. (1980). *China Men*. New York: Knopf.

Kingston, Maxine Hong. (1976). *The Woman Warrior: Memoirs of a Girlhood among Ghosts*. New York: Alfred A. Knopf.

Lee, H. Julia. *Understanding Maxine Hong Kingston*. South Carolina: University of South Carolina Press, 2018.

Ludwig, Sämi. *Concrete Language: Intercultural Communication in Maxine Hong Kingston's The Woman Warrior and Ishmael Reed's Mumbo Jumbo*. New York: Peter Lang, 1996.

Said, W. Edward. (1978). *Orientalism*. New York: Vintage Books.

Shi, Liang. (2002). *Reconstructing the Historical Discourse of Traditional Chinese Fiction*. New York: Edwin Mellen Press.

Smith, Sidonie. (1987). *A Poetics of Women's Autobiography, Marginality and the Fiction of Self- Representation*. Bloomington: Indiana University Press.

Wong, Sau-ling Cynthia, ed. (1999). *Maxine Hong Kingston's The Woman Warrior: A Casebook*. New York: Oxford University Press.

AUTHOR'S BIO

LIANG SHI is a Professor of Chinese at Miami University. His research interests cover classical Chinese thought, cross-cultural studies, Chinese fiction, and contemporary Chinese cinema. His publications include *Mirror Rubbing, Lala and Les: Chinese Lesbian Cinema, Reconstructing the Historical Discourse of Traditional Chinese Fiction*, and multiple articles.

4 A Study of Chinese Cultural Memories in Chinese American Literature[1]

Ping Yi, Chengdu University of Traditional Chinese Medicine

ABSTRACT

Ethnic literature has attracted increasing attention in literary circles, including Chinese American literature. Chinese history and culture are constantly deconstructed and reconstructed in the writings of Chinese American writers. Their works reflect the lives of Chinese Americans and their descendants against the background of mainstream American culture while retaining an indelible mark of Chinese culture. These Chinese cultural memories have a great impact on the values, ideas, and world outlook of Chinese immigrants. This paper studies Chinese cultural memories in Chinese American literature through close reading of the text.

KEYWORDS

Chinese American literature; Confucian ideology; Chinese cultural memory; New Historicism; the third space; the theory of Yin and Yang

INTRODUCTION

Chinese American writing dates back more than 100 years, having originated in the middle of the 19th century. In it, traditional Chinese culture and folk customs are constantly translated, deconstructed, and reconstructed, making Chinese American literature a unique cross-cultural form that prospered in the middle of the 20th century. A large number of Chinese-American literary texts have been recognized and published by mainstream American publishing houses. Meanwhile, the literary works of Chinese American writers such as Jade Snow Wong, Maxine Hong Kingston, Frank Chin, Amy Tan, and Gish Jen have had extraordinary repercussions in American society and won various honors in American literary circles. Consequently, an increasing number of American universities have set up centers for studying Chinese literature, and Chinese American texts have also entered classrooms in the United States, becoming required reading at American colleges and high schools. Chinese American writers create their works in English, depicting their life in the United States, but their works are distinguished by Chinese folklore and legends, Chinese cuisine, the effects of traditional Chinese medicine, the theory of Yin and Yang, and the five elements.

TRADITIONAL CHINESE FOLKLORE IN THE WOMAN WARRIOR

The New Historicism theory of literary criticism "rejects both traditional historicism's marginalization of literature and New Criticism's enshrinement of the literary text in a timeless dimension beyond history" (Tyson 2006, 291). In his article "Professing the Renaissance: The Poetics and Politics of Culture," Montrose defines New Historicism "as a reciprocal concern with the historicity of texts and the textuality of history" (Montrose 1989, 20), and re-figures the relationship between verbal and social formations "between the text and the world" (Montrose 1989, 23). As for "the textuality of history," Montrose endows two layers of meaning:

> Firstly, that we can have no access to a full and authentic past, a lived material existence, unmediated by the survival of textual traces of the society in question – traces whose survival we cannot assume to be merely contingent but must rather presume to be at least partially consequent upon complex and subtle social processes of preservation and effacement; and secondly, that those textual traces are themselves subject to subsequent textual mediations when they are construed as the "documents" upon which historians ground their own texts, called "histories." (Montrose 1989, 20)

Most Chinese American writers ironically apply traditional Chinese folklore, mythology, folk customs, and family stories. *Donald Duk* by Frank Chin, *The Woman Warrior: Memoirs of a Girlhood among Ghosts* and *China Men* by Maxine Hong Kingston are full of heroes and historical legends from ancient China.

In the second part of *The Woman Warrior*, "The White Tigers," Kingston rewrites the story of Fa Mulan. In Chinese history, the story of Fa Mulan stems from a poem "The Ballad of Mulan," which emerged in the period of the Northern and Southern Dynasties (420–589 CE), and was modified by poets during the Sui Dynasty and Tang Dynasty. In "The Ballad of Mulan," Fa Mulan replaces her father in the army, because he was too old and her brother was too young. The story reflects the Confucian value of filial piety. However, in *The Woman Warrior*, after hearing her mother telling the story of Fa Mulan, the narrator is so impressed and fascinated by the great myth of the heroine that she dreams: "when I grow up, I will be a woman hero like Fa Mulan" (Kingston 1976, 17) and that she will take back their lost laundries in New York and California. In this way, Chinese filial piety is transformed into American individualism, feminism, and entrepreneurial spirit. Besides the story of Fa Mulan, Kingston adds another historical story – that of Yue Fei, a national hero who defended against enemy invasion in the Southern Song Dynasty. His mother tattooed the words "faithful service for the country" on his back as a sign of his ambition to defend his country. Fa Mulan and Yue Fei originally belong to different dynasties, but Kingston empowers the heroine in *The Woman Warrior* with masculine strength from Yue Fei to state that a woman can undertake the same duty as a man.

In the fifth part of *The Woman Warrior*, "A Song for a Barbarian Reed Pipe," a talented poetess Ts'ai Yen is rewritten by Kingston. Ts'ai Yen, known as Cai Wenji by Chinese readers, lived during the Eastern Han Dynasty and the Three Kingdoms Period. During the war at the end of the Han Dynasty, she was kidnapped by the Huns and taken away to the North when she was only 23 years old. She was forced to marry the chieftain, and gave birth to two sons. She did not return to the Han territory until Cao Cao came to ransom her twelve years later. On her return, she recorded her story in a long autobiographical poem called "Hujia Shibapai," which Kingston translates as "Eighteen Stanzas for a Barbarian Reed Pipe" in *The Woman Warrior*. Kingston rewrites the story of Cai Wenji by imagining her singing songs in the desert, ending her story with a nostalgic note of living in an alien land, away from home. It was not easy for Cai Wenji to adjust to life in the North. In addition to the difference in lifestyles and diets, there were also language obstacles and culture shock. For example, when Cai Wenji first heard the Hun flutes, she did not understand their music, and thought of it only as a barbarous art, until she was able to appreciate its plaintive beauty. She then created her own song that matched the tone of the flutes in the desert night. The episode suggests that she began to find the balance between different cultures. The cultural position of Cai Wenji mirrors that of Kingston, who entered mainstream American literary circles by writing an Americanized story with Chinese sources. It is an allegory that embodies the meaning of cultural interaction and multiculturalism. It also expresses Kingston's wish to cross the boundary between two races and two cultures, and to create a synthesis between white American culture and Chinese culture.

Regarding the Chinese culture and traditions in *The Woman Warrior*, especially, the rewritten story of Fa Mulan, a number of male Chinese American writers, such as Frank Chin, Benjamin Tang, and Paul Chan, did not approve, and defined Kingston as "a contemporary representative of a 'fake' Chinese-American tradition-misogynist, eroticized, and inauthentic" (Wong 1996, 51). In *The Big Aiiieeeee: An Anthology of Chinese and Japanese American Literature*, Frank Chin leveled the pointed criticism that Kingston was perpetuating the stereotype of a misogynistic and exotic Chinese society catering to Western readers. According to Chin, Kingston "rewrites the heroine, Fa Mu Lan, to the specs of the stereotype of the Chinese woman as a pathological white supremacist victimized and trapped in a hideous Chinese civilization" (Chin 1991, 37). Frank Chin also criticized the image of Fa Mulan in *The Woman Warrior*: "It is an imagination informed only by the stereotype communicated to her through the Christian Chinese American autobiography" (Chin 1991, 46).

The dispute between Maxine Hong Kingston and Frank Chin actually revolves around the reconstruction and rewriting of traditional Chinese folklore and legends, and unconscious or deliberate cultural misreading. American critic Harold Bloom first proposed the concept of misreading in his book *The Anxiety of Influence*, pointing out that it can be "creative revision" (Bloom 1980, 4). Gideon Toury explained misreading as "a kind of activity which inevitably involves at least two languages and two cultural traditions" (Toury 1995, 200). In 1982, in her essay "Cultural Mis-readings by American Reviewers," Kingston disparaged her critics for imposing on her the task of representing a so-called "authentic" Chinese, with standards set by other Chinese-American authors. Kingston retorted, "why must I 'represent' anyone besides myself?" (Kingston 1982, 59) As a standard ABC (American-born Chinese), having been educated in the Western system and working in American society, Kingston upheld American values, such as individual equality and freedom. She stressed that her identity is neither Chinese nor white American, but distinctly Chinese American: "I have been thinking that we ought to leave out the hyphen in 'Chinese-American,' because the hyphen gives the words on either side equal weight, as if linking two nouns ... It looks as if a Chinese-American has double citizenship, which is impossible in today's world" (Kingston 1982, 60). She also declared herself to be an American writer: "I am an American. I am an American writer, who, like other American writers, wants to write the great American novel" (Kingston 1982, 57).

WRITING CULTURAL MEMORY: "THIRD SPACE" LANGUAGE IN THE JOY LUCK CLUB

Suffering from the cultural clash between the East and the West and racial discrimination, postcolonial theorist Homi Bhabha put forward the concept of the "third space" and "hybridity." (Bhabha 1996, 38) He stated, "For me the importance of hybridity is not to be able to trace two original moments from which the third emerges, rather hybridity to me is the 'third space', which enables other positions to emerge." (Rutherford 1990, 211) In his view, hybridity provides the "marginalized" culture with the possibility of entering the dominant culture. After that, Hoogvelt defined hybridity as "celebrated and privileged as a kind of superior cultural intelligence owing to the advantage of in-betweens, the straddling of two cultures and the consequent ability to negotiate the difference." (Hoogvelt 1997, 158) As a result, we can say that the "third space" is an expression of cultural intermingling, which mixes the characteristics of two cultures.

Chinese American literature exemplifies the features of the "third space." Most parents of Chinese American writers are first-generation Chinese immigrants. Chinese is their main language in daily life. However, the mainstream American education that Chinese American writers received in their childhood allows them to write in English. The bilingual influence means that their English texts are often mixed with Chinese *pinyin*.

Since different languages express different cultural information and represent different cultural identities, language is an insurmountable barrier between first-generation Chinese immigrants and second-generation ABC. Coming to the United States as adults, the mothers in *The Joy Luck Club* grew up with Mandarin Chinese as their native language, and English as foreign. They emigrated at the cost of giving up their mother tongue, which makes them lose not only their connection with the language but also with the culture it carries. Their poor English indicates not only their difficulty learning a foreign language, but also their resistance to American culture represented by English. As soon as they arrived in the United States, they were deprived of many rights. They were detained in an immigration office for three weeks, and even had to "hide those shiny clothes" (Tan 1989, 6). One "wore the same brown-checked Chinese dress until the Refugee Welcome Society gave her two-hand-me-down dresses, all too large in sizes for American women" (Tan 1989, 6). In their view, using English instead of Chinese would completely isolate them from their native culture, so the mothers speak Chinese at home and tell stories in it in to preserve the memories of their native culture. The mothers attach the utmost importance to the Joy Luck Club each week. On that occasion, they dress up in traditional Chinese dresses with stiff stand-up collars and blooming branches of embroidered silk sewn over their breasts (Tan 1989, 16). They eat delicious Chinese food, such as a "steaming pot of wonton," "a large platter of *chaswei*, sweet barbecued pork cut into coin-sized slices," and "finger goodies – thin-skinned pastries filled with chopped pork, beef, shrimp, and unknown stuffings" (Tan 1989, 20). They also enjoy playing Chinese *mah jongg*. Most importantly, they have someone to talk to, listen to, and even to vent their frustrations in their own unique language – half in their own dialects, the other half in Chinese English. This unique *pidgin* English reflects the mothers' confusion about their own identity, and is also a strategy to preserve the memory of the motherland and their native culture.

In *The Joy Luck Club*, the mothers hide their pasts from their daughters, They are reluctant to share their painful histories with them, because many of the stories are humiliating and agonizing. For example, Ying-ying could not bear to think of the time when she was abandoned by her husband during her pregnancy, and the time when she killed her baby out of anger. Out of guilt and sorrow, Suyuan Woo found it difficult to tell her daughter how she had deserted her twin daughters during the war. In addition to the unspoken pain and secrets between mothers and daughters, there is an irreparable gap between the daughters of American-born Chinese and their mothers in the language they use in their daily life. For the mothers, the special *pidgin* English with Chinese is a manifestation of adaptation to a foreign culture as much as a proof of self-existence. The daughters were raised and educated in the United States, and they speak fluent American English. Although the daughters can understand some Chinese, they are impatient with their mother's half-English-half-Chinese language. What their mothers have done with this special language makes the daughters feel strange and even embarrassed. The different languages used by the mothers and daughters result in different values. Language hinders understanding and exacerbates the conflict between them. Because of the language barrier and cultural conflicts, it is hard for mothers to pass on their beliefs and values to their daughters. The character Jing-mei points out on more than one occasion that she cannot communicate with her mother in the same language. Jing-mei speaks to her mother in English, while her mother answers in Chinese. On account of the language barrier, the "daughters grow impatient when their mothers talk in Chinese, who think they are stupid when they explain things in fractured English" (Tan 1989, 31).

With unique "the third space" language and storytelling techniques, Amy Tan makes the mothers in *The Joy Luck Club* into preservers of ancient Chinese myths, folklore, family history, and traditional culture. Moreover, history and memories can be reconstructed through the narration of the mothers. Just as Bhabha states, "the hybridity subverts the binary opposition between the self and the other, between the inside and the outside" (Bhabha 2004, 156). In his view, hybridity provides the "marginalized" culture of Chinese Americans with the possibility of entering mainstream American culture. It also endows the daughters with a cultural heritage to pass on.

THE REAPPEARANCE OF CONFUCIANISM: THE THEORY OF YIN AND YANG IN TYPICAL AMERICAN

A system of ethical regulation, Confucian ideology has played a dominant role in traditional Chinese culture since the 14th century. To a large extent, traditional Chinese culture is based on a value system crystallized in Confucian ideology, which regulates moral and ethical principles and the relationships between individuals and groups. It emphasizes family, groups, national unity, and harmony. In its turn, Confucian ideology has impacted the values, morals, and world outlook of Chinese immigrants.

In Chinese tradition, there is no doubt that a son's success brings not only fame to his family but also glory to his ancestors. In *Typical American*, Ralph – the only son of the Changs – was constantly reminded that it was his duty to honor his family and ancestors after completing his studies. On his way to the United States, he set two goals for himself: "he was going to be first in his class, and he was not going home until he had his doctorate rolled up to hand his father" (Jen 1991, 5). Therefore, when Ralph obtains his doctoral degree after a great deal of hardship, he is so excited that he cannot help crying with joy. At the graduation ceremony, he says, "I just hope my father, mother, could be here … They would have been so proud!" (Jen 1991, 119) Ralph wants his parents to witness the solemn moment when their son fulfils his promise of bringing honor to the family, and to share the joy of success with him. When he returns home, his wife Helen hangs his diploma in the living room, near their wedding portrait and the photograph of him with his parents and sister – a vivid representation of the concept of honor and disgrace deeply influenced by Confucianism.

The theory of Yin and Yang has an even more profound influence on *Typical American*. The theory first appeared in the *Book of Changes*, showing the binary opposition of things. At the same time, Yin and Yang are combined with eight objects in nature to form the Eight Diagrams. In the *Dao De Jing*, Lao Zi states that Yin and Yang are the attributes of all things in the universe. Yin is female, and is dark and tangible; Yang is male, and is light and intangible. Everything is a balance between the two, which was reflected in the characterization of Ralph's sister, Theresa. To begin with, Jen gives Theresa Yang physical attributes that are not common for Chinese people, such as a long, chiseled face, a big mouth, a full face of freckles, a head of brown hair. "Her father had insisted on giving the children cow's milk, with the result that Theresa turned out a giantess – five seven!" (Jen 1991, 47) She has an English name, plays baseball, and strolls when she walks, sometimes even with her hands in her pockets like boys. Educated at a conventional school and influenced by Western culture, Theresa upholds the values of independence and achieving success on her own. With her efforts and diligence, Theresa is accepted into an American medical school, and becomes a doctor. In order to succeed in her career, she works so hard that she spends almost all her time at the hospital. "How long her training had gone on already; when would there be an end to it? Days at a time, she was gone, and when she returned she sometimes went straight to bed without washing her face or brushing her teeth" (Jen 1991, 139). In fact, she turns out to be Ralph's savior several times, and the Changs' guardian angel. The first time is when Ralph becomes "unidentified" due to visa problems shortly after arriving in the United States, and decides to commit suicide. Theresa manages to find her troubled brother in the park. She encourages him to complete his masters and doctoral studies, and get tenure at the university. The second time is when Ralph mortgages his house in the suburbs. Theresa not only takes out all her savings, but also works a part-time job in the clinic at the expense of her vacation to earn money for him. The final time is when Ralph's Chicken Palace fails, and his wife Helen has an affair with his friend Grover. In traditional Chinese culture, the unity of the family is highly valued. "She was in many ways Americanized, but in this march, wasn't this what she'd longed for? Reunification, that Chinese ideal, she could not eat an orange without reciting to herself, as she did at New Year's, *quan jia tuan yuan* – the whole family together" (Jen 1991, 265).

On the other hand, Theresa also embodies Yin attributes. She yearns for love, and longs to have her own family and children. Her beautiful dress and girlish charm on blind date bring out her femininity. She would rather bear name-calling and being spurned by the Chinese community than having things made difficult for her loved ones. Born into an intellectual Chinese family with an enlightened father and a virtuous mother, Theresa had a happy childhood and a good education. Under the influence of Confucianism, she embodies the traditional virtue of benevolence, a strong sense of responsibility and accountability for family, and a spirit of self-sacrifice. Witnessing Ralph's depression triggered by her excellence, Theresa lies and says that her scholarship has been canceled in order to appease his sense of superiority. She embodies Confucian feminine virtues in which women have to follow "Three Obediences and Four Virtues," and to obey the men in the family. Believing that Ralph's success can bring glory to the Chang family as he is the only son, Theresa endeavors to help him succeed. For example, she introduces him to her friend Helen, who becomes his wife. Later, she does all of the housework and takes care of the baby so that Ralph can concentrate on his studies. She also unwittingly becomes the lover of Ralph's boss, Old Chao, so that Ralph can obtain tenure at the university.

Yin and Yang are not in complete opposition to each other. As in a *tai chi* diagram, there is Yang in Yin and Yin in Yang. They are mutually dependent. The combination of the two in Theresa makes her a representation of traditional Chinese culture as well as Western female independence. She is androgynous, with an independent personality and traditional Chinese feminine virtues. She embodies the best combination of Chinese and American cultures. Gish Jen once said in an interview, "I didn't write about identity, for I was a bicultural person, and I understood that I have been blessed with a lens through which I can look at the world" (Carole 2004, 43).

CONCLUSION

Facing two different cultures, Chinese American writers certainly have double cultural identities and visions. It is obvious that Chinese American writers are different from native Chinese writers and also different from white American writers in their cultural perspectives. In their writing, Chinese cultural memory is constantly translated, deconstructed, and reconstructed, which is not only a highlight of their work, but also an enrichment of world literature. Through the rewriting of cultural memory, Chinese American writers rediscover themselves and reconstruct their personal identities. This transformation of Chinese cultural memories allows Chinese American writers to "cross the barriers of ethnic minorities and make their works accepted by American society" (Zhang 1999, 17), as well as enhancing the diversity of American literature.

ENDNOTES

[1] This research was supported by Center for American Studies at Southwest Jiaotong University (No. ARC 2020008)

REFERENCES

Bhabha, K. Homi. (1996). Cultures in Between. *Questions of Cultural Identity*. ed. S. Hall and Du Gay. London: Sage Publications.

Bhabha, K. Homi. (2004). *The Location of Culture*. London: Routledge.

Bloom, Harold. (1980). *The Anxiety of Influence*. London: Oxford University Press.

Carole, Burns. (2004) Off the Page: Gish Jen. *Washington Post*, 11 (1), 40–45.

Chin, Frank et al, eds. (1991). *The Big Aiiieeeee: An Anthology of Chinese and Japanese American Literature*. New York: Meridian1.

Hoogvelt, A. (1997). *Globalization and the Postcolonial World: The New Political Economy of Development*. Baltimore: John Hopkins University Press.

Jen, Gish. (1991). *Typical American*. Boston: Houghton Mifflin/Seymour Lawrence.

Kingston, Maxine Hong. (1976). *The Woman Warrior: Memoirs of a Girlhood Among Ghosts*. New York: Random House.

Kingston, Maxine Hong. (1982). Cultural Mis-Readings by American Reviewers. *Asian and American Writers in Dialogue: New Cultural Identities*. ed. Guy Amirthanayagam. London: Macmillan.

Montrose, Louis A. (1989). Professing the Renaissance: The Poetics and Politics of Culture. T*he New Historicism*. ed. Harold Aram Veeser. New York: Routledge.

Rutherford, J. ed. (1990). *Identity: Community, Culture, Difference*. London: Lawrence and Wishart.

Tan, Amy. (1989). *The Joy Luck Club*. New York: Ballantine Books.

Toury, Gideon. (1995). *Descriptive Translation Studies and beyond*. Philadelphia: John Benjamins Publishing Company.

Tyson, Lois. (2006). *Critical Theory Today: A User-Friendly Guide*. New York: Routledge.

Wong, Sau Ling Cynthia. (1996). *Chinese American Literature*. New York: Cambridge University Press.

Zhang, Ziqing. (1999). Chinese American Literature Coexistence and Prosperity with Asian American Literature (General Preface). Gish, Ren. *Typical American*.

AUTHOR'S BIO

PING YI is a Professor at the College of Foreign Languages at Chengdu University of Traditional Chinese Medicine. She holds a Doctoral Degree in English Language and Literature from Sichuan University. Her research interests include American literature and culture, Traditional Chinese Medicine culture, and English teaching. Her published works include *Imagination and Representation: Chinese Traditional Culture in American Chinese Literature* (2017, Chengdu: Sichuan University Press), A *Multi-Perspective Interpretation of 20*[th]*-century Theory of Novels and Literary Classics* (2017, Chengdu: Sichuan University Press) and *The Study of Cultural Identity: Multi-dimensional Construction and Writings* (2019, Chengdu: Sichuan University Press).

5 On American Sinologist James Evert Bosson's Medio-translation in China

Xin Huang, Southwest Jiaotong University

ABSTRACT

Overseas Sinology, including overseas Tibetology and Mongology, is a mirror of Chinese culture, so medio-translation research within overseas Sinology can reflect on itself from the perspective of others, and is also a form of cultural feedback. James Evert Bosson (1933–2016) was an American Sinologist whose outstanding contribution mainly focused on Tibetology and Mongology. Bosson's research has cross-border significance, but the study of his medio-translation and his research in China has been marginal and even neglected. This article examines the forms of Bosson's medio-translation and his influences in China, and proposes that his Mongology and Tibetology were a product of his adaptation to the social and historical context of the United States, and to the characteristics of American Sinology in the middle and late 20th century.

KEYWORDS

James Bosson, Medio-translation, American Sinologist

INTRODUCTION

According to his obituary by the East Asian Research Center at the University of California, Berkeley, James Evert Bosson (1933–2016) was an American Sinologist whose contribution mainly focused on Mongology and Tibetology, and who had an important impact on the study of New Qing History in the United States. Bosson's achievements in Mongology are mainly concentrated in several groundbreaking works: *A Buriat Reader* (1962), *Modern Mongolian: A Primer and Reader* (1964), *Highlights of the Manchu-Mongolian Collections* (2003), and *Mongolia: The Legacy of Chinggis Khan* (1995), coauthored with Patricia Ann Berger, Terese Tse Bartholomew, and Heather Stoddard. Due to Bosson's outstanding achievements in Mongology in the United States, the Mongolian People's Republic awarded him the 'Order of the Polar Star' in 2014. His outstanding contribution to Tibetology mainly focuses on an examination of the fragments of the Tibetan classic *Sakya Gnomic Verses*, and a translation of the Mongolian *Sakya Gnomic Verses* into English. However, there is no systematical medio-translation research on Bosson and his contribution in China, which is out of proportion to his outstanding contribution to Mongology and Tibetology, and his translation of *Sakya Gnomic Verses*. For this reason, this article probes Bosson's medio-translation and his research in China.

I. The Medio-translation of Bosson's Research on Tibetology in China

In his early years, Bosson studied under the Tibetan scholar Turrell Wylie (1927–1984). In 1963, he joined the University of California, Berkeley to teach Mongolian, Manchu, and Tibetan. He also studied and translated many Mongolian, Tibetan, and Manchu texts, and many modern and contemporary linguists in these fields have learned from him. Bosson's outstanding contribution to Tibetology is reflected in his English translation and research on *Sakya Gnomic Verses* – a famous Tibetan classic by Kunga Gyaltsen (1182–1251). Bosson gives his English version the title of *A Treasury of Aphoristic Jewels: The Subhsitarstnanidhi of Sa Skya Pandita in Tibetan and Mongolian* (hereinafter referred to as *A Treasury of Aphoristic Jewels*), which was published by Indiana University Publications in 1969. (Huang 2020a, 337–338) Bosson's Tibetology is valuable in both translation studies and Tibetology, and deserves systematic study. The research on Bosson's medio-translation is found in monographs, translations, textbooks, and academic papers (including master's and doctoral papers and conference articles).

A. Medio-translation by monographs, translations, and textbooks

Chinese scholars such as Wang Hongyin (2016), Li Zhengshuan (2016), Wang Zhiguo (2016), Otogon (2010), Chen Qingying (1997), and Chen Xiaoqiang (1993) have all medio-translated Bosson's English version of *A Treasury of Aphoristic Jewels* in their monographs, textbooks, or translations.

1. According to the available literature, the earliest medio-translation of Bosson and his research on Tibetology was performed in 1993 by Chen Xiaoqiang – an expert on ethnic history, who introduced the Czech Sinologist and Tibetologist Joseph Kolmash (1933–) to Chinese scholars. Chen Xiaoqiang records Bosson in the postscript of the Chinese version of *The Spirit and Wisdom of Life: A Tibetan Lama*. The medio-translation by Chen is as follows:

   Original note: The quotations of the poems in the text are all from Bosson' s translation of *A Treasury of Aphoristic Jewels*, Indiana University, Bloomington, 1969 (Uralic and Altaic Series, V. 92). (Chen 1993, 319)

   At the same time, Chen's translation makes a brief review of other versions of *Sakya Gnomic Verses*. It also points out that the version by Bosson is a complete translation – 457 stanzas in total.

2. In the third chapter of the monograph *A Survey of Translation of the Chinese Ethnic Classics: Efforts Towards Anthropologic Poetics of Translation (Part One)*, Wang Hongyin (1953–2019), a professor from Nankai University, not only explains the basic content of Bosson's *A Treasury of Aphoristic Jewels*, but also emphasizes that Bosson's version is edited in Mongolian-English and Tibetan-English respectively. Wang Hongyin (2016) observes that Bosson's version is indeed a commentary translation and prose translation, and that Bosson's purpose is to "probe into the problems of how to translate between Tibetan, Mongolian and English." In the medio-translation, Wang Hongyin makes the following comments on Bosson's prose translation:

   Because it is a prose translation, the translator does not need to consider the rhyme and rhythm, and can also choose the words with philosophical and psychological connotations, so the translation reflects a more profound and accurate philosophy ... In the comment process, the translator adds some analogies appropriately in the version, a kind of combination of Chinese and Indian philosophy that embodies the complete oriental wisdom, thus he enriches the quality of the poems of *Sakya Gnomic Verses*. (Wang 2016, 154)

Similar to Wang Hongyin's comments on Bosson's translation, scholars such as Huang Xin (1978–) and Yan Xiaoying (1979–) hold that "in Bosson's version the cultural connotations are reproduced completely and the origin relationship between Tibetan Buddhism in China and Indian Buddhism is reflected in an implicit way." (Huang & Yan 2018, 156) Since this medio-translation by Wang in 2016, Bosson's prose-translation of gnomic verses has been discussed in detail and accepted by most Chinese scholars interested in the translation of Chinese ethnic classics. From the perspective of Chinese culture, the medio-translation of Bosson's version of *A Treasury of Aphoristic Jewels* asserts that Tibetan Buddhism in China is a localized Buddhism with Chinese characteristics. Such cultural feedback brought by the medio-translation of the overseas Sinologists and Tibetologists resonates with the fact that medio-translation is also a kind of cultural exchange and mutual learning, like Bosson's version about Tibetan Buddhism.

3. Li Zhengshuan (1963–) and his team are the main force in medio-translation of Bosson and his English version of *A Treasury of Aphoristic Jewels*. The first section of Chapter 5 in their *A Concise Course Book on Classic Translation into English* is about the English translation of Tibetan gnomic verses, in which Bosson was mentioned at the beginning. (Li & Wang 2016) The 178-page textbook was published for English majors by Shanghai Jiaotong University Press in 2016. Although the content about Bosson is rather brief, the wide audience of the textbook indirectly exerts a radiation effect of Bosson and his research in China through such medio-translation. In addition, when Li Zhengshuan combs the English versions of *Sakya Gnomic Verses,* he has medio-translated Bosson in the preface of his own translation, which was published as *Tibetan Gnomic Verses Translated into English* by Changchun press in 2013. Since 2013, the medio-translation of Bosson and his English version of *A Treasury of Aphoristic Jewels* has increased sharply, which will be discussed later.

4. Wang Zhiguo (1975–) medio-translates the publication information of Bosson's *A Treasury of Aphoristic Jewels* when he comments on Li Zhengshuan's English version of *Sakya Gnomic Verses* published in 2013. But unfortunately there are no more comments about Bosson and his translation in Wang Zhiguo's introduction. Nevertheless, he comments on the versions of Tibetan gnomic verses, saying that "the English translations (including Bosson's) of Tibetan gnomic verses open up a multi-dimensional translation space of ethnic literature from ethnic culture to literary texts, and then to world literature, thus making it possible for ethnic culture to enter the hall of world literature." (Wang 2016, pp. 107, 112) This brief comment is in line with Wang Hongyin's purpose for translating Chinese ethnic classics – to move ethnic literature and culture from the edge to the center, so that the whole world can understand, recognize, and accept them.

5. Although Otogon's monograph *Research on Mongolian Literature Unearthed in the Northern District of Mogao Grottoes in Dunhuang* focuses on textual research on the newly unearthed Mongolian documents in the northern district of the Mogao Grottoes in Dunhuang, Otogon (2010) repeatedly quotes Bosson's translation of *A Treasury of Aphoristic Jewels* in his book's appendix when he discusses the fragments of a printed sutra in Mongolian of Phagspa script in the Mogao grottoes, and includes a 10-pages an appendix about Bosson's version.

The medio-translation of Bosson's version in the fifth chapter, *The Fragments of Printed Sutra of Sakya Mottoes in Mongolian Quadratic Script Unearthed in the Northern Section of Mogao Grotto* mainly involves the fragment-research of Bosson's *A Treasury of Aphoristic Jewels*. Here is an example to illustrate that Otogon's view quotes from Bosson's version:

Fragment TIII D322: D1 clearly shows the page numbers 10 and 11 respectively. This fragment shows that each folio contains twenty lines, and with three lines per stanza this allows six and two-thirds stanzas on each side. By comparing the fragments with the MS published by Ligeti one can approximately reconstruct the length of the Phagspa edition. From this one can calculate the length of the entire book to have been approximately seventy folios. (Otogon 2010, 123–124)

In order to facilitate the readers to trace the source and obtain more information from it, Otogon also "links" one complete endnote to each quotation in his medio-translation. The endnote to the quotation above, for example, allows the reader to expand the research of another Bosson paper – *A Rediscovered Xylograph Fragment from the Mongolian Phagspa Version of the Subhāsitaratnanidhi*, issued in Central Asiatic Journal (Volume 6, 1961). It is no exaggeration to say that Otogon's medio-translation successfully establishes the authority of the trilingual Mongolian-Tibetan-English translation of Bosson's *A Treasury of Aphoristic Jewels*, and provides readers with more information, which is beneficial in broadening the horizons of Chinese scholars. Later Zheng Binglin (1956–), a professor of Dunhuangology from Lanzhou University, transcribes Bosson's views into his book *Series of Ethnic History and Culture in Ancient Northern China: Ethnic Studies of Dunhuang* (Zheng 2012). Then, after a second medio-translation by more scholars, Bosson and his research on Tibetology have been widely introduced in China. Thus, his academic influence also becomes cross-border, from translation studies to Tibetology, and then to Dunhuangology.

B. Medio-translation by academic papers

Until May 2020, there were 45 references in total by the CNKI cross-database full text retrieval with "Bosson" and "*Sakya Gnomic Verses*" as keywords, which include five master's dissertations or doctoral theses, and five Chinese conference articles. The literature mentioned above are cited 127 times in total, and downloaded 6,834 times. The following will elaborate on these articles.

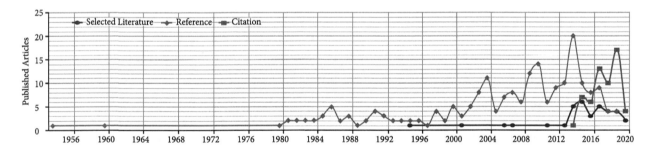

Figure 1: The General Trend of the Medio-translation of Bosson and his English Version in China

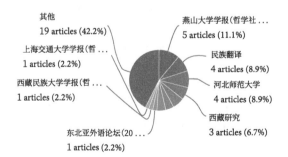

Figure 2: Distribution of Articles by Source

Figure 3: Distribution of Articles by Institution

1. Academic papers studying the medio-translation of Bosson and his research on Tibetology began in 1988. That year, W. Hogjiltu (1949–) medio-translated Bosson in his article of *A Literature Review of Mongolian Quadratic Scripts* in the *Journal of Inner Mongolia University*. However, in this article, Hogjiltu only mentioned that Bosson published his article *A Rediscovered Xylograph Fragment from the Mongolian Phagspa Version of the Subhāṣitaratnanidhi* in Central Asiatic Journal, Vol. 2, 1961. Thus, the time of the medio-translation of Bosson and his research on Tibetology by means of academic papers is slightly earlier than that by monographs mentioned above.

    The medio-translators are divided into two categories, namely scholars in the field of Mongology, and scholars in the field of the translation of Chinese ethnic classics. In 2014, the number of articles in print peaked at about 20 (see Figure 1 for details) because Li Zhengshuan's research team appeared in 2013, and their project *Research on the English Translation of Tibetan Gnomic Verses* (2013) was founded by the Ministry of Education of China.

    The main subjects of medio-translation are gnomic verses. There are 37 articles (about 82.2%) related to Bosson's version of *A Treasury of Aphoristic Jewels*, and the remaining eight articles (about 17.8%) focus on Bosson's research on Mongology. From the source distribution (see Figure 2 for details), we can see that these articles are mainly found in academic journals that have relevant columns such as ethnic research or classics research, such as *Journal of Yanshan University* (five articles), *Journal of Sichuan Minzu College* (three articles), *Minority Translators Journal* (four articles), *Mongology Information* (two articles), *Tibetan Studies* (three articles) and *Journal of Xizang Minzu University* (Philosophy and Social Sciences Edition, one article). In terms of institution distribution (see Figure 3 for details), they are mainly from Hebei Normal University, Sichuan Normal University, Tibet University, and Xizang Minzu University. Among the authors, Li Zhengshuan and his research team published the most papers – 16 articles by Li himself.

    Eleven articles (about 24.4%) are funded by the National Social Science Fund of China (NSSFC) and some other funds, which reflects the achievements of medio-translation of Bosson and his version of *A Treasury of Aphoristic Jewels* in China, and also speaks to the fact that China has promoted the development of medio-translation and related research through its favorable policies and financial support.

2. Among the translation studies of ethnic Chinese classics, Li Zhengshuan and his research team for *Sakya Gnomic Verses* are major force who medio-translate Bosson's research and translation in Tibetology. More than 20 of the 37 articles on translation studies of Chinese ethnic classics came from this team. Among them, three team members should be highlighted, who have medio-translated Bosson or Bosson's version of *A Treasury of Aphoristic Jewels* in their master's dissertations or doctoral theses. They are *A Translation Report to Ordinary Wisdom from the Principle of Faithfulness and Equivalence*, *A Comparative Study of Three English Versions of Sakya Gnomic Verses: From the Perspective of Functional Equivalence Theory*, and *A Study of Translation of Sakya Gnomic Verses*, (Zhao 2015; Geng 2016; Wang 2015) However, among the 37 papers, only Wang Miqing (2015) and Huang Xin (2018, 2020b) have medio-translated Bosson and his version of *A Treasury of Aphoristic Jewels* in great detail, while others only briefly introduced the translation history of Tibetan gnomic verses, or provided literature reviews of the translation of *Sakya Gnomic Verses*. As can be seen, the medio-translation of Bosson and his research on Tibetology is still in a relatively "marginal" position.

3. The first Chinese scholar to medio-translate Bosson's English version of *A Treasury of Aphoristic Jewels* in a doctoral thesis is Wang Miqing (1967–). In her thesis, *A Study of Translation of Sakya Gnomic Verses*

(2015), Wang introduced Bosson's translation of *A Treasury of Aphoristic Jewels* in two subsections of about 22 pages. Her medio-translation covers five aspects, namely the overview of the translation, translator profile, translation background, translation purpose, and translation strategy. Wang Miqing (2015) believes that Bosson aimed to "explore the language conversion," and that his translation style is a "prose-translation." In addition, a young scholar Huang Xin has published two academic articles in the journal *Tibetan Studies* utilizing communication theory and translation theory, discussing how Bosson handles the cultural-loaded words and his translator subjectivity respectively. The conclusions from the two articles by Huang Xin (2018; 2020b) are:

a. Bosson chooses the Mongolian *Sakya Gnomic Verses* to translate due to its archaeological value.
b. Bosson is very different from literary translators, and his version indirectly shows the academic tradition of American Sinology (or Chinese Studies), paying attention to the current situation and solving practical problems. The so-called "Chinese Culture Vogue" from the 1950s to the 1970s in the United States and the prevalence of Tibetology and Mongolology called for the translation and dissemination of Chinese culture, Tibetan Buddhism in particular.
c. The translation strategy – "literal translation" or foreignization adopted by Bosson when he deals with the cultural-loaded words means that the version involves a purely linguistic translation method.

Thus, we can summarize that Wang Miqing and Huang Xin's medio-translation greatly promoted the dissemination of Bosson and his translation of *A Treasury of Aphoristic Jewels* in China.

II. Medio-translation of Bosson's Research on Mongology in China

As mentioned in the introduction to this article, Bosson was an expert in Mongology and a member of the Executive Committee of the International Mongolian Society. In his early years, he studied under Nicolas Poppe (1897–1991), an American scholar of the Mongolian language. Bosson's achievements in the field of Mongology are manifested in several books: *A Buriat Reader* (1962), *Modern Mongolian: A Primer and Reader* (1964), *Highlights of the Manchu-Mongolian Collections* (2003), and *Mongolia: The Legacy of Chinggis Khan* (1995). He also edited *The Mongolia Society Bulletin* (1965–1967), the journal of the Mongolian Society. In 2014, he was awarded the 'Order of the Polar Star' for his contribution to Mongology in the United States. It should be emphasized here that all of this information about Bosson comes directly from Sinological materials in the United States, rather than the medio-translation in China. From this we can conclude that the medio-translation of Bosson and his Mongology in China still lags behind and is in a marginal position.

A. Medio-translation by monographs, translations, and textbooks

Shi Yun (1980), Zhou Jianqi (2004), Qiao Ji (2011), Shen Weirong and Hou Haoran (2016), and the Institute of Ethnology and Anthropology of CASS (1988) mention Bosson's Mongology in their books. However, except for the relatively detailed medio-translation by Shi Yun and Zhou Jianqi, others are only brief introductions. For example, in their book *Text and History: The Making of Tibetan Buddhist Historical Narratives and Construction of Sino-Tibetan Buddhist Studie*s, Shen Weirong and Hou Haoran only mention that Professor Bosson had studied the fragments of the Phagspa scripts in his version of *A Treasury of Aphoristic Jewels* (Shen & Hou 2016). Qiao Ji (1941–) in his book *The Whole History of Mongolian: Religious* mentioned that "Bosson's study of *Die Mongolica der Berliner Turfansammlung* is almost perfect" (Qiao 2011). Another example is that *Mongolian Literature Directory* (second volume) compiled by the Institute of Ethnology and

Anthropology in 1988 only mentions the paper *Some Notes on the Dialect of the Khorchin Mongols* coauthored by Bosson and B. Unensechen (1916–). The following is some medio-translation:

1. As early as August 1980, the *Introduction to the Mongolia Society* was translated and collected by Shi Yun (1924–1994), an ethnic historian. He recorded that Bosson was one of the first 60 members when the Mongolia Society was founded in 1961, and in the membership list Bosson is included as "James E. Bosson, Ankara, Turkey" (Shi 1980). From Shi Yun's translation, we can also surmise that Bosson was elected as a director by the Second General Membership Meeting of the Mongolia Society in 1965, and the Third General Membership Meeting in 1967. Bosson was also an editor of the journal of *The Mongolia Society Bulletin* from 1965 to 1967 (Shi 1980). The medio-translation by Shi Yun is very influential in Mongology because it is consistent with that of the Obituary for Bosson issued by East Asia Research Center at the University of California, Berkeley in 2016 (Mongolia Initiative 2018; Huang 2020a).

2. In 2004, Zhou Jianqi (1927–2011), an Mongology expert, translated and published the *Introduction to Altaic Linguistics* written by Nicolas Poppe (1897–1991), a famous American scholar of the Mongolian language, and also a teacher of Bosson. In his translation, Zhou mentioned Bosson and his research on Mongology several times, such as on page 14, 15, and 17 of the index. When Zhou medio-translated Bosson's Mongology, he commented:

About the study of Buriat, Khorchin, Khalkha and other Mongolian dialects, the readers are advised to expand their reading of Bosson's *A Buriat Reader (1962)*, prepared as a companion volume to Poppe's *Buriat Grammar*. According to Bosson, a student, after having learned the thirty lessons in *Modern Mongolian: A Primer and Reader* (1964), will be able to read anything coming from the Mongolian People's Republic; And *Some Notes on the Dialect of the Khorchin Mongols* (1962) is indexed in *Uralic and Altaic Series*, Bloomington, Indiana. (Zhou 2004)

It can be concluded that Bosson's academic influence on Mongology began with the help of his tutor Nicolas Poppe, and was then spread in different languages by translators in China and abroad. For Chinese scholars interested in Mongolian dialects, this end-around or indirect method not only helps them study Mongolian, including its dialects, but also promotes the spread of Bosson's research on Mongology in China. Therefore, this medio-translation can be seen as the cultural feedback that is needed in the development of traditional Chinese culture. Of course, cultural feedback can also be called converse-socialization. It is an inevitable phenomenon in the social transformation period, and a basic condition for a nation or society to move forward, too. Thus, in a transitional period, the medio-translation of Bosson's research on Mongology by Zhou is also a phenomenon of cultural feedback from overseas Sinologists, Tibetologists, and Mongologists.

B. Medio-translation in academic papers

Based on the available documents, we find that most of the medio-translation of Bosson's Mongology in China has the following characteristics:

1. Literature sources are mainly academic journals sponsored by universities or the Federations of Social Science Associations in Northwestern areas or Chinese border areas, such as the *Journal of Inner Mongolia University for Nationalities*, *Journal of Donghua University*, *Mongology Information* and *Journal of the Western Mongology*, and *Journal of Lanzhou University*. The institutions for medio-

translation are mainly universities or research institutes with Mongology departments, among which Inner Mongolia University, Lanzhou University, and Inner Mongolia Normal University are the most prominent.

2. The earliest medio-translated papers appeared in Taiwan in 1984. Taiwan's International Conference on Chinese Frontiers called Bosson a "Mongolian scholar" when he attended, and published the meeting minutes in *Bulletin of the Institute of China Border Area Studies*, No. 15, in 1984. In 1985, this conference information was reprinted on the Mainland by *Materials and Information for Mongology*, No. Z1. In the reprinted material, the information that "Bosson J. E., Professor of Oriental Languages at the University of California, Berkeley, and director of the University of California, Sweden (Mongology) … has submitted a research paper on Mongology entitled *Some Early Swedish Contributions to China Border Area Studies* (English manuscript)" is medio-translated again (Xin 1985).

3. The themes of medio-translation mainly focus on three aspects: fragments of Mongolian of Phagspa script, the interpretation and transliteration of specific Mongolian words in the Middle Ages, and information about Mongology in the United States. For example, Siqin Chaoketu (1986) believes that in Bosson's version of *A Treasury of Aphoristic Jewels* published in 1969 there exist some mistakes with the Latin transliteration of adverbs in classical Mongolian literature. Scholars such as W. Hogjiltu (1988), Otogon (2007), and Qiao Ji (2011) mention Bosson in their literature reviews of the Mongol language in square (Phagspa) scripts, or their research on Mongolian literature. In the overview of Mongology in the United States, most Chinese scholars, including Bai Mengxuan (1998), medio-translate Bosson as "a first-class Mongolian linguist, an excellent scholar trained by the Mongolian Research Center of the University of Washington … Bosson himself has trained many excellent Mongolian students, such as Jan Olaff Swantesson (1944–), a linguist and Mongolian scientist of Lund University in Sweden" (Bai 1998). However, regrettably, Bai does not medio-translate Bosson's research on Mongology in her paper.

4. There is no special or systematic medio-translation of Bosson's Mongology in China. In addition to medio-translation comprising only a few words and phrases, like those mentioned above, Bosson and his research achievements are given mostly as the "other" identity or in attachments, meaning that the medio-translation is marginalized. For example, When Jia Jianfei (2009) mentioned Professor Mark C. Elliott, a leading figure in the study of New Qing history in the United States, he gave only a one-sentence introduction to Bosson: "Bosson is a teacher of Mark C. Elliott." Another example is Dr. Li Ruohong (2003), vice president of the Harvard-Yenching Institute, USA. When she medio-translated E. Gene Smith, an expert in Tibetan literature in the United States, she mentioned Bosson in an annotation as "one of the most outstanding inner-Asian linguists," and "a classmate of E. Gene Smith" (Li 2003, 97).

III. Reflection on the Medio-translation of Bosson and his Research in China

A. Slow Movement to the Center

Although there are a few Chinese scholars who have medio-translated Bosson from the perspective of Manchu and Chinese borderland studies – for example, Liu Yanchen (2007) briefly mentioned that Bosson was engaged in the teaching of Manchu, especially his research on Manchu "Gacuha"[1] – Altanochir (2014), a researcher from the Chinese Frontier Research Institute of CASS, quoted Bosson's point of view five times in order to prove the authenticity of the records related to Johann Christophe Schnitzker's escort of the Tulichen Mission in the Qing Dynasty in his analysis of Sino-Russian relations in the 18th century.

However, compared with the medio-translation of overseas Sinology, Chinese scholars' medio-translation of Bosson and his English version of *A Treasury of Aphoristic Jewels* lag behind, and has marginal status. In 1965, Bosson completed the Tibetan-Mongolian-English translation of the *Sakya Gnomic Verses* in his doctoral thesis. In 1969, it was published as a monograph by Indiana University. In China, Shi Yun (1980) began the medio-translation in his monograph in 1980, and Li Zhengshuan's research team appeared in 2013, thus the medio-translation lags far behind in both time and richness of content. In another example, the study of the English translation of Tibetan Gnomic verses began in the 1830s, and *Sakya Gnomic Verses* appeared in English in 1833.[2] In the 1960s and 1970s, the "Chinese Culture Vogue" (especially Tibetan Buddhism) in the United States further promoted the translation and dissemination of Tibetan gnomic verses there (Li & Zhao 2019).

Moreover, we may conclude that it was a long time before Bosson and his English version of *A Treasury of Aphoristic Jewels* began to receive a little attention in China, if we judge from the history of the medio-translation of *Sakya Gnomic Verses*. The first English translation by Alexander Csoma de Kőrős appeared in 1833, Bosson in 1965, Tarthang Tulku in 1977, John T. Davenport in 2000, and Li Zhengshuan in 2013. The formation of a research team for the translation of *Sakya Gnomic Verses* in China was established in 2013, and then all versions (including Bosson's *A Treasury of Aphoristic Jewels*) were medio-translated. Finally, increasing numbers of scholars joined the translation of Chinese ethnic classics and the study of Sinology overseas. The scholars engaged in medio-translation include classic translators with foreign language backgrounds, and Tibetan or Mongolian scholars with ethnological research backgrounds. Although there is a tendency for slow movement to the "center," Bosson in medio-translation is just a "professor of Mongolian language and literature" or "an English translator of *Sakya Gnomic Verses*." Therefore, there is still a great space for Chinese scholars to medio-translate Bosson and his research.

B. Self-reflection on adapting to the times

In comparison, the medio-translation of Bosson's research on Tibetology, represented by his *A Treasury of Aphoristic Jewels*, eventually achieved something more than his research on Mongology. This may be due to China's policy in the new era – strengthening translation and research into the translation of Chinese ethnic classics to spread national culture. In recent years, the medio-translation of Chinese ethnic literature and culture has attracted increasing attention, forming a medio-translation model of moving from the "edge" to the "center." Overseas Tibetology and Mongology are all mirrors of traditional culture, through which we can perform better self-reflection. The medio-translation of overseas Sinology is a phenomenon of academic exchange and mutual learning between China and Western countries, as well as a form of cultural feedback.

With the powerful support of national policies and funds, the research on ethnic literature and culture has shown a diversified trend, and the translation and research of Chinese ethnic classics have begun to bear fruit. In 2010, the National Social Science Fund of China launched the 'Chinese Academic Translation Project', some ethnic classics such as *Sakya Gnomic Verses* (*Sajiageyan,* 萨迦格言), *Manas Epic* (*Manasi,* 玛纳斯), *Brotuo Epic* (*Buluotuoshishi,* 布洛陀史诗), *Gesar* (格萨尔), *A General History of Tibetan Medicine* (*Zangyiyaotongshi,* 藏医药通史) and *The Secret History of the Mongols* (*Menggumishi,* 蒙古秘史) have begun to receive attention from academia, and the number of provincial and national-level projects related to the translation of Chinese ethnic classics is increasing year by year. All of this has boosted the medio-translation of Bosson and his research in China.

As another example, Dunhuangology is a key discipline at Lanzhou University, whose Master Degree program and Doctoral program were established in 1983 and 1998 respectively. It has cooperated with the Institute of Chinese Culture of the University of Michigan for talent cultivation and academic research. Therefore, it is natural that Bosson – as a well-known Mongolian scholar from the University of California, Berkeley – will be medio-translated or introduced into China. Thus, it is evident that the preferential policies and financial support of the state have promoted the development of the translation of classics and the medio-translation and research of overseas Tibetology and Mongology. Research in this field can be regarded as a response of Chinese scholars to the cultural imperative of adapting to the times. Medio-translation research in overseas Tibetology and Mongology is similar to the study of other fields in Sinology: they can all self-reflect from the perspective of others. It is one of the ways of modernization for Chinese civilization, by jumping out of one's own cultural circle: medio-translating overseas Tibetology and Mongology to domestic readers, and reflecting on oneself through the contrast between the "edge" and the "center," or through their interactive and changing relations.

C. Understanding the motivation from the center

Bosson devoted himself to Tibetology and Mongology, and achieved so many remarkable achievements that he was awarded the 'Order of the Polar Star' by the Mongolian People's Republic in 2014, and he was gradually medio-translated into China. To some extent, what Bosson did also reflects his adaptation to the context of American society and history, and the theme of the times. In turn, his adaptation is similar to the cultural mission of the Chinese translation circle. The reasons why the rapid development of Oriental Studies in the United States became the "center" can be divided according to internal and external perspectives, which are as follows.

The internal factors include two aspects: firstly, after the accumulation of research by a large number of Orientalists before the Second World War, Oriental Studies in some American universities, such as John Kings University and Harvard University, began to develop greatly, which laid a solid foundation for those research institutions to become the center of Oriental Studies (Wu 2017). Secondly, after the attack on Pearl Harbor in the Second World War, the US authorities began to realize that they did not place enough emphasis on Oriental Studies, so they began to pay more attention to it, and adopted many measures to promote it, including congressional legislation,[3] the establishment of a coordination mechanism, and raising fiscal expenditure. All of these things created favorable conditions for Oriental Studies, including Mongolology and Tibetology. As a consequence, after the Second World War, American Oriental Studies developed very rapidly, and the "academic environment and technical conditions for scientific research were very rich" (Deliger & Chen 2004, 242). For example, Columbia University, Indiana University, University of California, University of Washington, and various scientific research institutions established a considerable number of research centers and sub-institutions. As far as Mongology in the United States is concerned, "some academic research methods, development programs and research scopes are ahead of the world's Mongolian academic community" (ibid). It was during the Second World War, when he was in high school, that Bosson became familiar with the Mongolian textbooks published by Swedish missionary to Mongolia Folke Boberg (1896–1987), and as a result he became interested in Mongology. Under the guidance of Hugh Nibley (1910–2005), he obtained a bachelor's degree from Brigham Young University in 1954, and was then admitted to the University of Washington as a graduate student in Far Eastern Languages and Literature, where he studied with the Mongolian linguist Nicolas Poppe (Mongolia Initiative 2018; Huang 2020a).

The external factors for America to become once the center of Mongolian study are: after the Second World War, a group of Oriental scholars moved to the United States, including Mongolian scholar Nicolas Poppe and Belgian missionary Mostaert Antoine (1881–1971). Nicolas Poppe carried out research at Washington State University as the leader of Mongology. Mostaert Antoine entered Harvard University and collaborated with Francis Woodman Cleaves (1919–1995), who promoted the university's Mongolian and Oriental Studies departments. Coincidentally, Bosson was a postgraduate majoring in Far Eastern Languages and Literature at the University of Washington, and Nicolas Poppe was his teacher during that time. In addition, the Rockefeller Foundation in the United States funded the establishment of nine Tibetology research centers in the United States and Europe. Thubten Jigme Norbu (1922–2008), a living Buddha of the Gelug Sect, moved to Bloomington, Indiana in 1965 and became a professor of Tibetology at Indiana University, where he began to train Tibetan scholars. He mentored prominent Tibetologists such as Christopher Beckwith (1945–) and Elliot Sperling (1951–), making Bloomington an important Tibetology center in the central United States. In 1969, Tarthang Tulku (1934–) established the Tibetan Nyingma Meditation Center at the University of California, Berkeley, which helped to introduce Tibetan tradition and Buddhism to the international community. All of these things inevitably had an impact on Bosson's academic research. In addition, between 1961 and 1963, Bosson also studied the Altaic language in depth in Turkey, funded by Fulbright, which laid the foundation for him to move into Mongology and Tibetology.

CONCLUSION

J. E. Bosson made outstanding achievements in Tibetology and Mongology, but compared with other overseas Sinologists, the medio-translation of his work and research in China is quite scant and marginalized. In the current upsurge of overseas Sinology or Chinese Studies, we must explore the beginning and end of the interactive transformation of the "center" and the "edge," and recognize the complex relationship between overseas Sinology and the reconstruction of Chinese academic culture (Zhang 2010). Bosson's dedication to Mongology and Tibetology reflects his adaptation of the original Tibetan classics to the social and historical context of the United States and the spirit of the era. The medio-translation of Bosson and his contribution, in return, reflects Chinese scholars' adaption to the new era. Overseas Sinology, including the medio-translation of Bosson, as further cultural feedback, can be used to enhance the enunciative power of China's academic study, and to reduce aphasia in some research fields. For most overseas Sinologists, including overseas Tibetologists and Mongolists, although ethnic literature and culture can only "acculturate" them rather than "sinicize" them, Chinese ethnic literature and culture can at least become the objects to which they pay attention in the "center" or "edge" of their research. What they have done will more or less promote cultural exchange between China and their own countries. This kind of bridging function can be seen as "borrowing the sail to cross the sea" for the spread of Chinese culture all over the world.

FUNDING

This research was financially supported by the National Social Science Fund of China (Project No. 17XYY018) and by the Center for American Studies at Southwest Jiaotong University (Project No. ARC2020004).

AVAILABILITY OF DATA AND MATERIALS

The data generated or analyzed to support the findings of the literature statistics with cross-language search in section two is openly available on CNKI. All other data that supports this study has been clearly cited, and is included in the published articles or books in the References section.

ENDNOTES

[1]   A tool often made from the knuckles of sheep, pigs, deer, and cattle, and used by women and children of the Mongolian, Manchu, and other ethnic groups.

² The first English version of *Sakya Gnomic Verses* was by Alexander Csoma de Kőrős (1784–1842) – a Hungarian Tibetologist – in 1833. The translation is called *A Brief Notice of the Subhashita Ratna Nidhi of Saskya Pandita*, which is derived from the Tibetan version of *Sakya Gnomic Verses*.

³ *The National Defence Education Act* was passed by the US Congress in 1958, which included Tibetan language studies. The University of Washington also set up the Tibet Studies program, which was co-chaired by Bosson's teacher, Nicolas Poppe, and Chinese-American scholar Fang-kuei Li (1902–1987).

REFERENCES

Altanochir. (2014). "The Swede Johann Christophe Schnitzke and his Account on the Mission of Tulichen. *Borderland Studies of China*, 2 (00), 297–310.

Bai, M. X. (1998). A Brief Introduction to Jan Olaff Swantesson, a Swedish Linguist. *Mongolian Studies Information*, 17 (04), 62. doi:CNKI:SUN:MGXX.0.1998-04-012.

Bosson, J. E. (1969). *A Treasury of Aphoristic Jewels: the Subhsitarstnanidhi of Sa Skya Pandita in Tibetan and Mongolian*. Bloomington: Indiana University Publications.

Chen, X. Q. (1993). The Spirit and Wisdom of Life: a Tibetan Lama. In School of Tibetology of Minzu University of China (Ed.). *Tibetan studies*. Beijing: China Minzu University Press.

Deliger & Chen, Y. M. (2004). Mongolian studies in the United States. In Baolige (Ed.). *Mongolian studies yearbook*. Hohhot: Inner Mongolia Academy of Social Science.

Geng, L. J. (2016). *A comparative study of three English versions of Sakya Gnomic Verses: From the perspective of functional equivalence theory*. Shijiazhuang: Hebei Normal University.

Huang, X. & Yan, X. Y. (2018). A comparative study of English versions of *Sakya Gnomic Verses*: On the translation of culture-loaded words from the communication perspective. *Tibetan Studies*, 169 (03), 152–160. doi:CNKI:SUN:XZYJ.0.2018-03-019

Huang, X. (2020a). James Evert Bosson (1933–2016). *Central Asiatic Journal*, 63 (01–02), 337–338. https://doi.org/10.13173/centasiaj.63.1-2.0337.

Huang, X. (2020b). The subjectivity of translator in Tibetan classic: *Sakya Gnomic Verses. Tibetan Studies*, 171 (02), 79–86. doi:CNKI: SUN:XZYJ.0.2020-01-010.

Jia, J. F. (2009). An interview with Mark C. Elliott on Qing history. *International Social Science Journal (Chinese Edition)*, 26 (2), 62–67. doi:CNKI:SUN:GJSK.0.2009-02-020.

Li, R. H. (2003). An introduction to American Tibetologist: Kim Smith and his new book. *China Tibetology*, 16 (2), 97–100. doi:CNKI:SUN:CTRC.0.2003-02-012.

Li, Z. S. & Wang Y. (2016). *A Concise Course Book on Classic Translation into English*. Shanghai: Shanghai Jiaotong University Press.

Li, Z. S. & Zhao C. L. (2019). The Promotion Effect of Translating Tibetan Gnomic Verses on Constructing Tibetan Economy and Culture in Different Periods. *Journal of Xizang Minzu University*, 40 (2), 70-76+156. doi:CNKI:SUN:XZMZ.0.2019-02-01.

Liu, Y. C. (2007). Teaching and Research of Manchu History in American Universities: A Case Study of Harvard University. *Manchu Minority Research*, 23 (01), 49–53. doi:CNKI:SUN:MZYY.0.2007-01-010.

Mongolia I. (2018). James E. Bosson (1933–2016). *Journal of Central Asiatic Journal*. 61 (1), 191–192. https://doi.org/10.13173/centasiaj.61.1.0191

Otogon. (2007). Fragments of Sakya mottoes in Mongolian Quadratic Script Unearthed in the Northern Section of Mogao Grotto. *China Tibetology*, 20 (04), 58–68. doi:CNKI:SUN:CTRC.0.2007-04-008.

Otogon. (2010). *Research on Mongolian Literature Unearthed in the Northern District of Mogao Grottoes in Dunhuang*. Beijing: The Ethnic Publishing House.

Qiao, J. (2011). *The Whole History of Mongolian: Religious*. Hohhot: Inner Mongolia University Press.

Shen, W. R. & Hou, H. R. (2016). *Text and History: the Making of Tibetan Buddhism historical Narratives and Construction of Sino-Tibetan Buddhist Studies*. Beijing: China Tibetology Publishing House.

Shi, Y. (1980). *Introduction to The Mongolia Society*. Hohhot: Chinese Association of Mongolian History.

Siqin, C. K. T. (1986). On the Adverb Iɣ-a in Middle Mongolian. *Minority Languages of China*, 08 (01), 58–63. doi:CNKI:SUN:MZYW.0.1986-01-009.

Hogjiltu, W. (1988). A Research Overview of Mongol Language in Square (Phagspa) Scripts. *Journal of Inner Mongolia University*, (04), 85-92+83. doi:10.13484/j.cnki. ndxbzsb.1988.04.012.

Wang, H. Y. (2016). *A Survey of Translation of the Chinese Ethnic Classics: Efforts Towards Anthropologic Poetics of Translation (part one)*. Dalian: Dalian Maritime University Press.

Wang, M. Q. (2015). *A Study of Translation of Sakya Gnomic Verses*. Shanghai: Shanghai International Studies University.

Wang, Z. G. (2016). *Translation of Tibetan Classics: Internal and External Communications*. Dalian: Dalian Maritime University Press.

Wu, R. H. (2017). Review of American Mongolian studies. In Naranbilig (Ed.). *Mongolian studies yearbook*. Hohhot: Inner Mongolia Academy of Social Science.

Xin, X. (1985). International China Border Academic Conference Held in Taiwan. *Materials and Information for Mongology, 06* (Z1), 118-119+113. doi:CNKI:SUN:MGXX.0.1985-Z1-026.

Zhang, X. (2010). Some Opinions of Chinese Ancient Civilization and Chinese Studies. *Journal of Tsinghua University (Philosophy and Social Sciences)*, 25 (06), 19–21. doi: 10.13613/j.cnki. qhdz.001929.

Zhao, C. L. (2015). *A Translation Report to Ordinary Wisdom from the Principle of Faithfulness and Equivalence*. Shijiazhuang: Hebei Normal University.

Zheng, B. L. (2012). *Series of Ethnic History and Culture in Ancient Northern China: Ethnic Studies of Dunhuang*. Lanzhou: Gansu Ethnic Publishing House.

Zhou, J. Q. (2004). *Introduction to Altaic Linguistics*. Hohhot: Inner Mongolia Education Press.

AUTHOR'S BIO

XIN HUANG is an associate professor, and a supervisor of postgraduates and PhD candidates at Southwest Jiaotong University. He mainly focuses on the translation of ethnic classics and Tibetology. He has presided over five national and provincial research projects, and has published more than 20 academic papers. He won third prize in the '14th Excellent Educational Research Achievements in Sichuan Province'.

6 The Embodiment of Local Culture in Howard Goldblatt's Translation of *Red Sorghum*

Xie Ye, Southwestern University of Finance and Economics

ABSTRACT

Renowned American translator Howard Goldblatt has made a great contribution to the spreading of Chinese literature, especially the work of Mo Yan. Goldblatt's translations have been instrumental in allowing Mo Yan to win the Nobel Prize for Literature. In his translations, Goldblatt makes use of his comprehensive knowledge of Chinese tradition to achieve a balance between smooth reading in the target language and retaining the local color and cultural essence of the original novel. This paper explores how Goldblatt translates local cultural elements and manages culture differences in *Red Sorghum*.

KEYWORDS

Howard Goldblatt; Local culture; *Red Sorghum*

1. INTRODUCTION

The literary achievements of Mo Yan in the Western world rely heavily on his translator, Howard Goldblatt. In Mo's work, there are many local expressions from his hometown and Chinese traditional culture, and the translation of these cultural elements greatly determines whether the English version is a success or not. Even-Zohar (1990, 1–6) suggests that the role that cultural elements play in the translated literature can be either central or peripheral, primary or secondary (Munday 2001, 110). If it is primary, the translator should be concerned more with the linguistic and cultural features of the source text. Whereas if it is secondary, the translator should emphasize the literary conventions and cultural features of the target system (Gentzler 1993, 117). According to this theory, Goldblatt mediates the peculiarity and strangeness of Chinese culture for English readers in his translation with different translation strategies. Through Goldblatt's various translation techniques, the cultural identity and differences in Mo Yan's original work are ingeniously transplanted into the English version. This paper classifies Goldblatt's four translation strategies to reveal how he renders the cultural elements in Mo Yan's original work of *Red Sorghum* in his English version.

2. TRANSLATED VERSIONS OF MO YAN'S WORKS

Translated texts have the potential to enter a literary tradition as cultural intruders – carriers of foreign values infiltrating that cultural system. When a cultural system is mature, self-sufficient, and confident, domesticating translation is often adopted. However, translation is also undertaken for the purpose of bringing about new ideas or changes. When a literary tradition is young, weak, or in a crisis, translated literature may assume a central position, taking part as a cultural tool "in the process of creating new, primary models" (Even-Zohar 1990, 1–6). In such circumstances, foreignizing translation achieves the purpose of renovating an indigenous literature. Therefore, the power relations between different cultures often decide which translation method is used. In the English version of *Red Sorghum*, Goldblatt adopts different translation methods to convey the richness of Chinese culture.

Mo Yan – winner of the 2012 Nobel Prize for Literature, and one of the most prominent contemporary Chinese novelists – has had many of his works translated into other languages around the world. Among them, six have been translated by Howard Goldblatt. A lot of research has been done on the translation of *Red Sorghum*. Hu (2008, 22) studies the cultural misreading in Goldblatt's English translation. Wu Yao and Wu Jianlan (2018, 109–110) have analyzed the translation strategies in *Red Sorghum*, namely, foreignizing and domesticating translation. However, Goldblatt's rendering of local color has not been sufficiently studied, which is the task of this paper.

3. LOCAL COLOR RENDERED IN ENGLISH

All of the following translation samples are selected from the first two parts of the novel *Red Sorghum*, namely 'Red Sorghum' and 'Sorghum Wine'.

3.1 Translations of folk sayings in Northeast Gaomi Township

Folk sayings are expressions of common experiences or observations created by the masses. They are not only linguistic phenomena, but also cultural road marks. As a representative of local literature, *Red Sorghum* is densely scattered with folk sayings. The following are some examples:

1. 奶奶说他见了水比见了亲娘还急:
   Grandma said that the sight of the river excited him more than the sight of his own mother.
2. 心急喝不了热黏粥:
   Greedy eaters never get the hot gruel.
3. 北斗勺子星——北斗主死, 南斗簸箕星——南斗司生, 八角玻璃井——缺了一块砖, 焦灼的牛郎要上吊, 忧愁的织女要跳河 ...:
   The ladle of Ursa Major (signifying death), the basket of Sagittarius (representing life); Octans, the glass well, missing one of its tiles; the anxious Herd Boy (Altair), about to hang himself; the mournful Weaving Girl (Vega), about to drown herself in the river ...
4. 不看僧面看佛面, 不看鱼面看水面, 不看我的面子也要看豆官的面子上, 留下吧 ...:
   If not for the sake of the monk, stay for the Buddha. If not for the sake of the sake of the fish, stay for the water. If not for my sake, stay for little Douguan.
5. 上知天文下知地理:
   They understood the ways of the heavens and the logic of the earth.

6. 杂种出好汉，十个九个都不善:

   Eight or nine out of every ten bastard kids turn out bad . . .

7. 三分像人七分像鬼:

   Three parts human and seven parts demon.

8. 鸡走鸡道，狗走狗道，井水不犯河水:

   Chickens can go their own way, dogs can go theirs. Well water and river water don't mix.

9. 狐狸吃不到葡萄就说葡萄是酸的: . . .

   accusing them of sour grapes.

10. 嫁鸡随鸡嫁狗随狗:

    Marry a chicken and share the coop, marry a dog and share the kennel.

11. 无恩不结夫妻，无仇不结夫妻:

    Man and wife, for better or for worse.

12. 人生一世不过草木一秋:

    Human existence is as brief as the life of autumn grass.

13. 凤凰和谐: Do the phoenix dance;

    鸳鸯凤凰: Share their love like mandarin ducks or Chinese phoenixes

14. 索性一不做二不休: There was no turning back.

    破财消灾: Financial losses, lucky bosses.

15. 说的有鼻子有眼哩: The details were lurid.

16. 茂不茂，吕不吕: That's terrible singing.

17. 积德行善往往不得好死，杀人放火反而升官发财:

    Charity for the sake of karma doesn't mean you'll die in bed; murder and arson are a sure path to the good life.

18. 鲁班门前抡大斧，关爷门前耍大刀，孔夫子门前背'三字经'，李时珍耳边念'药性赋':

    Wield an axe at the door of master carpenter Lu Ban, or wave his sword at the door of the swordsman Lord Guan, or recite the Three Character Classic at the door of the wise Confucius, or whisper the 'Rhapsody on the Nature of Medicine' in the ear of the physician Li Shizhen.

19. 智者千虑，难免一失: Even the wisest man occasionally falls prey.

20. 一盏省油的灯: No economy lantern.

The cultural elements in a text can be translated using either the domesticating or foreignizing method, as famously put forward by Venuti (2010, 811–812). Foreignizing translation means that the translator leaves the author in peace, as much as possible, and moves the reader towards him; in domesticating translation, the translator leaves the reader in peace, as much as possible, and moves the author towards him. These 20 folk sayings are translated in both ways. Among these samples, sentence 1, 2, 3, 4, 8, 12, 13, and 18 retain their local colors in translation in terms of metaphor and phrasing. For example, sentence 8 retains the original folk metaphors of "chicken," "dogs," "well water," and "river" to indicate that people should only care about their own business. Goldblatt can apply foreignizing translation to this sentence because direct word-to-word translation is perfectly comprehensible for the readers. However, for some phrases, whose meanings are obscure in target culture, domesticating translation or the combination of these two kinds of translation is necessary. Sentence 16 is an example. Since 吕 and 茂 refer to two local opera dramas rarely known to foreigners, domesticating translation is adopted to eliminate the strangeness of the original work for target readers.

3.2 Translation of names and appellations

In *Red Sorghum*, people's names take on rich local colors as well. There are many nicknames and curse names such as "鬼子" and "小舅子." Goldblatt translates them as "Japs" and "the prick," which successfully conveys the disdainful attitude of the speakers. The following are examples of translated names:

刘罗汉: Arhat Liu, named after Buddhist saints; 九儿: Little Nine; 大咬人: Man-Biter; 单五猴子: Five Monkeys Shan; 小白羊: Little White Lamb; 曹梦九: Nine Dreams Cao; 曹二鞋底: Shoe Sole Cao the Second

It's obvious that these names retain their local colors in translation, while still being comprehensible to foreign readers. In the case of Arhat, the related provenance is followed. As for Five Monkeys Shan and Little White Lamb, both nicknames retain their animal names, which match the characters' images and reflect their close relationship as a couple.

Apart from names, how people address others of their own choice is also of interest. In the English version, "老伙计" is translated as "foreman," which adds the connotation of "head" or "leader." In this case, the Chinese name itself does not emphasize the leadership status, but the English version takes the context into consideration and translates it as "foreman."

Sometimes, for the sake of comprehensibility, more general honorific appellations are used to signify the social status of the person, instead of using a direct translation of the local-colored form of address. For example, 长官: your honor; 掌柜的: barkeep; 主家: client; 老总: Sir; 青天大老爷: His honor, the upright magistrate!

These translations adapt to Western expressions. In some cases, Chinese tends to use "爹" or "娘" to express begging or ridicule, instead of referring to one's own biological father and mother. This transfer of meaning needs to be embodied in translation, for instance, "亲爹, 别打我了" and "让你娘一顿好打." Here, "爹" and "娘" are ingeniously translated by Goldblatt as master and mistress, which underscores the relationship between the speaker and listener appropriately, and wisely avoids the direct translation of "father" and "mother," which would cause misunderstanding.

3.3 Translation of nouns with local features

In this novel, one of the most impressive translations is "fistcake," which is a new word created by Goldblatt to translate "抃饼." He renders the Chinese "吃大饼时要用双手抃住往嘴里塞, 故曰 '抃饼'" as "since they stuff the rolled flatbreads into their mouths with both fists, they are called 'fistcakes.'" The translated version shifts the focus from the gesture to the fists. Wang believes that the translated version comes into being because the structural part of "抃" is closely connected with fists, which responds to the following contexts of "bandits" and "greenwood hero," who both use fists as weapons to attack others (2013, 275–279).

Among the translations of local-colored objects, "炕" is translated as "kang" rather than "bed" to retain the local flavor. 炕 is a special kind of bed in the northern China, which can be heated during winter. It has no counterpart in the Western world, so the translator adopts the strategy of transliteration to authenticate the local object.

The following are some examples of domestic translation: 大辫子: pigtail; 泥神: clay statues; 糟木头: the stinking blockhead; 纸钱: bank notes; 厢房: side rooms; 臭火: shiny dud; 现大洋: silver dollar. For others, Goldblatt retains the Chinese features as much as possible, but at the same time explains them in translation to make them comprehensible for foreigners, such as: 争窝子: fighting over the nest; 抢支七长八短, 土炮、鸟枪、老汉阳 …: Their motley assortment of weapons included shotguns, fowling pieces, aging Hanyang rifles …; 草鸡: who turns chicken. In the example of Hanyang rifles, the English version explains what Hanyang is by adding that it is a category of gun.

3.4 Other translations

Apart from the categories above, some translated words and phrases are exemplary but hard to classify. They divided into three parts here for analysis: the first part is comprehensive categories; the second part studies the translation of the Chinese word "天"; and the third part discusses the translation of Chinese characters.

1. 你挂彩了: You're wounded; 面无惧色: There was no fear in his eyes; 让你长长眼色: Just giving you a taste; 老子不吃他的: Well, that's not my style; 人生禅机: the mysteries of life; 风平浪静: No wind, no waving motion; 她打的什么谱: Who does she think she is? 你姓甚名谁: What is your name? 偷窥者: peeping Toms; 披麻戴孝: wear mourning clothes; 九流: low-class rowdies; 头头是道: have it all figured out; 千叮咛万嘱咐: had told her; 心跳如鼓: heart was racing; 逢年过节: on all the holidays; 我们那地方的手艺人家: the craftsmen from our neck of the woods; 仙风道骨: in the presence of immortals; 芸芸众生: doomed creatures; 萍翻桨乱: restless and uneasy; 雨打魂幡: set their souls adrift; 花拳绣腿: fists and feet flying; 打瘪了的喇叭: the bend mouth of his trumpet; 青天白日之下: in broad daylight; 恍若隔世: seemed to belong to another world.

   In the above translations, English culture is melded with Chinese tradition, and foreignizing translation that retains the local expression is welded to domesticating translation that explains the connotation for comprehensibility. At the same time, the above translations also underscore cultural differences that were taken into consideration in the process of translation. For example, "下九流" is translated as low-class rowdies. In old Chinese society, people were divided into upper, middle and lower social classes, each with nine professions. Goldblatt directly translates "下九流" as low-class rowdies, avoiding translating "九" directly, which wouldn't make sense to foreign readers. Thus the English version erases the burden of reading by omitting the detailed nine categories, but as a result, it also fails to show the specific connotation of this aspect of traditional Chinese culture. In the case of "面无惧色" (there was no fear in his eyes), "让你长长眼色" (let you taste), and "嗅到死神的气息" (see the angel of death), "面" face, "眼色" eye and "嗅" smell are translated and modified into "eye," "taste" and "see" respectively for the sake of English idiomatic expression. The switch of senses implies cultural differences as well as differences of idiomatic expressions in two languages, and may give some inspiration for translation in terms of sense organs.

2. This part is concerned with the translations of "天" in English: 老天爷, 保佑我吧: "Old man in heaven, protect me!"; 天经地义: it's their due; 天王老子: Lord of Heaven; 天哪: My god; 天凑地合: marriages are made in heaven; 你死后升了天: You exist in heaven; 以为我家通神入魔, 是天助的买卖: assume that she was communing with spirits to seek divine assistance for the business; 天上的蝌蚪文: the script of heavenly tadpoles; 听天由命: resign yourself to your fate; 天理良心: Heaven has no eyes.

   In fact, "天," is an important Chinese concept, and has been studied by many scholars. Among them, Feng Youlan elucidated five different meanings attached to the word "天," namely, the physical *Tian* sky, the ruler *Tian* emperor, the fatalistic *Tian* fate, the naturalistic *Tian* natural course, and the patriarchal and ethical *Tian* as a heavenly course. In the above examples of translation, "天" is translated as "heaven" 天道 most of the time. The truth is that heaven in Western culture, as God's domain, is a place of salvation where the blessed enjoy their eternal bliss. *Tian* in "天理良心" refers to the patriarchal and ethical *Tian* without any relation to the physical *Tian*, which could be approximately translated as heaven in the Western sense.

3. 一会儿排成个"一"字, 一会儿排成个"人"字: from a straight line one minute to a V the next.

    "一" and "人" are Chinese characters that have no corresponding English letters with the same shapes. In the translated version, a straight line is used to indicate "一"; V indicates "人" because the upturned V resembles the original shape that the author wants to express. Besides, "八字步" is translated the same way as "V imprints." This translation highlights Goldblatt's ingenuity in not sticking to the original but creatively inventing his own in his domesticating strategies.

4. CONCLUSION

This paper has analyzed Howard Goldblatt's translation of cultural elements from four kinds of translated materials. In terms of his translation strategies, domesticating and foreignizing translation are both used, and they sometimes work together. In his translation, Goldblatt strives to retain the local colors of Chinese expressions through his foreignizing strategies, at the same time explaining them and domesticating them to make these expressions comprehensible to readers of a foreign culture. This paper only considers Goldblatt's translation of the first two parts of Mo Yan's *Red Sorghum*. Further studies based on a broader material on Goldblatt's translation of local colors would be of great interest to readers and translation scholars.

REFERENCES

Even-Zohar, I. (1990). Polysystem Studies. *Poetics Today, 11* (1), 1–6.

Gentzler, E. (1993). *Contemporary Translation Theories*. London: Routledge, 117.

Hu, Y (2008). *Cultural Misreading of Literary Translation Based on Howard Goldblatt's Translation of* Red Sorghum. Central China Normal University, 22.

Munday, J. (2001). *Introducing Translation Studies*. London & New York: Routledge, 110.

Venuti, L. (2010). The translator's invisibility: a history of translation studies. *Translation Review, 69* (4), 811–812.

Wang, W. (2013). Reflections on the English Translation of Dialect in the *Red Sorghum Family*. *Foreign Chinese*, 30 (04): 275–279.

Wu, W., & Wu, J. (2018). Analysis of Domestication and Foreignization – A Case Study of *Red Sorghum Family*. Overseas English, (01): 109–110.

AUTHOR'S BIO

YE XIE gained her Masters from Southwestern University of Finance and Economics (SWUFE), majoring in Foreign Linguistics and Applied Linguistics. She is interested in semantics, cognitive linguistics, and corpus research. In 2020, her two papers "A Corpus-Based Analysis of the Usage of Reporting Words assert and claim in BAWE and CEE" and "An Analysis of Classroom Language Based on the Cooperative Principle" were published respectively in the book *Corpus Approach to Language Studies: From Theoretical Linguistics to Applied Linguistics,* and *The International Journal of Languages, Literature and Linguistics.*

7 Constructing an Ideological Cultural Toolkit in Chinese Language Classrooms

Ye Tian, University of Pennsylvania

ABSTRACT

In this study, the formal curriculum and enacted curriculum of a second-year Chinese language course at an American university are examined to illustrate that school knowledge is not neutral but reflects dominant ideologies, and that Chinese language education in the US is no exception. Like many other Chinese language courses, this course outfits students with various cultural tools that are ideological and the result of conflicts among different interest groups. Students, as active agents, use the tools they have available to them, such as language, knowledge from the curriculum of their Chinese language class and from other courses, and prior sociocultural experiences, to understand China. These cultural tools, imbued with varying degrees of power and authority, compose a hierarchical toolkit, in which certain tools are more privileged than others. All of these cultural tools both enable and constrain how students think and talk about China, as their affordances and constraints convey different ideological messages about Chinese culture and society. Meanwhile, students can master, appropriate, or resist these cultural tools in thinking and talking about China.

KEYWORDS

Images of China, Curriculum, Cultural tools, Official knowledge, Mediated action

A CURRICULUM THAT PROVIDES IDEOLOGICAL KNOWLEDGE

In the field of teaching Chinese language and culture in the US, one of the leading concerns is about possible ideological indoctrination of language learners via Chinese language programs. For example, some scholars consider Confucius Institutes to be a soft ideological or diplomatic arm of a strong Chinese state (Stambach, 2015). They are suspicious that the Confucius Institutes are designed to increase China's "soft power" and help China project an image of itself as a benign country among students (Kluver, 2014; Paradise, 2009). Similarly, when examining the courses teaching Chinese culture at US colleges, scholars also warn that studying China with a so-called "neutral stance" that is "untainted by national and ideological interests" often results in training students to use a "normative standard" to look at China unfairly as "the variations, deviations, or specificity of that cultural entity" (Wang, 2020, 5).

Drawing on Apple's theory (1992, 1993, 2000, 2004) of a school curriculum as ideological knowledge, this research paper uses a case study to exemplify that, for better or worse, ideological indoctrination of Chinese language learners via Chinese language programs is inevitable. In fact, no school knowledge is purely neutral or objective, but is the product of cultural, political, and economic conflicts, tensions, and compromises.

This paper showcases the representations of China in the curriculum and pedagogy of an intermediate level Chinese language course offered at an American university. Data gathered include the textbook, observer field notes of instruction taken over a 16-week period, and interviews with two language instructors and all eight students who were enrolled on the course.

The formal curriculum and the enacted curriculum of this second-year Chinese language course reflected the "selective tradition" illustrated by Apple's research (1992, 1993, 2000, 2004). A curriculum is not ideologically neutral; it always reflects and conveys a certain ideology (e.g. sociocultural values, understandings, beliefs, and attitudes) to its target. When instructors make their curriculum choices, they basically "select" for the existence of such ideology in their classroom. In this particular Chinese language course (and also in most Chinese language courses in the US, according to my decades of teaching experiences), positive representations of China and positive attitudes towards China that convey a pro-China ideology, are designed, selected, legitimized, and taught. This process is accomplished through the mediated activity of the enacted curriculum.

As the core part of the formal curriculum, the textbook used by this Chinese language class – *A New China* – establishes a positive image of a new China and encourages a positive attitude towards China for American college students. Similar to many Chinese language textbooks, *A New China* celebrates China's long history and rich civilization (e.g. the Great Wall, tourist attractions, Chinese cuisine, table etiquette, and face-saving culture). Moreover, this textbook introduces the idea that China has undergone dramatic and positive changes in almost all aspects as a result of the rapid development of the economy since the economic reform of the late 1970s. For instance, the textbook shows that Chinese people's living standards and material conditions in China are improving every day (e.g. more private cars and household appliances, and excellent highway and dormitory conditions). Chinese people live a prosperous and relaxing life (e.g. small parks, night markets, and zoos). Communication with the world, especially the Western world, has become more frequent, which has caused China's social system and values to become more and more Westernized (e.g. less communist influence, fewer propaganda slogans and more commercial advertisements, a capitalistic economic system, improving gender equality, and fewer restrictions on freedom of speech). The fact that it is Beijing, and not "backward" rural areas, that is often used to represent China in the textbook helps to establish China as progressing towards a more Westernized, modern, and prosperous nation.

Some negative representations of China can be found in the textbook, such as relatively backward material conditions (e.g. no dryers, traffic jams, and dirty restrooms), uncivilized behavior (e.g. not waiting in line, and bad driving habits), and unenlightened political ideology (e.g. censorship). But compared to the actively promoted positive portrayals of China, these negative representations are limited to only a few aspects. Furthermore, when evaluating these negative representations of China, whether they are aspects that are different from the West or elements that still lag behind developed countries, the textbook leads its readers to three choices: a) to take a pluralist multicultural perspective, b) to consider China's special historical, cultural, political, social, and economic conditions, or c) to recognize China's huge progress. Using these strategies, the textbook spares no effort in advocating that American college students should hold a more tolerant and understanding attitude towards China. Thus, the formal curriculum (that is, the content of the textbook) reflects and enables a pro-China ideology by privileging positive representations of China and attitudes towards it, while also providing (but understating) negative representations and attitudes.

A CURRICULUM THAT OUTFITS STUDENTS WITH CULTURAL TOOLS

The formal curriculum enables and supports the production of positive images and representations of China. The enacted curriculum utilizes the knowledge of China in the textbook and in the supplementary materials provided by instructors to outfit students with a variety of cultural tools to understand China. In this cultural toolkit, positive representations of China (and thus a pro-China ideology) are legitimized and privileged over negative representations of China. As a result, the enacted curriculum of this second-year Chinese language class conveys to students a highly ideological and pro-China form of knowledge.

Specifically, the positive image of China in the textbook is privileged in their classrooms due to the instructors' traditional audio-lingual pedagogy and textbook-centered teaching philosophy. Most supplementary materials also convey similar positive representations of China and positive attitudes towards China to students. Besides the few negative descriptions of China in the textbook, supplementary materials also contain several negative representations of China (e.g. severe traffic conditions, and the poor state of education in the countryside). The existence of the negative descriptions of China in both the formal and enacted curriculum exemplify Wertsch's concept of privileging, which address "the issue of the organization of mediational means in a dominance hierarchy" (1991, 124). In line with Wertsch, it is easy to see that the curriculum of this Chinese language class (and, again, of many other Chinese language courses) is not about privileging only the positive representations while eliminating others, but instead is about creating a hierarchy of representations in students' toolkits. In this toolkit, certain tools are viewed as more legitimate or more appropriate than other tools.

This hierarchy of knowledge of China in students' cultural toolkits is reflected in many aspects. First, the larger quantity of positive representations of China compared to the limited negative representations of China in both the formal and enacted curriculum definitely provided students with more available resources, or cultural tools, in their toolkit to understand China in positive ways, thereby enabling a pro-China ideology. In other words, though negative representations of China that are contained in the curriculum are found in students' toolkits, they are not strong enough to disrupt the positive representations that are privileged in the curriculum.

Second, the verbal representations of China in class that are conveyed in the everyday communications between the instructors and students also shape students' views regarding the usefulness or appropriateness of these cultural tools. For example, instructors can use different response words to invalidate a student's own negative comments on China. Wertsch (1998) states that cultural tools are differentially imbued with cultural "power and authority," which are provided by the sociocultural setting in which they are produced or used (65). This explains why "certain knowledge is publicly available and openly taught while other forms of knowledge are not" (Wertsch, 1998, 66). Wertsch exemplifies this point with the teacher-student discourse in formal instructional settings. He states that the traditional classroom is often organized around "I-R-E" sequences (a teacher initiates a question, a student replies, and the teacher evaluates the answer). In this discourse sequence, because the teacher initiates the question and evaluates the response, he or she "occupies a position of authority" (Wertsch, 1998, 69). The "I-R-E" sequences are one of the key features of the audio-lingual pedagogy (Kumaravadivelu, 2006; Rivers, 1983), which is applied in most Chinese language classes in the US. In this second-year Chinese language class, the instructors' preferred instructional method imbued positive representations of China with authority and social legitimacy, signaling to students that these positive representations are a more useful and appropriate cultural tool than negative representations of China.

In fact, it is very common to find that a student's negative comments about China receive an impatient and critical response from the instructor, even though the instructor may claim that he or she does not care what students say about China as long as they can use the grammatical elements correctly. However, it is very common for instructors to spontaneously defend China when they hear something negative about it. Their discouragement or even harshly critical responses to the negative representations of China give power and authority to positive representations of China, and contribute to the production of a hierarchy of usable knowledge about China in students' toolkits, wherein negative information about China is positioned as less desirable and useful. These negative responses give students a clear indication that the positive representations of China in the textbook are more useful. Or, in Apple's (1992, 1993, 2000, 2004) framework, the positive representations of China and the pro-China ideology contained in these presentations are socially legitimized by the instructors in their classes.

Third, students' knowledge of China from other resources is often undervalued. These resources may include personal experiences, family background, and other courses related to China, and they are also part of students' cultural toolkits. Most students have some knowledge of China beyond the curriculum of this second-year Chinese language class. However, this knowledge is generally limited or superficial. Moreover, the instructors' teacher-centered and textbook-centered teaching methods (which are the two common consequences of the audio-lingual teaching pedagogy) determine that classroom instruction is always focused on the content of the textbook. In other words, in the process of language teaching and learning, information about China from the textbook is privileged over the knowledge that students have gained from other sources.

Thus, this process structures students' China-specific cultural toolkits hierarchically from the most accessible, useful, sensible, and appropriate representations, to those that are less so. Negative representations of China are still available to students (e.g. students may still know and remember the dirty restrooms or the severe traffic situation in Beijing), but they are less likely to use that negative information about China when they talk and think about China.

A CURRICULUM THAT ENABLES A PRO-CHINA IDEOLOGY

Wertsch (1991, 1998, 2002) highlights the fact that cultural tools have an inherent functional dualism. When discussing how individuals mediate their minds and actions to find meaning in that relationship, Wertsch states that cultural tools, which include many forms (e.g. narrative, knowledge of texts, language, technology, and specific textual resources) provide "affordances" as well as impose "constraints" (1998, 40). In other words, cultural tools are both enabling and constraining resources that are used by the agents (Wills, 2001). Wertsch (1991, 1998, 2002) reminds us that in the examination of any cultural tool, we must pay careful attention to the semiotic resources that both enable and constrain the mediated actions of the agent.

In the case of this second-year Chinese language class, as stated above, the curriculum contributes various cultural tools and resources to students' China-specific cultural toolkits. All of these cultural tools inevitably enable a particular way in which students could understand China while constraining alternatives. For instance, the specific representations of China and attitudes towards China provided in the curriculum is a cultural tool. This cultural tool enables a pro-China ideology (e.g. China is in the process of modernizing and improving; China's Westernization represents a huge progress) and constrains the negative ones (e.g. only a few limited aspects of China could be improved). When evaluating these negative representations of China, the curriculum also enables a positive attitude towards China while constraining the critiques of China's problems. The formal curriculum repeatedly advocates that American college students should observe the negative representations of China with an understanding and tolerant attitude. Westerners should seek to understand China's problems by considering China's special historical, cultural, political, social, and economic conditions. Thus, this cultural tool – the specific representations of China and attitudes towards China provided in the curriculum – enable a specific pro-China ideology while providing fewer resources for constructing a negative view of China.

The extra example sentences, visual images, and authentic language materials provided by the instructors are also different types of cultural tools that contribute to students' toolkits of China. All of these cultural tools afford, support, or enable positive understandings of China and positive attitudes towards it, while constraining alternative negative ones. For example, when learning the grammar pattern "more and more" ("越来越" in Chinese), students are repeatedly taught to say that "Chinese people's living standards are not as good as American people's living standards. However, in five years Chinese people's living standards will catch up with American people's living standards" and "Beijing's air is getting worse day by day. However, Beijing is getting more modern year by year. Chinese people's salaries are getting higher year by year. China's household appliances are becoming more common year by year." When learning about the night markets, attractive images of Beijing's night views and Chinese food constrain negative attitudes towards China that students might have gained from the textbook or their personal experiences, and instead promote a positive understanding of China. They enable the same positive representations of China as their correlating lessons in the textbook: China is a country that has a rich historical heritage and food culture, and its people live happily in a stable, relaxed, and prosperous society. Indeed, a few supplementary materials, or cultural tools, conflict with the pro-China ideology of the textbook. These cultural tools enable negative understandings of China while constraining positive ones, but they are not privileged in students' China-specific cultural toolkits.

Thus, most cultural tools in students' toolkits enable positive representations of and positive attitudes towards China, and constrain negative representations and attitudes. Although students have access to all the tools in their toolkits, for most students, the ones that could convey a positive image of China are more appropriate than negative knowledge of China. When students draw on their cultural toolkits to think about China, the toolkit constrains the negative pieces of information and makes them less accessible and available than others, perhaps to make them seem less rational and "accurate" than others. This is how the curriculum structures students' cultural toolkits hierarchically to make positive representations of China most accessible and usable. That is, in line with Apple, the curriculum embodies and communicates a pro-China ideology because the positive representations of China and the positive attitudes towards China are privileged and viewed as being the most appropriate or correct, meaning that they are socially legitimized in this particular Chinese language class, and also in most Chinese language courses.

THE POSSIBLE IDEOLOGICAL EFFECTS OF THE CURRICULUM ON DIFFERENT STUDENTS

Students have been outfitted by the curriculum of this second-year Chinese language class with cultural toolkits, but how do they use the resources in the toolkits to talk and think about China? What are the possible ideological effects of the enacted curriculum on different students? The answer is that different students use the various resources available to them, including the curriculum as well as other resources, to talk and think about China in different ways. This finding also fits Wertsch's statements that cultural tools are usually unequally distributed among different students because certain "mediational means" are "viewed as being more appropriate or efficacious than others in a particular sociocultural setting" (1991, 124). As a result, students use the same cultural tools differently. Wertsch (1998, 2002) uses the terms "mastery, appropriation, and resistance" to describe these different processes and results. Mastery indicates knowledge of how to utilize a cultural tool to accomplish an action with ease. Appropriation pertains to the process of integrating knowledge (an attitude, or a point of view) from other social and cultural resources into one's own pre-existing cultural toolkit. An individual can also master a cultural tool without appropriating it, but a successful mastery of the cultural tool would engender a positive appropriation, which would indicate that the individual can spontaneously and creatively use the cultural tool in different situations. Moreover, Wertsch (1998, 2002) highlights that appropriation often implies resistance, which means that an individual, or an agent, does not always accept the cultural tool or use it. In many instances, resistance or even rejection (as the rule rather than an exception) is more common than the appropriation. In summary, mastery, appropriation, and resistance all constitute the relationships between agent and mediational means.

- Mastery

A successful Chinese language class often leads to students' mastery of cultural knowledge about China from both the formal curriculum and the enacted curriculum. Representations of China, especially the privileged positive representations of China in the curriculum, as cultural tools, have been repeatedly "filling" students' toolkits following the dominant method of instruction in classrooms. In other words, students are successfully outfitted with these cultural tools and resources about China. Thus, they are able to easily remember, retell, and reproduce information specific to China when they answer the instructors' questions in class, when they perform oral presentations, and when they talk with Chinese people.

- Appropriation

Although students master knowledge of China in the curriculum in a similar way, there is variation in their manners of appropriation of the cultural tools provided by the curriculum. It is normal that some students are much more dependent on the curriculum, because they do not have enough information about China from other sources to challenge or resist the privileged knowledge of China in the curriculum. When these students talk about the potential usefulness of the curriculum, they tend to draw spontaneously on the positive representations of China provided by the curriculum. In particular, their attitudes towards China are often consistent with the positive attitudes towards China that are privileged in the curriculum.

- Resistance

It is also not rare that some students also master the content of the curriculum but have access to other cultural tools that they believe are more "appropriate or efficacious" (Wertsch, 1991, 124) than those that limit their peers, that is, mainly the curriculum. Examples of these tools are: more profound personal experiences, more extensive knowledge about China from other courses, a deeper Chinese heritage or cultural background, and more developed critical thinking skills. When thinking about China, these students sometimes resist using the cultural tools provided in their Chinese language class, and turn to other cultural tools. Occasionally, when the cultural tools provided by the curriculum conflict with other cultural tools, these students might use their personal cultural tools in order to reject the privileged positive representations of China and positive attitudes towards China.

In some rare cases, for students who already have a set of opinions about China from other cultural tools beyond the curriculum, the curriculum provided might not be able to add any new knowledge about China for them, or might not be able to change their understandings of and attitudes towards China. In other words, in these cases, we can find all three relationships between a student (agent) and the mediated means: mastery, appropriation, and resistance. The student can master the cultural tools specific to China provided by the curriculum very well. He/she can appropriate the cultural tools provided by the curriculum when there is no conflict with other cultural tools that he/she already has. However, when conflicts occur, he/she tends to resist and even reject the cultural tools provided by the curriculum.

CONCLUSION

In summary, the case of this second-year Chinese language class exemplifies that the curriculum of many Chinese language courses provides students with various cultural tools to understand China. The cultural tools that enable a positive understanding of China and positive attitudes towards China while constraining negative ones are privileged over the cultural tools that enable the negative ones while constraining the positive ones. One of the major ideological effects of the curriculum of these courses is that it enables a pro-China ideology while constraining an anti-China ideology, with privileged representations supporting an image of China as a progressive, modernizing, and Westernizing country. This pro-China ideology also consists of students' positive attitudes towards China, which is also enabled by specific cultural tools (e.g. positive representations of China and positive attitudes towards China provided by the curriculum). The curriculum enables students to grasp a set of specific information about China together, into a consistent entirety of knowledge.

China has been experiencing dramatic changes in the past 30 years, yet it is still quite different from any Western country with which American students may be familiar. It is not easy for a second-year-level Chinese language textbook to describe such a complex country for its students, let alone to help students understand China in its entirety. Instead of providing different methods for understanding particular culture, events, customs, actors, history, or policies in different settings, the privileged positive representations of China and the positive attitudes towards China in the curriculum, serve as the basic tool in presenting and interpreting China, which has enabled a simplistic, yet unified pro-China ideology in the student's understanding of China. Students' mastery and appropriation of (and resistance to) these cultural tools vary according to their dependency on this language course for their knowledge about China. For many students, the Chinese language course makes a huge difference in terms of how they are outfitted to think about China. This case study exemplifies how Chinese language instructors, researchers, and legislators should examine whose interests are reflected in the politics surrounding the production of knowledge about China within Chinese language courses. This study also sheds light on the possible ideological effects of the curriculum on students' understanding of China and attitudes toward it.

REFERENCES

Apple, M. W. (1992). The Text and Cultural Politics. *Educational Researcher, 21* (7), 4–11.
Apple, M. W. (1993). The Politics of Official Knowledge: Does a National Curriculum Make Sense? *Teachers College Record, 95* (2), 222–241.
Apple, M. W. (2000). *Official knowledge: Democratic education in a conservative age.* New York, NY: Routledge.
Apple, M. W. (2004). *Ideology and Curriculum* (3rd ed.). New York, NY: Routledge Falmer.
Kluver, R. (2014). Introduction: The Confucius Institute as a Communicative Phenomenon. *China Media Research, 10* (1), 1–3.
Kumaravadivelu, B. (2006). *Understanding Language Teaching: From Method to Postmethod.* (ESL & Applied Linguistics Professional Series). Mahwah: Taylor and Francis. https://doi.org/10.4324/9781410615725
Paradise, J. F. (2009). China and International Harmony: The Role of Confucius Institutes in Bolstering Beijing's Soft Power. *Asian Survey, 49* (4), 647–669.
Rivers, W. M. (1983). *Communicating Naturally in a Second Language: Theory and Practice in Language Teaching.* New York: Cambridge University Press.
Stambach, A. (2015). Confucius Institute Programming in the United States: Language Ideology, Hegemony, and the Making of Chinese Culture in University Classes. *Anthropology & Education Quarterly, 46* (1), 55–70. doi:10.1111/aeq.12087
Wang, B. (2020). The Study of Chinese Culture in American Classrooms. *China-US Journal of Humanities,* (5), 1–7.
Wertsch, J. V. (1991). *Voices of the Mind: A Sociocultural Approach to Mediated Action.* Cambridge, MA: Harvard University Press.
Wertsch, J. V. (1998). *Mind as Action.* New York, NY: Oxford University Press.
Wertsch, J. V. (2002). *Voices of Collective Remembering.* Cambridge, U.K.; New York, NY: Cambridge University Press.

AUTHOR'S BIO

YE TIAN is the Interim Director of the Chinese Language Program at the University of Pennsylvania. Previously, he taught Chinese at various institutions including Harvard University, Middlebury College, and Bucknell University. With a PhD in Education, Society, and Culture from the University of California, Riverside, his research is centered on Chinese language education, with an interest in educational technology, and a focus on investigating Chinese language education through sociocultural and historical frameworks and methodologies. His refereed journal articles include "The Error Tolerance of Machine Translation: Findings from a Failed Teaching Design" in *Journal of Technology and Chinese Language Teaching 11* (1), 19–35; and "From Greek/Latin to Chinese: What We can Learn from the First Chinese Teacher at Harvard" in *Curriculum History*, *18* (1), 54–70.

8 The Effect of the Power Distance Dimension on Cultural Differences between China and the United States

Jane Kuo, University of California, San Diego

ABSTRACT

Integrating cultural components and cross-cultural comparisons has long been an integral part of a second language acquisition course. By applying "Power Distance," an influence dimension within Geert Hofstede's study of cultural dimensions, this paper examines what differentiates vertical societies from horizontal ones. The usage of honorifics, modesty, and euphemistic expressions in the Chinese and American cultures will be juxtaposed and compared. Analysis of historical origins will also be performed in order to identify the reasons underlying the cultural differences between these two countries.

KEYWORDS

cross-culture, power distance, honorifics, historical origin

INTRODUCTION

Culture is a complex and comprehensive concept. The culture in which individuals are raised affects their social interaction and societal communication styles. Since culture influences the rules and norms that guide human behavior within a culture, it has an enormous impact on all aspects of society. When people interact with others in society, they observe various behavioral patterns that are based on the norms, rules, and values of that society (Gudykunst, 1996).

Moreover, people in different countries have different cultural norms and values. Since norms and values are the fundamental baselines that determine people's views and actions, cross-cultural comparisons have long been a focus of interest and study by researchers and educators. Foreign language teachers have also been aware of the importance of teaching cross-cultural comparisons on their language courses.

Hofstede conducted a cross-cultural study in the late 1960s and established that inequality, power, and authority are measured in organizational structures. Each structure's limits of acceptance are defined by the allowance of authority and inequality to remain in place. Based on the degree to which cultures encourage power or responsibility, organizations can vastly differ in their systems, ranging from centralized and bureaucratic (vertical) to participative and equitable (horizontal).

Applying Hofstede's "Power Distance" dimension as a theoretical framework, the purposes of this paper are to examine which cultural factors differentiate a vertical society from a horizontal one, and illustrate the reasons underlying the differences between China and the US It is hoped through the comparison of the "Power Distance" difference between these two countries, educators will have a better understanding of the causes that lie behind their different cultural values, attitudes, and behavior.

CULTURE IN LANGUAGE LEARNING

The relationship between language and culture is intricate and interdependent. Thus, the identification of the cultural factors within foreign language teaching is a very complex issue. Many foreign language experts have become aware of the importance of incorporating cultural factors in language courses since ACTFL (American Council on Teaching Foreign Language) recommended the standards and guidelines for teaching foreign languages.

ACTFL 5CS STANDARD AND ACTFL WORLD LANGUAGE 21ST CENTURY SKILLS

"The World-Readiness Standards for Learning Languages" is a national standard for foreign language education guidelines. It was formulated by the joint efforts of the AED (American Education Department) and ACTFL in 1996 and revised in 1999.

The purpose of those standards is to create a direction that guides curriculum design and instruction implementation. As a goal, the standards aim to prepare learners to apply the language skills beyond the instructional setting and attain a strategy for global competence in the future (ACTFL, 1999).

WHAT ARE ACTFL 5CS?

The ACTFL formulated the core content of standards – also known as the "5Cs" – that include Communication, Cultures, Connections, Comparisons, and Communities. The goal of integrating these 5Cs into language teaching is to help learners develop competence for communicating effectively and interacting efficiently without misunderstanding (ACTFL, 2011). ("On the Web, Standards for Foreign Language Learning in the 21st Century").

Since the formulation of these guidelines, the 5Cs standards for teaching foreign languages have received extensive attention and research in foreign language education. Particularly, foreign language teachers have become increasingly aware that understanding a society's culture is an integral component of discerning the cultural values embedded in language.

One of the 5Cs standards set by the ACTFL is cultural comparison. Its definition is "learners use the language to investigate, explain, and reflect on the concept of culture through comparisons of the cultures studied and their own." By this research process of cross-cultural comparison, learners can better grasp the differences of values and concepts between their native language and the target language (ACTFL, 1999).

TEACHING CULTURE IN CHINESE AS A SECOND LANGUAGE

In the 1970s, language teachers began to address the importance of incorporating culture in teaching Chinese as a foreign language. They proposed that language teaching and cultural teaching were inseparable, and inspired numerous research studies on what and how cultural components should be incorporated in language teaching (Qiao, 2009; Chen, 1992; Zhang, 1990; Tian, 1997).

However, these studies were centered on choosing which cultural components should be incorporated into language courses. Some courses that introduce Chinese culture involve a wide range of subjects, such as ancient Chinese architecture, painting, cooking, Buddhism, which have no direct relevance to the language curriculum. Hu (1993) advocated that more appropriate and pertinent cultural content should be introduced into Chinese language teaching.

BIG "C" VS. LITTLE "C"

Depending on the field of research, the definition of culture can vary widely.[1] To better incorporate appropriate cultural components, language teachers should first understand the definition of culture and what culture should be taught.

In regards to language learning in a broad sense, culture refers to "the sum of spiritual and material civilization created by mankind." In a narrow sense, culture generally refers to customs, norms, and practices in a society (Shu, 1996).

According to Lee (2009) and Peterson (2004), culture can be categorized into two general types: big "C" culture and little "c" culture. Big "C" culture refers to culture that is most visible and created by mankind in the course of social and historical development. It represents a set of facts relating to art, history, geography, fashion, music, literature, architecture, holidays, and regional cuisines (Lee, 2009; Peterson, 2004). Since the cultural elements of big "C" are the more overt forms of culture, they would be first discovered and learned.

Little "c" culture, by contrast, refers to culture that incorporates the routine aspects of life, and it is invisible. It includes people's common social habits, such as communication styles, verbal and non-verbal language symbols, customs, rituals, lifestyle, and behavioral norms. Some little "c" cultures may just exist for a short time, yet people in a society cannot carry out smooth communication without understanding it. The aspects of culture included in little "c" culture should be the content of the second language teaching[2]. Culture components such as paper cutting or martial arts are big "C" cultures that may not be suitable for the domain of teaching Chinese as a second language.

THE IMPORTANCE OF CROSS-CULTURAL COMPARISONS

Other than the appropriateness of cultural selection, cross-cultural comparison of cultural factors also influences communication styles. Therefore, it is important to assess the cultural similarities or diversities inherent in two cultures or societies. For example, etiquette rules required in one country may be awkward in another culture, therefore etiquette rules are not universal, which means there is no universal agreement about their rules or standards. According to Byram (1997), cultural learning is seen as a comparative process in which learners are encouraged to be aware of their own culture and contrast it with the target culture.

In addition, teaching linguistic abilities (namely lexicon and grammar) are essential. Merely having linguistic competency may not be sufficient to carry out smooth communication. As a result, a miscommunication caused by cultural inappropriateness can at times be more embarrassing and damaging than using incorrect expressions (Grosse, 2019).

Therefore, teaching cultural components would be equally crucial and must be included in the curriculum. Teachers should also be very cautious in selecting proper cultural components that not only fit the students' level of language proficiency but also their maturity. Furthermore, teachers should be familiar with each student's cultural background, and should be able to offer reasonable clarification underlying any cultural differences. However, foreign language teachers should bear in mind that the content of cultural teaching in second language acquisition is certainly different from teaching students whose mother tongue is Chinese. (Hu, 1993)

HOFSTEDE'S CROSS-CULTURAL STUDY

While working for IBM in the late 1960s, Geert Hofstede, a Dutch anthropologist, noted that cultural differences among various countries had huge business consequences for international firms (Kuo, 2004). In 1968 and 1972 he defined four dimensions of cultural difference and conducted a questionnaire survey of 116,000 IBM employees in more than forty countries around the world. The four original dimensions of culture difference employed in his survey were "power distance" (large or small), "individualism versus collectivism," "masculinity versus femininity," and "uncertainty avoidance." The results of his findings were published in his book titled *Cultural Consequences* in 1980.

In 1991 Professor Michael Bond of the Chinese University of Hong Kong conducted a study on the comparison of Eastern and Western cultures. Based on Bond's research findings, Hofstede added a fifth dimension, "long-term orientation"[3], which reflects Confucian values[4].

In 2010, Hofstede added a sixth dimension, "laissez-faire and restraint," to his model based on Michael Minkov's (2010) analysis of World Values Survey data. Since the publication of *Cultural Consequences*, Hofstede's theory has inspired vast research in the study of cross-cultural communication, not only in the field of corporate culture but also in language instruction (Kashima & Kashima, 1998) and social behavior (Wheeler, Reis & Bond, 1989).

However, most studies used the "individualism vs. collectivism" dimension, and few were based on other dimensions, such as "power distance." In this paper, "power distance" is used to explain different language expressions, such as honorific versus humble forms and real-world behavior.

THE CHARACTERISTICS OF POWER DISTANCE

Hofstede defines the dimension of "Power Distance" as the degree of equality distribution in a given society and its workplaces (Hofstede, 1980). The characteristics of a large power distance index within a society or organization are 1) centralized authority, autocratic leadership, and paternalistic management; 2) hierarchical structure with vertical levels that members accept as part of the social order; 3) less powerful members accept that power has its privileges; 4) more powerful members perceive their subordinates as unequal; and 5) subordinates fear the high ranking or more powerful members. With these characteristics, members in large power distance societies recognize that everyone within the group has a proper place, which needs no further justification. Thus, they accept and tolerate the fact that power is distributed unequally.[5]

Contrastingly, the characteristics of small power distance cultures are: 1) decentralized authority; 2) a horizontal or flat organizational structure; 3) members are rights-conscious; 4) members' lack of acceptance of authority, and questioning of authority; and 5) members' tendency toward egalitarianism. People in small power distance societies strive for power equalization and demand justification for power inequalities.[6]

Hofstede studied the impact of culture on organizations from a social perspective. Based on the characteristics of this dimension, the degree of unequal distribution of power in societies and organizations can be judged differently. The fundamental issue addressed by this dimension also affects how a society handles civic and social inequalities when they occur. Studies by Hofstede showed that the power distance index in Eastern cultures is relatively high, and people usually respond to inequality with tolerance or by ignoring it. The index found in Western cultures is low, and a deeply rooted "consciousness of right" in its citizens drives them to resist the inequality of power distribution. [7]

Confucianism – the core of Chinese cultural concepts – advocated the distinction between respect and modesty. In China, with its orderly society, rules must be followed, and hierarchies restrict social movement. Traditionally, the Chinese tend to give greater value and pay more attention to authority, title, seniority, and age. For example, when subordinates meet their superiors, they frequently show their respect both in language and behavior.

On the contrary, Americans do not value the power of authority as much. They give more credence to the exertion of individual ability and achievement. Americans value personal freedom and are less willing to be restricted and constrained. They tend not to obey orders from superiors or the government unless their leaders are just and fair. This characteristic is related to the spirit of how the nation was founded, and may be a key factor to why the American social hierarchy is relatively fluid.

CULTURAL VALUES AND HIERARCHICAL CONCEPTS REFLECTED BY APPELLATION TERMS

Language expressions are based on social norms, which are reflected and restricted by traditional values, attitudes, habits, and social customs (Hu, 1993). Honorific Chinese expressions or humble words of appellation, greetings, praise, and euphemisms refer to expressions that can articulate self-deprecating, respectful, and polite mannerisms. Honorific expressions embody various hierarchical concepts, and play an important role in distinguishing and forming interpersonal relationships. A long-standing moral standard that the Chinese have abided by is 礼 "li" (rite or propriety") and the corresponding virtue was 尊人卑己, meaning "respecting others and humbling oneself."

The practice of "respecting others and humbling oneself" has been a traditional virtue that the Chinese have upheld, and the polite (yet tactful on some occasions) attitude of this virtue has been reflected in the language. The common usage of honorific forms, also known as courtesy titles, such as 您 "nin" and 贵 "gui" would be a good example to indicate that China is a hierarchical society. In showing respect to a person, instead of using 你 "ni," it is customary to use the honorific form of 您 "nin," meaning "you," similar to the outdated "thou" in English.

When addressing people in the United States, the standards of title are Mr., Mrs., Ms., Professor, Dr., Reverend, and Your Honor (to a judge). In China, honorific appellations before the name of a person such as "Manager XYZ" or "President XYZ" are seldom used. "Mr./Ms. XYZ" would be more appropriate than "Manager XYZ," and first names over last names and job titles are commonly used.

There are many honorifics versus humble expressions in Chinese. The following tables show some examples.

Table 1: Examples of Honorific and Humble Expressions.

	尊人 Respect others	卑己 Humble oneself
Last name	贵姓	敝姓
Residence	府上、贵宅	寒舍、舍下
Father	令尊、令堂、尊父	家父、家严
Mother	令慈	家母、家慈
Son	令郎、令公子	犬子、小犬
Daughter	令媛、令千金	小女
Organization	贵(校、店、公司)	敝(校、店、公司)
Gift	贵重厚礼	薄礼
Publications	大作、尊著	拙作、小作
Opinion/viewpoint/suggestions	高见	浅见、愚见

Humility and respect for others were the minimum requirements of courtesy in past eras. Honorifics were widely used in ancient China, especially among the upper class. However, in modern Chinese, many of these terms are no longer used. Moreover, during the "New Culture Movement" and other movements to promote vernacular Chinese and the removal of traditional culture, polite expressions in classical Chinese also significantly declined in modern times. Nevertheless, modern Chinese still retains many honorifics, especially in written language. The rule of thumb is one must use modest and respectable words with seniors and higher-ranking members unless you are familiar with them. It is considered to be rude if the proper expressions are not used. People who do not humble themselves are often regarded as arrogant and this can lead to life or work failure.[8]

The following tables depict the different language expressions in greetings between China and the United States.

Table 2: Greetings in Chinese and English

中	美
您贵姓?	What is your (honorary) last name?
免贵, 姓...	Xxx
请问, 尊姓大名	May I have your (honorary full) name?
你好 您好!	How do you do? How are you, Sir?
很高兴认识您!	Very pleased to meet you.
幸会幸會!	Honored to meet you.
久仰久仰!久仰大名!	I've heard so much about you. (Literally: It has been so long since I heard your great name.)

The following table depicts typical expressions of thanks in Chinese.

Table 3: Expressions of Thanks

中	美
承蒙賜教,不勝感激	*Being deeply grateful for your instruction* *Much indebted to* *Much obliged for your instruction* (Thank you for your guidance and support, I appreciate it.)
受益匪浅 惠我良多	Of great gain Benefited greatly

The following are humble expressions in Chinese that demonstrate that one's knowledge and efforts are limited and not worth mentioning.

Table 4: Modest Expressions in Chinese

中文	英文
抛砖引玉	Throw a brick to attract jade back.
添砖加瓦	To do one's bit to help
绵薄之力	To do one's best to help but not contributing much
马齿徒增	Having accomplished nothing at old age; be old but unfit for anything (Not accomplished despite old age)

Note: Most English translations have varying degrees of deficiencies in reflecting the traditional Chinese culture as implicated by self-effacing language. The words that cannot be translated are due to the reflection of different social and cultural backgrounds in societies (Zhao, 1992). Many idioms and probes are a crystallization of the wisdom of a culture, therefore the meaning may be lost in translation. Moreover, improper translation can result in misunderstanding.

HISTORICAL ORIGINS

Cultural values vary among countries in their close relationship to the historical origin of a country. The following section explains why China and the United States have different power distances from the perspective of historical origin.

China

Compared to the US, China's history is much longer, and it has experienced monarchy and feudalism. It was during the long feudal era that the concept of hierarchical ethics was formed. The ethics and morals that were upheld for thousands of years include the value of social order in society. This is not only the core of Confucian hierarchical society but also the foundation of the Chinese nation. According to the ideology of Confucius and Mencius, each person's status and civil rights within society are predestined, and hierarchy differences are inherent and eternal.

The USA

The United States was greatly influenced by Christianity in its founding. Americans believe in personal freedom and the pursuit of happiness before God. George Washington once said, "To govern a country appropriately, it's impossible without God and the Bible." In the eyes of the new colonists, only God could be the almighty ruler and have absolute judgment. Therefore, only when people transcend all authority and communicate directly with God, can they gain the power to independently judge things and moral standards. This strong religious sentiment nurtured the foundation of the American people's idea of equality and inspired efforts to pursue and value freedom.

The most famous phrase from the Declaration of Independence is, "All men are created equal," when America gained independence in 1776. Americans believe that they are "endowed by their Creator with certain unalienable rights, that among these are life, liberty, and the pursuit of happiness."[9] Thus, there is a long history of protest movements and civil rights conflicts in response to perceived violations of rights.

Charted below are some examples of major protest movements in America.

Table 5: Timeline of Equality Movements in the US

Year	Events
1954–1968	Civil Rights Movement
1964	The US "Civil Rights Act" passed
1960–up to now	Feminist Movement
1980–2009	LGBT (Q) Rights Movement
2011	Occupy Wall Street Movement
2020	BLM (Black Lives Matter)

The various human rights movements listed above have been efforts to narrow the gap of inequality and reduce the hierarchical differences in American society. The pursuit of individual freedom, social equality, and economic parity are key elements that fuel egalitarian campaigns that emphasize equality across gender, region, economic status, and political beliefs.

"Mask Battle"

At the time of writing, the United States is the country with the most severe cases from the COVID-19 pandemic, and its number of confirmed cases and deaths ranks number one in the world.

Although there is enough scientific evidence to prove that wearing a mask can prevent the spread of the virus, some Americans still just don't want to wear masks. Not only is there resistance in wearing them but also protests against others doing so. Those who oppose wearing masks believe it violates their rights and civil liberties.

In the United States, there have been many incidents of protests such as burning masks and violence. The "mask battle" is another incident that reveals the importance of human rights in the ethos of America. It also shows a confrontation between those who defend public safety in the United States and those who believe in personal freedom. The battle reflects the clear characteristics of individual rights awareness and the weak hierarchical system in Western culture.

CONCLUSION

Through cross-cultural comparisons in a language course, students can gain insight into a country's cultural knowledge and discern the contrasts and dissimilarities between their own culture and that of others. They can also deepen their understanding of the underlying causes that are distinguished from cultural values.

Hofstede's cross-culture theory claims that China's hierarchical structure is more vertical than that of the US. Honorifics are the reflection of a hierarchical society's cultural values and attitudes. This study applies Hofstede's "Power Distance" dimension, examining the different usages of honorific expressions between China and the United States. It confirms Hofstede's finding that China is a hierarchical society with a vertical structure, whereas the hierarchy of the US is relatively flat.

In addition to the "Power Distance" dimension, are there any other variables worthy of further cross-cultural research? With the impact of globalization, exchanges and conflicts among countries have become more frequent. Following this trend, cultural context will need to determine the dominance and importance of one culture over another, and how different modes engage with each other. The outcome will define the values and beliefs that will influence the future of global exchange and communication.

ENDNOTES

1. There are as many as 164 definitions of culture according to anthropologists, Kroeber and Kluckhohn in 1952.
2. https://coerll.utexas.edu/methods/modules/culture/01/which.php
3. It was first called Confusion dynamism.
4. https://geerthofstede.com/related-scientists/michael-harris- bond/
5. https://www.andrews.edu/~tidwell/bsad560/HofstedePowerDistance.html
6. http://home.sandiego.edu/~dimon/CulturalFrameworks.pdf
7. The power distance indexes of China and the US are 80 and 40, respectively.
8. https://stedu.stheadline.com/sec/article/869/%E6%82%85%E8%AE%80%E4%B8%AD%E6%96%87-%E8%AA%9E%E6%96%87%E8%87%AA%E5%AD%B8-%E8%A9%9E%E7%9A%84%E5%B0%8A%E8%88%87%E5%8D%91%E5%92%8C%E8%B-2%B4%E8%88%87%E8%B3%A4
9. (https://bensguide.gpo.gov/declaration-of-independence-1776)

REFERENCES

Bond, M. (1991). Geert Hofstede. https://geerthofstede.com/related-scientists/michael-harris- bond/Byram, M. (1997). *Teaching and Assessing Intercultural Communicative Competence.*
  Google on Google play. https://books.google.com/books
Chen, Guanglei (1992), Cultural Integration in Language Instruction, *Journal of Language Teaching and Linguistic Studies*, (3).
Hu, Mingyang (1993), Cultural Factors of Teaching Chinese as a Second Language, *Journal of Language Teaching and Linguistic Studies*, (4).
Grosse, C. (2019). *The global Manager's Guide to Cultural Literacy.* Cambridge Scholars Publishing.
Gudykunst, W. B., Ting-Toomey, S., & Nishida, T. (Eds.). (1996). Communication in Personal Relationships Across Cultures. Sage Publications, Inc.
Hofstede, G. (1980). Culture's Consequences: International Differences in Work-Related Values, Beverly Hills, CA: Sage.
Kashima, E.S. & Kashima, Y. (1998). Culture and Language: The Case of Cultural Dimensions and Personal Pronoun Use. *Journal of Cross-cultural Psychology*, (29), 461–486.
Kuo, Jane (2004), The Influence of Power Distance on Organizational Culture and Communication – A Cross-culture Comparison of China, Japan, and United States, *Journal of American-Chinese Society and Culture*, (7), 89–99.

Lee, K-Y. (2009). Treating culture: What 11 high school EFL Conversation Textbooks in South Korea Do, English Teaching: Practice and Critique, (8), 76–96.

Minkov, M. (2010). Cross-Cultural Analysis: The Science and Art of the World's Modern Societies and Their Culture Books. book google.com

Peterson, B. (2004). Cultural intelligence: A guide to working with people from other cultures, http://www. Amazon.com

Qiao, Tan (2009), Research on Teaching Chinese as a Second Language within the Last 30 Years Regarding Cultural Integration, *Kaoshi Zhoukan*, (47).

Tian, Guimin (1997), The Importance of Cultural Transmission in Teaching Chinese as a Second Language, *Nankai Xuebao*, (6).

Shu, Dingfang (1996), Language and Cultural Relations and Issues of Cultural Introduction in Beginning Stages of Foreign Language Instruction, *Foreign Language World* (1), 11–17.

Wheeler, L., Reis, H.T., & Bond, M.H. (1989). Collectivism-Individualism in Every Social Life: The Middle Kingdom and the Melting Pot." *Journal of Personality and Social Psychology*, (57), 79–86.

Zhang, Zhanyi (1990), On Communicative Culture and Knowledge Culture, *Journal of Language Teaching and Linguistic Studies*, (3).

Zhang, Zhanyi (1992), Cross-Cultural Communication and Discussion, *Journal of Language Teaching and Linguistic Studies*, (4).

Zhao, Xianzhou (1992), Reconsidering Cultural Integration, *Journal of Language Teaching and Linguistic Studies*, (3).

https://coerll.utexas.edu/methods/modules/culture/01/which.php

https://www.andrews.edu/~tidwell/bsad560/HofstedePowerDistance.html

http://home.sandiego.edu/~dimon/CulturalFrameworks.pdf

https://stedu.stheadline.com/sec/article/869/%E6%82%85%E8%AE%80%E4%B8%AD%E6%96%87-%E8%AA%9E%E6%96%87%E8%87%AA%E5%AD%B8-%E8%A9%9E%E7%9A%84%E5%B0%8A%E8%88%87%E5%8D%91%E5%92%8C%E8%B2%B4%E8%88%87%E8%B3%A4

https://bensguide.gpo.gov/declaration-of-independence-1776

A Brief Talk on the Differences between Chinese and American Cultures https://www.wenmi.com/article/pzmgzg02bzsd.htm

AUTHOR'S BIO

Professor JANE KUO is the former director of the Chinese language program at the University of California, San Diego, and Professor Emeritus of Thunderbird School of Global Management at Arizona State University. During her tenure at Thunderbird, she developed a business-focused Chinese language curriculum for both MBA and EMBA programs. Over the years, she also conducted numerous seminars on business-specific Chinese language and cross-cultural communication skills for executives at Fortune 500 companies, including Motorola and Intel. Professor Kuo is widely recognized as a pioneer in business Chinese instruction and has authored *New Pathway*, the best-selling *Open for Business: Lessons in Chinese Commerce for the New Millennium* and *Start-up Business Chinese*. She also co-authored *Business Negotiation: Theory and Practice*. She has served as a board member of the national Chinese Language Teachers Association-US and was a founding board member of CLTA's Southern California regional chapter.

9 Conjugating "Chinese" in Sinophone Cinemas

Rujie Wang, The College of Wooster

ABSTRACT

The paper is a brief study of cultural identity as trans-nationalized in seven narrative films from Hong Kong, Taiwan, and Chinese diaspora cinemas. It is an exercise of making the critical distinction between culture and civilization. As is evident in these films, (national) culture is a set of metaphysical qualities used to distinguish a people whereas civilization is set of shared experiences in which people participate globally. The former is aristocratic by nature and the latter democratic. Within this framework, the films are critical elaborations of a national culture rooted in language and traditions. The lives of these characters are defined, more than anything else, by their ambivalence towards both cultural tradition and global civilization. In these sinophone films of recent decades, cultural identity is being negotiated but not necessarily at the expense of or to the exclusion of other cultural traditions. The stories suggest, among other things, that the Chinese are outgrowing their cultural self-definitions that are often aristocratic and ethnocentric. This study helps document the subtle changes in Chinese humanity that happen at the frontiers of a global civilization. The films thus constitute a democracy of perception, subjecting Chinese culture to different interpretations.

KEYWORDS

Taiwan cinema, Hong Kong cinema, Chinese diaspora, cultural negotiation, sinophone film

"Even though there were periods of so-called conquest dynasties or foreign rule, the cultures of foreign nationalities were continuously coming into and overlapping with China, just as the culture based largely on the Han ethnicity continuously melded with other cultures and underwent changes. The cultural tradition based on Han culture, however, extended across time in this region, forming into a clear and distinct cultural identity and [the] mainstream."

– Ge Zhaoguang (p. 19)

"The nation, too, is not only a social but also a metaphysical being; the nation, not 'the human race' as the sum of the individuals, is the bearer of the general, of the human quality; and the value of the intellectual-artistic-religious product that one calls national culture, that cannot be grasped by scientific methods, that develops out of the organic depth of national life – the value, dignity and charm of all national culture, therefore, definitely lies in what distinguishes it from all others, for only this distinctive element is culture, in contrast to what all nations have in common, which is only civilization. Here we have the difference between individual and personal, civilization and culture, social and metaphysical life. The individualistic mass is democratic, the nation aristocratic."

– Thomas Mann (p. 179)

Perhaps nowhere is this idea of "national culture" more palpable and problematic than in the films analyzed below, made in Taiwan, Hong Kong, and Chinese diaspora communities. As attempts at transcultural negotiations, they show just how cultural identity gets reconstructed to include the idea of social democracy. In other words, these stories underscore what Thomas Mann refers to as the distinction between culture and civilization. The fictional characters represent, among other things, very complex emotions, torn between a cultural identity rooted in traditions and a global civilization predicated on the notion of freedom for those able to endure the unbearable lightness of being. Thorsten Botz-Bornstein sheds light on this ambivalence with his idea of civilization as a form of hyperreality, "a condition common in technologically advanced cultures where virtual reality has made possible the endless reproductions of fundamentally empty appearances." (Botz-Bornstein, p. 1) To the extent this claim is true, it is not hard to understand those living in developed Chinese cultural spheres. For them, the idea of "*zhong guo*" (中國) is bound to be very different from what it used to mean centuries ago within Chinese culture. "That which is situated in the center of the two (Heaven and Earth) is known as 'the middle kingdom.' Those who dwell on the edges of heaven and earth are known as 'the four outlanders.' The four outlanders are on the outside. The 'central kingdom' is on the inside." That metaphysical, aristocratic, and ethnocentric idea of "China" is obsolete in the eyes of many Han Chinese who "dwell on the edges" or in territories that Song literati member Shi Jie (1005–1045) would have considered as being occupied by "the four barbarians" (四夷). For many in Taiwan, Hong Kong, and overseas, "China was not necessarily the center of the world, and the four barbarians came from civilized countries. In fact, in the eyes of these so-called barbarians, China may be one of the 'Four Barbarians.'" (Ge Zhaoguang, p. 48)

I chose these films because they all have parts where English is spoken and therefore are not exactly Sinophone films ("Singlish" or Chinese-Anglo cinema). They represent a variety of "China" that is a home, country, or culture, in contrast to the homes, countries, or cultures that are the host societies for many overseas Chinese. In other words, the films seem driven by a deep anxiety over one's cultural identity to one degree or another – something that has preoccupied the Chinese for centuries. That sense of apprehension about being bereft of one's identity was already tangible in the ominous remark by Qing minister Guo Songtao (郭嵩燾, 1818–1891), made upon his return from touring Europe, that "The way they [the Westerners] view China is the same as how China used to view 'the barbarians.' It is sad that there have not been literati in China who understand this."[1] In light of the changes in geopolitics that have shaped Taiwan, Hong Kong, and overseas Chinese communities, it is imperative to take seriously what Mann refers to as the "difference between individual and personality, civilization and culture, social and metaphysical life." It is to this difference that the selected films speak directly – in English, Mandarin, and various local dialects – while expanding the "metaphysical being" that is Chinese culture.

Contemporary scholars such as Wang Hui (汪暉), Zhang Longxi (張隆溪) and Lydia Liu (劉禾) have all aptly pointed out that Asia, for the most part, is an ideological construct created by the Europeans more than anything else. This gives us some historical context for transcultural negotiations in film or elsewhere in which Asia is implicated. This is because "Modernity for the Orient is primarily its subjugation to the West's political, military, and economic control. The modern Orient was born only when it was invaded, defeated, and exploited by the West. This is to say that only when the Orient became an object for the West did it enter modern times." (Yoshimi Takeuchi, pp. 147–8) This view is echoed by Edward Said who argued that the "Orient" is the product of European imagination and cultural biases. "Asia," including China, thus emerges from what Henry Rosemont refers to as "the conceptual framework of rights, within which human beings are seen as free, rationally choosing autonomous individuals." (Nadeus, p. 111) This same cultural discourse also "subsumes human differences under the totalizing category of national identity . . . in legitimizing Western imperialist expansion and domination of the world." (Liu, p. 48) What this means is that in the past two centuries in which the West has subjugated Asia through war and trade, "China" often exists as a problem. Fukuzawa Yukichi (福沢諭吉), for example, seriously entertained the possibility of "leaving Asia" (*Datsu-A Ron*, 1885, 脱亞入歐). To him, cultural identity boils down to a matter of choosing friends. "Those who cherish bad friends cannot escape the fate of being branded as a bad person. My heart and determination lie in the refusal of bad friends." The "bad friends" is a reference to China (Shina) and Korea (Chosen) with which Fukuzawa wanted Japan to sever cultural ties. "Unless we [Japan] want to prevent the coming of this Western civilization with a firm resolve, it is best that we cast our lot with them. If one observes carefully what is happening in the present world, one should realize the futility of preventing the onslaught of Western civilization. Why shall we not float with them (the West) in the same ocean of civilization, sail the same waves, and enjoy the fruits and endeavors of civilization?" (Fukuzawa, p. 15) Nowhere is this rhetorical question more relevant than in the social problem films in which the viewer realizes his or her cultural identity in the self-awareness of the fictional characters as Chinese or Asian.

To differing degrees, the theme of identity crisis is present in all the films that transvalue Han Chinese traditions in the context of European civilization. As such, they are but variations of recent events such as independence or de-sinicization (去中國化) movements in Hong Kong and Taiwan. They can also be seen as continuations of the May Fourth radicalism to abolish Chinese writing in order to save the country (漢字不死中國必亡), mediated by a "new rhetoric [that] is deceptively simple: since China's backwardness had deep roots in Chinese polity, society, and culture, the total transformation of Chinese-ness is a precondition for China's modernization." (Tu p. 5) The films stage that transformation of identity in a series of "hyper-realities" in which "it is impossible to distinguish reality from fantasy." (Botz-Bornstein, p. 3) Most Chinese today are used to thinking of themselves as related by abstract affinities such as universal human rights rather than kinship and friendship. The films invite them to exercise their right to choose a civilization or redefine their own and ultimately they represent the dynamism of the Hegelian dialectic, reacting critically to an old symbolic order (thesis), waking up to a new cultural myth or higher truth of reality (antithesis), and reconciling themselves with a mode of existence to be defined as becoming (synthesis). These critical steps of the "creative self-negations and destructions"[2] (Zhang, p. 73) taken by those during the May Fourth movement, Communist Revolution, Cultural Revolution, and Deng's reform also go on in the hearts and minds of those, Chinese citizens or not, living beyond China's borders that used to circumscribe their identity.

British Hong Kong was one of the areas where the Chinese could become "modernized" and even "civilized." In an article titled 'Barbarism – Civilization', published in one of China's first English language newspaper the *Canton Register*, the global progress of the Anglo-world is invoked as evidence that British civilization is far more superior to Chinese despotism:

By what right are the aborigines of North America and New Holland driven from their indisputable homes by the governments of the United States and Great Britain? By no other than that barbarism must vanish before civilization, ignorance succumb to knowledge: such appears to be a law of nature, or rather, the will of God! (Stan Neal, p. 62)

One such record of "barbarism vanishing before civilization" or "total transformation of Chinese-ness" is *The Unwritten Law*, (1985) directed by See Yuen Ng, a.k.a. Wu Siyuan (吳思遠). In this courtroom drama, social justice prevails under Christian precepts and triumphs over the barbarity of the colonized. Trial by jury was designed to settle criminal matters where the fate of the individual on trial is in the hands of his or her peers and not those who happen to be in power. The female lead Liu Hui-lan is a prostitute, charged for killing a sadistic playboy Zeng Yonglin who gets sexual pleasure from torturing women. The characters who exemplify the Christian virtues of hope, charity, and love are the male lead Liu Zhipeng, his mother the prostitute, and Mother Maria at the orphanage where he is brought up. The story ends with Liu Hui-lan exonerated and free.

The film is a window into the minds of Hong Kongers living under Western subjugation. It begins in England when Liu Zhipeng, in cap and gown, graduates from the London School of Law, with Latin honors of summa cum laude. He grows up in a Christian orphanage in Hong Kong, under the loving care of Mother Maria. His job as a solicitor in Hong Kong puts him in the position to defend Huilan, whom he does not know is his biological mother who abandoned him. By winning the case for his mother, he not only glorifies the works of Mother Maria but also celebrates the ethos of Christianity. When Mother Maria is ordered to testify under oath whether Zhipeng is the son of Huilan, a legal maneuver on the part of the prosecutor to disqualify Zhipeng as the lawful representative for Huilan, Maria's adamant denial "No" helps secure the acquittal for Huilan. This untruth is not a lie because, in Christian theology, all people are God's children and it is through His divine grace that Christians achieve salvation and redemption. The concept of equality before God triumphs in a repressive and corrupt society in which people are treated according to their social status. An Asian messianic figure of the Enlightenment, Zhipeng understands not only the letter but also the spirit of the law to achieve justice and bring mercy to the poor. This tribute to European civilization is in perfect accord with the view of Robert Morrison (1782–1834), Anglo-Scottish Protestant missionary in Macau and Guangdong, father of Anglo-Chinese literature, "The general principles of our religion give a tone of elevation and dignity to the human mind which is not felt here …. They the Chinese do not associate something approaching equality for the worship of their gods. The multitudes of people in this country are truly, in a moral and religious view, as 'sheep without a shepherd. (Gao Hao p. 580) To Director Ng, Europe represents the highest stage of world civilization and Hong Kong a benighted place where sheep need a shepherd to lead them out of darkness. Some Chinese settlers and colonists, however, had a view much less sanguine on the encounters between Asian peoples and European powers. One Cheoke Hong Cheong protested loudly what he saw as racial discrimination by the British Australians:

Is it possible the Parliament of Victoria and the other colonies can enact that even a British subject, if of the Chinese race, and just because he differs from the European in the colour of his skin, is therefore to be treated as a felon? Then, again, is it possible that common human rights accorded to other civilized people are to be denied to us? That it is to be a crime, punishable by hard labor, if man or woman of the Chinese race travel over the line separating any of the colonies without a permit, which might not be obtainable? If such is to be then we protest in the sight of heaven that this is a crime, not as committed against us only, but against the great Creator of all "who made of one blood all nations of men." (Marilyn Lake, p. 387)

In Ng's commendatory version of British colonization, justice, and racial equality prevail over evil. As a sinner and Chinese, Huilan is saved by the grace of God, a footnote to the civilizing mission of the white man to bring light to those kept in the darkness of ignorance and barbarity.

As a British colony and a huge metropolis that was once only a fishing village, Hong Kong is a typical migrant city with a diverse population. To many residents, Hong Kong is a gateway to freedom and endless opportunities. Shot in 1996 when the colonial rule was coming to an end, *Comrades, Almost A Love Story* by Peter Chen (陳可辛, 1962–) is a nostalgia film. "On the surface," says critic Gan Tian (p. 26), "the film is about a process in which two Mainlanders try to achieve HK identity but there is no reason why it is not also a process of finding one's history and identity on the part of the local residents. . . . The crazy spirit of Li Qiao struggling to change her life no matter what epitomizes the spirit of Hong Kong immigrants, old and new, who would not take it lying down. This is why the film triggers nostalgia among Kong Kongers hoping to establish and revise their history." The twists and turns of the romance between Li Qiao and Li Xiaojun take the viewer on a tour oscillating between the heaviness and lightness of being a Chinese in British Hong Kong. The products of this historical moment, the two youth cannot erase their past in the Mainland even when convinced, as Li Qiao is, that "This is Hong Kong; everything is possible here!" Their struggles as Chinese emigrants delineate the itinerary of a round trip from disclaiming to reclaiming their cultural identity. "If I wanted to marry a Chinese," Li Qiao says to Li Xiaojun, "I wouldn't have come to Hong Kong." For her, Xiaojun is her alter ego that is attached to her like the shirt of Nessus. He triggers in her the kind of negative narcissism in people like Bo Yang and Lu Xun who felt as though culturally implicated by Chinese traditions but powerless to resist the white mythologies of race. The true nature of their romance is nothing other than their shared desire to destroy their past and be different, which pushes them apart but also draws them together. They cannot be together until the two can accept each other and themselves, which they do at the end of their self-discovery odyssey from China's borders to the Statue of Liberty in New York Harbor.

The film transnationalizes Chinese identity and offers an encyclopedic treatment of overseas Chinese experiences as migrants. The two main characters testify to the fact that "the mobility of laborers makes these people culturally lost, socially uprooted, and politically impotent in the public life of their destination societies. . . . While the problem of identity arises everywhere with globalization; international immigrants are doubtless among those who meet the most serious challenges in this regard, as they have to abandon their own language, culture, and religion in settling into new destinations." (Wu, pp. 188–9) The romance of the two immigrants expands the Chinese imagination and extends the Chinese vision from the Mainland where the two lovers begin their odyssey all the way to the New York Harbor where they are nothing like who they were years ago except for their passion for Teresa Deng's songs. The two protagonists disseminate a changing version of Chinese identity, recording the moments when a Chinese person steps onto foreign soil, learns the language of the host-country, deals with immigration matters, and feels overwhelmed by homesickness and love. The voyage taking Xiaojun and Li Qiao from China to America allows new experiences to happen, but only as variations of what they have experienced in the past, as if in déjà vu.

Hong Kong as a conglomerate of different cultures is never Chinese enough for China or Western enough for Europe. It is a composite of both but like neither. Wayne Wang's *Chinese Box* is characterized by a playfulness about Hong Kong's identity. Comprising both English and Chinese, the film is an interesting exercise of deconstruction through which it rejects the essentialist notion of culture in favor of a global civilization. As the title suggests, identity is really like a set of boxes with graduated sizes, which the viewer sees open one after another at the very beginning, with no substance inside. The story reveals a set of interlocking relationships that change with the dynamics of geopolitics. As the white colonizer, John Spencer perfectly exemplifies the British rule in Hong Kong before 1997, genuinely concerned with the interests of the natives such as Jean and Vivian. He does not realize that his presence as a white colonizer biases his investigation as a reporter. Despite his compassion for the conquered races, John feels he is losing his grip on reality. As the colonized, both

Jean and Vivian learn the art of mimicry in all its forms to accommodate the racial stereotypes and prejudices of the West against them.

In the film, what matters is not the truth of reality but the apparatuses of perception. The story is about an unstable hyperreality that will soon be subverted when Hong Kong reverts to China. John is often frustrated with the information he gets from the natives because he does not know what to believe. When viewing a video clip of Jean talking about herself, John's friend Rick positions the projector in such a way that her face gets shown over John's to create a hybrid cultural identity. The uncanny image of two faces overlapping, one Chinese and one white, reveals the violent history of colonial subjugation and cultural domination. The violence of European colonialism that John represents also created new forms of inequality. The politics of self-representation were not any less complex with the end of British rule, as there are now going to be issues about how pure Hong Kong residents are as Chinese rather than as British subjects. While some in Hong Kong perceive the Mainland as a politically less evolved and culturally inferior place, some Mainlanders such as Mr. Zhang also feel a sense of superiority over the Hong Kong residents whose Chinese-ness has been compromised during the colonial occupation. Mr. Zhang feels embarrassed to be seen in public with Vivian and would introduce this former prostitute only as his secretary to his business associates.

The film could not have been made at a more opportune moment to observe the dynamic and complexity of cultural politics. In 1997 when the British colonial rule of Hong Kong was coming to an end, not only was the history and law of Hong Kong going to be rewritten, individual Hong Kongers also needed to rethink their lives in relation to the changes to come. Hong Kong's history is subject to different interpretations, either as a satellite state of European civilization wherein the Chinese natives enjoy self-autonomy or even independence, or as lost Chinese territory that the motherland is now reclaiming from the colonizing foreign powers. The battle over the right to interpret history is dramatized when Jean gives an oral account of her past, in which she was madly in love with her boyfriend William. But when John brings this white man to confront his past, William has no recollection of ever being in love with an Asian woman and does not remember Jean. All these individual boxes of personal memory or identity are being put into larger boxes of national and international history.

The geographic distance between Hong Kong and the Mainland is infinitesimal but the distinction between culture and civilization is significant. Take for example *Happy Together* (春光乍洩, 1997) by Wong Kar-wai. The definition of national culture as Thomas Mann understood it is relevant in the story where three homosexual young people travel to South America to escape their identities as defined within Chinese culture. Their problematic relationships are characteristic of the tension (hostility) between Hong Kong, Taiwan, and China. The change of venue in Buenos Aires is a quest for freedom denied at home. For Lai Yiu-fai (黎耀輝), Ho Po-wing (何寶榮) and Xiao Chang (小張), the sojourn in Argentina is a way to revolutionize how they normally experience Hong Kong or Taiwan, to stage an antithesis of the original thesis. They would rather cope with the unbearable lightness of being nothing (and free) than carry the burden of a national culture as their identity.

To an extent, the story is about self-exile or escapism, but it is also about the homecoming that happens at the end. The film begins with Lai's and Ho's passports being stamped which, according to Carlos Rojas, "[A passport] is a symbol both of one's identity and of the contingencies that underlie that identity. ... The passports, in other words, symbolize Hong Kong and China's own attempt to figuratively "start over." (Rojas, p. 516) As British subjects, Cantonese speakers, and male homosexuals, their relationships are contentious or even poisonous, characteristic of the complex relationships between Great Britain, Hong Kong, Taiwan, and China as different temporalities converge. They are at the mercy of larger historical forces and cultural trajectories over which they have no control. Regardless of where or how far they travel, they are inextricably connected to the local culture that continues to shape their growth, like the saying "you can take the man out of the ghetto, but you cannot take the ghetto out of the man." Like Hong Kong in 1997 being pulled apart by the divergence of Great Britain and China as two world powers, the gay relationship is so volatile and precarious that Lai, at one point, refuses to give Ho's passport (freedom) back to him so that he cannot run away. Their relationship is analogous to that between China, England, Hong Kong, and Taiwan: it is contentious and interdependent.

What is expressed here is the notion of civilization that is individualistic and democratic rather than aristocratic and metaphysical. The incompatibilities between Ho (who is volatile or tempestuous) and Lai (who tends to be calm, collected, and self-disciplined) are such that one critic goes so far as to compare the two with the Nietzschean dichotomy of Dionysius and Apollo. (Wang, p. 72) Their emotionally taxing love relationship in which Ho often returns to Lai only to leave again allegorizes the uncertain situation of Hong Kong's homecoming to China. Before going back to Hong Kong, Lai watches television in a motel room when the news of Deng Xiaoping's death is broadcast. His homecoming coincides with the death of China's paramount leader, an allegorical figure of patriarchal authority. Lai's apprehension about his return to reconcile with his father who may or may not forgive him for stealing money is an analogy to Hong Kong's anxiety as the crown colony of Great Britain is about to become an authoritarian-run Chinese Hong Kong. Their escapism is a temporary suspension from being in time and culture, Chinese or otherwise. The narrative shifts back and forth from black-and-white to colorful, documenting the difficulties and struggles of overseas Chinese to find and hold onto meaning in each fleeting moment. The film ends with Lai's train coming to a halt at the terminal in Hong Kong where another cycle of self-exploration awaits.

Chinese identity as defined within Confucian humanism is challenged the most, it would seem, within the discourse of human rights. For this reason, Ang Lee's *Wedding Banquet* (喜宴, 1993) is a very important film to study the art of "reproducing hegemonic national subjects" despite the liberalism that disrupts the traditional family as a Confucian construct. According to Sarah Olutola, Ang Lee displays queer liberation in such a way as to fulfill the regulatory functions of the patriarch. (Olutola, p. 94) It is Wei-tong's father, the retired army general, who conducts what Homi Bhabha refers to as "the process of transcultural negotiation." (Bhabha, p. 312) As one of the most populous world cities, New York City epitomizes global civilization where one is expected to experience cultural and ethnic diversity. Ang Lee's view of transcultural negotiation is presented through the figure of Father Gao when confronted with same-sex relations cross racial lines. He is a newer version of the philosopher-king, changing the famous remarks by Julius Caesar from "I came; I saw; I conquered" to "I came; I saw; I *learned*." William Leung is quite apt to point out that "In fact, it is the bedrock of Chinese culture – the father's paramount esteem for familial unity and continuity – that finally becomes the agent for healing the potential disruption and enables a kind of new family to emerge." (Leung, p. 31)

For Ang Lee, as some have argued, Chinese traditions contribute to world civilization and become trans-nationalized through globalization. "As contemporary Chinese and Taiwanese negotiate an increasing trans-national self and nation, the 'soy sauce jar' has begun to crack. Filmmakers like Ang Lee may use 'soy sauce' to flavor their dishes, but they juxtapose it with unexpected ingredients. There may be a danger, as bell hooks argues, that "within commodity culture, ethnicity becomes spice, seasoning that can liven up the dull dish that is the mainstream white culture. ... Ang Lee re-envisions Chinese civilization in a much more sympathetic light, as something that is highly versatile and adaptive. The 'soy sauce jar' that both represents and contains Chinese and Taiwanese national and trans-national identities, is figuratively broken to reveal a new sensibility while the fluid of the 'jar' is not discarded. Recognizing the unfinished nature of intercultural processes endows the individuals with a sense of agency and consequence." (Dariotis and Fung, p. 189) The film thus challenges the conventional philosophical paradigm that treats civilizations as if by nature separate, static, and distinctive. Mr. Gao's ethnicity and morals as a Confucian contribute greatly to a global civilization in which cultures are interdependent. His skills in dealing with the challenges of cultural and racial diversity in NYC are reminiscent of the traditional cultural ideals of "bringing the four barbarians into China (納四夷入中國) . . . to bring the many ethnic groups on its periphery into a single 'Chinese nation.'" (Ge Zhaoguang, p. 65)

As is with space, cultural differences can also be experienced *as* time. As Mann pointed out, "national culture" is by nature metaphysical, aristocratic, and intellectual, not subject to change. This is the reason why Rey Chow views Zhang

Yimou's representation as that of a "timeless China of the past . . . signified mythically." (Chow, p. 145) *What Time Is It There* (2001, 你那邊幾點) is "an allegory of the political situation in the post-generalissimo Chiang Kai-shek era" that defines Tsai Mingliang as a Taiwanese filmmaker. (Liao, p. 63) The death of Xiao Kang's father seems to rob everybody of their identity. This film, with its nostalgia for the bygone Chiang Kai-shek era, seems to be a tale of two cities (Taipei and Paris) except the vast distance between Asia and Europe reveals nothing meaningful in this post-Chiang age. Like identities, time zones are also man-made realities and cultural constructs that are arbitrary and artificial; they are only as true or meaningless as people make them. The point of the film is that cultures are as different from one another or as true as the time zones or people's inner spiritualities. Xiao Kang is lonely after his father dies and does not have a real life anymore other than as a street vendor of wristwatches. A pious Buddhist, his mother also becomes emotionally withdrawn and weary of waiting for her husband's spirit to visit her. Living under the same roof, the mother and son might as well be living in two different spiritual realms. Relationships may appear nonexistent for people related by blood but, at the same time, seem quite real for strangers. After a young woman – Chen Xiangqi – buys the wristwatch that he was wearing, Xiao Kang becomes attracted to her. She is going to Paris the next day, and Xiao Kang becomes fascinated with the seven-hour time difference between Taipei and Paris. He resets all his timepieces to Paris time so he can live in her time, which suggests that reality is being hollowed out through globalization. Plagued by nothingness, Xiao Kang only seems preoccupied with a place where he is not.

The crosscuts back and forth between the two cities connect things and people that have no inherent meanings to one another. Paris-Taipei romance is as nonexistent as the spirit of Xiao Kang's dead father. The young woman Chen Xiangqi has absolutely nothing to do in Paris because her life as a Taiwanese woman has no real meaning other than being seven hours away from Taipei, which is perhaps why she insists on buying a watch that can tell the times of two different places. Similarly, Taipei as a place or time zone that is no more home to Xiao Kang than Paris is to Xiangqi. After Xiangqi leaves Taipei, Xiao Kang tries to telepathically move himself to Paris by watching *The 400 Blows* (1959) in which his meaningless existence is reflected in Antoine Doinel's problematic childhood. In this distant land that Xiao Kang cannot afford to visit except through some cultural artifact like videotapes, Xiangqi lives a life not any different from Xiao Kang's life that is seven hours ahead of Taipei. On the surface, French culture and society cannot be more different from Taiwan, yet the homogeneity of modern civilization seems to render life everywhere so flat and empty that no one can achieve intimacy regardless of how close they are geographical to one another.

As global cities, Taipei and Paris offer nothing meaningful other than the unbearable lightness of being. People everywhere live in different "time zones" and personal bubbles. Xiao Kang's parents dwell in different spiritual realms even as his mother masturbates in the dark for fear that her dead husband will be frightened away by bright light. Meanwhile, in Paris, Xiangqi meets Cecilia Yip, a young woman from Hong Kong, only to realize that they do not make a good lesbian couple. Back in Taipei, Xiao Kang is seen having sex with a prostitute, but the intense physical act never brings the two any closer than Taipei is to Paris, with the prostitute stealing all his watches while he is asleep dreaming of Xiangqi in France. The story helps register different international time zones in which a person feels alienated from other individuals by his gender, sexual orientation, language, or religious creed. We realize the artificiality of civilization as opposed to the authenticity of culture (the old days of Chiang Kai-shek) when Xiao Kang's father oddly reappears at the end as if to undermine the reality of the characters in different localities in space and time. The montage sabotages time zones and sequences. With temporal linearity removed, the sequence and causality of events are gone, and individual identity evaporates. There is no "here," "there," "now" or "then." There is also no identity for the characters. The story is thus an exercise in deconstruction to expose the superficiality of modern life in which fantasies are mistaken for reality.

The lines separating one person from another seem hard to draw in America for obvious reasons. But even in this multiracial society or "universal nation," Chinese Americans still often feel as though they are being ". . . defined by our European heritage and institutions."[3] (Huntington, p. 9) This dominant definition of America's national identity becomes the nightmare for a Chinese immigrant family in *The Gua Sha Treatment* (2001). The controversy surrounding *Gua Sha Treatment* shows the relevance and validity of cultural institutions that do not necessarily originate in the West. A Chinese expat living in the US. Zheng Xiaolong (鄭曉龍) is interested in how ideals of democracy and liberty impact the life of overseas Chinese (-Americans). His story revolves around a case of child abuse when the accused do no more than *gua sha*, a traditional medicine treatment not recognized by the US legal system.

Based on a real event, the story demonstrates how "European heritage and institutions" can benefit as well as discriminate against people of Chinese descent in America. It is not just Chinese medicine that is called into question and put on trial, but the hierarchical Confucian values as well, such as loyalty, filial piety, obedience, and self-sacrifice. The hierarchy of these home values is rendered problematic and negotiated through the character of Datong (大同) whose name signifies universal harmony. To a degree, the drama is a sequel to earlier historical chapters of racial discrimination such as the Chinese Exclusion Act (1882–1943) in which the Chinese are described as "Asiatic barbarians." In the courtroom, Datong is called "barbaric" by a white nurse present at his son's birth when he tells her to save his wife if mother and son cannot both survive. He is caught committing perjury when standing in as the culprit for his father's questionable medical practice, an act exemplary of Confucian ethics.[4] In short, the film raises the self-awareness of Asian Americans whose cultural legacy is not well accepted or is badly misunderstood in the US. The legal battles that the Xu family goes through underline the problems of American national identity as Huntington understands them. If America is a Western nation defined by European heritage and institutions, do the Xus have to renounce part of their ethnicity, religion, and tradition to be respected? The film lends itself to a much larger conversation that began long ago on racial and civilizational differences.

The *gua sha* controversy is only a catalyst for debating the conscious values subscribed by many overseas Chinese such as Datong. The trial draws into the courtroom the literati tradition that is not well recognized in the dominant Eurocentric narrative of human rights. In his *The Essence of Chinese Civilization*, scholar Liang Shuming (1893–1988) defines Confucianism from a comparative perspective. Some of his critical observations provide a cultural prototype of which Xu Datong is one instance in America. In this philosophical treatise, Liang identifies what may appear a lack of civic spirit on the part of the Chinese, well elaborated in the film plot:

> Chapter IV: Chinese lack public life. Westerner's strength and our people's shortcoming. As it turns out every Chinese is a docile subject but, at the same time, every one of them is an emperor. Behind shut doors, he is an emperor to his wife and children. But once out the door, his propensity to be peaceful and accommodating comes out like second nature, a docile and pleasant man with his philosophy of taking losses as natural blows of life. But he has not cultivated the social skills to interact and negotiate with others in public settings, being neither haughty nor humble. Mr. Hu Shiqing is said to have been to every corner of the world, especially in the Americas and the South Pacific areas where there are pockets of overseas Chinese. He enjoyed talking about the overseas Chinese he had met, and came to this conclusion: that the overseas Chinese tend to outdo the expats of other nations as well as the natives. In nearly all walks of life, they outperform the rest, even in robbery or panhandling. However, these are personal skills and not the achievements of an organized group. Because of this inferiority in organizing themselves into a society and inability to receive legal protection from the state, they are doing worse than the overseas Japanese, and are bullied by the natives. This is the perfect example of the reason why in today's competitive world the Chinese are inferior and weak as a whole. … In addition, in his *The Travels in the New World*, Liang Qichao further elucidates the point that China has clans whereas the West has citizens; the Chinese have self-rule by clan or village but do not have a bourgeois society. From the very beginning, the West preferred governance by citizens whereas the Chinese favored tribal and communal governance. (pp. 66–7)

Nothing elucidates Confucian humanism better than Datong as a (Chinese) character. His problems underscore the fact that "China has clans whereas the West has citizens." What Datong does not understand and ignores at his peril is the spirit of democratic people for whom, in the words of Tocqueville (p. 409), "common opinion remains the sole guide" and whose similarity "gives them an almost unlimited trust in the judgment of the public." Datong's self-righteousness as a Confucian gentleman (*jun zi*, 君子) is aristocratic by nature, as he "aims at harmony, and not at uniformity" (君子和而不同小人同而不和). He expects that his beliefs and conducts are private matters not subject to social conformity so long as they do not challenge social harmony.

The court is not only where Datong has to prove that *gua sha* is a bona fide medical treatment. It is also where authoritarianism, despotism, or totalitarianism is on trial, which the Americans have fought against in favor of law and constitutional democracy. Born and raised in a different tradition, Datong is utterly unfamiliar with the cultural institutions of the country in which he now resides. He acts like a patriarch (father and monarch) at home and a docile subject outside. Contrarily, Americans belong to "Western self-ruled bourgeois society" (西洋之'市民'市制之自治) and abide by the law and public opinion when they interact. What is brought to light through this case of "child abuse" is how civil society and democracy operate in the pursuit of truth and justice. In the Confucian context, society is conceived of through the concept of the family. A family man, Datong expects himself to do no wrong in society if he conducts himself like a good son, father, and husband. His over-reactions throughout the legal proceedings dramatize Chinese cultural ineptitude while in such "democratic nations" where the order is maintained when elected officials legislate and enforce laws to settle disputes and protect public interests. To Zheng's credit as the director, the story comes to an intriguing ending when Judge Horowitz rescinds his earlier ruling against Datong. The end confirms the utopian vision of reform-minded political thinker Kang Youwei (康有為, 1858–1927), the author of *The Book of Great Unity / Universal Harmony* (大同書) which happens to be Datong's name. The drama reintroduces the idea of universal harmony and it reminds the viewer of the words of Chinese philosopher Fei Xiaotong (費孝通): "Each (culture) is beautiful by its own aesthetics; each also finds beauty through the aesthetics of the other; when different aesthetics coexist, there is great harmony." So, beneath this brief clash of civilizations that ends in temporary peace and harmony, the viewer sees also the recurring theme of a Confucian utopia, coexisting with the ideal of social democracy in America as a "universal nation." *Gua Sha* is one of the Sinophone films showing the dangers as well as rewards of transcultural negotiation in the contexts of colonialism, diaspora, emigration, exile overseas, global travel, and tourism.

The value of these Anglo-Chinese films lies in the fact that the directors transvalue the idea of *Zhongguo* (中國) through imaginaries, and allow cultures to coalesce. China in these stories is not a monolith or noun but a process or verb that people are learning to conjugate. This China resonates with the viewer when being translated back and forth between Chinese and English. In these hyperrealities, East-West "cultural differences" are presented to delineate the contours of a global civilization sutured together out of the fabrics of Confucianism, Christianity as well as the democratic values of individual freedom and equality. "China" is no longer just a metaphysical construct but also a sociological process, thanks to the film aesthetics of Ang Lee, Wong Kar-wai, Peter Chen, Zheng Xiaolong, Tsai Mingliang, Wayne Wang, and Wu Siyuan. To these filmmakers, the viewers owe their changing identity, as much as "later modern human beings are still being shaped by Shakespeare, not as Englishmen, or American women, but in modes increasingly postnational and postgender." This is the sense in which critic Harold Bloom regards Shakespeare as "the first universal author" and "an international possession, transcending nations, languages, and professions." To Bloom, the Shakespearean plays amount to "the invention of the human"[5] (Bloom, pp. xviii, 1, 2, 7, 10) with highly sophisticated individual characters, men and women capable of change who are no longer just hegemonic national subjects. Likewise, these Sinophone films reinvent the Chinese through memorable characters who speak Chinese and English as the languages of social change. As is true for Shakespeare, the filmmakers create new mythologies or modes of being that the Chinese have not thought of before.

The gap between Renaissance humanism in the West and this ever-changing identity among Chinese in the diaspora is getting smaller. That gap used to boggle the mind. For Yan Fu (1854–1921), the scholar and translator of Darwin's *Natural Selection*, the Chinese are a different species compared to Westerners, since their cultures are so diametrically opposed.

> China values the Three Bonds more highly, while the Westerners give precedence to equality. China cherishes relatives, while the Westerners esteem the worthy. China governs the realm through filial piety, while Westerners govern the realm with impartiality [*gong*]. China values the sovereign, while Westerners esteem the people. China prizes the one Way, while Westerners prefer diversity. . . . In learning, Chinese praise breadth of wisdom while westerners respect new knowledge. In respect to disasters, the Chinese trust fate, while Westerners rely on human strength. (Yan Fu, pp. 49–50)

Yet, this aristocratic idea of China as a "national culture," which idealizes what distinguishes one people from another, is constantly being renegotiated in the films to underscore what people all over the world have in common. The fictional Chinese characters seem to desire nothing better than what the Westerners want as they break with traditions to achieve equality and individual freedom. Time is on the side of change as people spread civilization to transcend their respective cultures. There have been plenty of films in Chinese cinema in which people fight for justice through Marxism and communism, building a republic modeled on the Western nation-state and joining the march of history dictated by global capitals and free markets.

Amazing things happen in these films in which Chinese traditions are being redefined in the context of European cultural institutions. It almost seems that the characters are created to debunk the notion that the Chinese are *culturally* predisposed to act differently from Westerners. This body of films reaffirm the point made by Liu Qing against cultural nationalism in favor of a cosmopolitanism.

> There has been a long history of homegrown theories of China as a unique culture. Since the late Qing period, there have been several revivals of the argument that have developed into a conclusion that can be summed up as the "unsuitable" logic: namely, because China is so special and unique, any non-native concepts, values, systems and praxis are unsuited to Chinese situations. There has been no shortage of this logic or lack of eloquence for it. For example, Western medicine is not suitable for China, because Chinese physiological constitution is different from that of the Westerner; free love is not suitable for China, because since antiquity the Chinese have advocated the ideal of extended family, marriage has never been between men and women as individuals but the merging of two families arranged by the parents and the matchmaker; "coed education is not suitable for China because the traditions would not consider appropriate for men and women to touch hands; "Marxism is not suitable for China because the generality drawn by the Jewish person about European traditions and social praxis cannot be valid for Chinese situations; "individual rights" are not suitable for China because the Chinese identity always stems from the collective and never been an atomized self; "market economy is not suitable for China because Chinese culture has always been community based, especially after the temperament of socialist experience that renders impossible the pursuit of money and profit as personal values. It is said that prior to fast-food giant McDonald's made an entry to China, the company consulted experts on its business prospect and the assessment was that it would be undoubtedly a total failure because the Chinese have their special and rich culinary tradition for flour-based food and would not eat hamburgers. As a result, McDonald's did not make the move well after KFC stepped into the fast-food market. To date, not only do we see Western medicine, McDonald's, coed

education and free love, Marxism and marketplace introduced into China, but also the taking roots and coming to fruition of these Western institutions. (Liu Qing, pp. 12–3)

In the narrative film above, we see a vast array of characters who achieve identity through "these Western institutions" when the traditional close-knit organic community (有機共同體) is all but extinct. They are ordinary citizens of civil society (公民社會), proprietors (業主), legal representatives (法人), tax-payers (納稅人), homosexuals (同性恋者) or celibate (獨身主義者).

The films record not only metamorphoses of the individual outgrowing their aristocratic and ethnocentric self-definitions but also a collective psyche in all – Chinese citizens or naturalized in their respective host societies – who find a sense of themselves as a people. The films have addressed the issues that the Chinese have experienced in the diaspora:

The untold suffering of the Chinese people – caused by Western imperialism, the Taiping Rebellion, the collapse of the Manchu dynasty, the internecine struggle of the warlords, Japanese aggression, the conflict between the Nationalists and the Communists, and the misguided policies of the People's Republic of China – contextualized the meaning of Chinese-ness in a new symbolic structure. Marginality, rootlessness, amnesia, anger, frustration, alienation, and helplessness have gained much salience in characterizing the collective psyche of the modern Chinese. (Tu, 1994, vii)

The filmmakers document important changes in Han Chinese self-awareness as they explore the frontiers of a global civilization, similar to what happened to American identity deeply rooted in Europe when "the advance of the frontier has meant a steady movement away from the influence of Europe, a steady growth of independence on American lines."[6] (Turner, p. 201) Thanks to these filmed cultural events, "Chinese nowadays are a new species. Therefore, we need to emphasize, that the Chinese who have been through the experience of the Twentieth-Century are *not* the ancient Chinese, overseas Chinese, those who identify themselves as part of cultural China, or people referred to as citizens of the world." (Zhang, p. 77) It would be equally correct to argue to the contrary, that contemporary Chinese *are* all these things. These films thus constitute a democracy of perception, subjecting Chinese culture to different interpretations.

As these film texts recede into the distance by the day, we gain new horizons in what it means to be Chinese. Chris Berry is quite right that "it is not so much China that makes movies, but movies that help to make China." (Berry, p. 3). That China is not only real but also justified as Nietzsche understands the human world, namely, "it is only as an aesthetic phenomenon that existence and the world are eternally justified" (. . . *nur als ästhetisches Phänomen ist das Dasein und die Welt ewig gerechtfertigt*). As philosophy and history meet in these films, there emerges a community of mind where the Chinese come to embrace new values and develop new conscious attitudes. If history is, to quote Hegel, ". . . the progressing self-determination of the Idea, the progressing self-development of Spirit" (Hegel, p. vii), then the directors should be credited as poets and seers who have helped redefine Chinese identity, frame by frame. The idea of China has gone through more changes in these Chinese/English language films over the past century than has been recorded in the historical records and scholarly works written in the past two millennia in both China and the West. Thanks to these films, the Chinese have awoken to their self-development in the world. It is only right that movie lovers and fans of Anglo-Chinese films pay homage to these filmmakers by saying, in the words of Hermann Hesse, "If I know what love is, it is because of you"

ENDNOTES

[1] "In recent years, when the king of Persia toured London, the British King awarded him medals of honors. *Times* newspaper reported rather disparagingly: "Why should the half-civilized deserve medals of honors?" To the Westerners, European countries that govern with the rule of law are civilized. Others like China, Turkey and Persia are half-civilized. The word "half" means half civilized. Countries in Africa are referred

to as "barbarian," just like the word "Yi Di" in Chinese, which is what the Westerners meant by uncivilized. During the time of Xia, Shang and Zhou dynasties, China alone was viewed as a place where there existed such rituals as dress code for mourning the dead, all those places far away from China were disparaged as "the barbarians." Since the Han dynasty, the culture of change through education has been steadily on the decline towards extinction, while the culture of law in Europe has been on the rise to prominence. The way they view China is the same as how China used to view the barbarians during the time of the Three Sage Kings. It is sad that there have not been literati in China who understand this.

2   "What I mean by the so-called affirmation of the whole is affirming their negation.... There is not necessarily logic in things linked together sequentially. Was not the history of over 2000 years overthrown overnight during the May Fourth movement? This is because there is a new logic. "New" here is not an adjective but a noun, the new as a subject by and of itself. With its own history, the history of the new is a whole thing that affirms a new set of contradictions. The history of the new continuously subverts, breaks through, revolts and self-destroys.

3   "We Americans" face a substantive problem of national identity epitomized by the subject of this sentence. Are we a "we," one people or several? If we are a "we," what distinguishes us from the "thems" who are not us? Race, religion, ethnicity, values, culture, wealth, politics, or what? Is the United States, as some have argued, a "universal nation," based on values common to all humanity and in principle embracing all peoples? Or are we a Western nation with our identity defined by our European heritage and institutions?"

4   *Analects*, Book VIII, chapter XVIII; "The Duke of She informed Confucius saying 'Among us here are those who may be styled upright in their conduct. If their fathers have stolen a sheep, they will bear witness to the fact.' Confucius said 'Among us, in our part of the country, those who are upright are different from this. The father conceals the misconduct of the son, and the son conceals the misconduct of the father. Uprightness is to be found in this.'" 叶公语孔子曰、吾党有直躬者、其父攘羊而子证正之。孔子曰、吾党之直者异于是、父为子隐子为父隐、直在其中矣。

5   "Shakespeare will go on explaining us, in part because he invented us.... Shakespeare's originality in the representation of character will be demonstrated throughout, as will the extent to which we all of us were, to a shocking degree, pragmatically reinvented by Shakespeare. Our ideas as to what makes the self authentically human owe more to Shakespeare than ought to be possible."

6   "At first, the frontier was the Atlantic coast. It was the frontier of Europe in a very real sense. Moving westward, the frontier became more and more American. As successive terminal moraines result from successive glaciations, so each frontier leaves its traces behind it, and when it becomes a settled area the region still partakes of the frontier characteristics. Thus, the advance of the frontier has meant a steady movement away from the influence of Europe, a steady growth of independence on American lines."

REFERENCES

Berry, Chris. (1998) "If China Can Say No, Can China Make Movies? Or, Do Movies Make China? Rethinking National Cinema and National Agency" in *Boundary* 2 25:3

Bhabha, Homi. (1990) *Nation and Narration*, Routledge, p. 312.

Bloom, Harold. (1998) *Shakespeare: The Invention of the Human*, Riverhead Books

Botz-Bornstein, Thorsten. (2011) "America against China: Civilization without Culture against Culture without Civilization?" in *Culture and Dialogue*, Vol. 1 No.2

Chow, Rey. (1995) *Primitive Passions: Visuality, Sexuality, Ethnography and Contemporary Chinese Cinema*, Columbia University Press.

Dariotis, Wei Ming and Eileen Fung. (1997). "Breaking the Soy Source Jar, Diaspora and Displacement in the Films of Ang Lee," in *Transnational Chinese Cinema: Identity, Nationhood, Gender*; ed. by Sheldon Xiaopeng Lu, University of Hawaii Press

Fei, Xiaotong. On The Contribution of Confucian Culture to A World Civilization; 费孝通《谈儒家文化对世界文明的贡献》

Fukuzawa Yukichi (福沢諭吉). (1885) *Datsu-A Ron*, transl. by Dwight Tat Wai Kwok https://tspace.library.utoronto.ca/bitstream/1807/18797/1/Kwok_Dwight_TW_200911_MA_thesis.pdf

Gan, Tian. (2017). "From Self-Esteem to Self-Despair: An Analysis and Comparison of *Comrades, Almost A Love Story* and *My Dear*; Film and Television News, 甘甜,"从自信到自卑:《甜蜜蜜》和《亲爱的》的比较分析":《影视观察》

Gao Hao, *The Amherst Embassy and British Discoveries of China in History*, 2014, vol.99 No.4

Ge Zhaoguang. (2018). *What Is China? Territory, Ethnicity, Culture and History*, translated by Michael Gibbs Hill, Harvard University Press

Guo, Songtao. The Diaries from London and Paris, in *Travel Logs of Western Countries, Collections by Guo Songtao*, vol.3 annotated by Lu Yulin, published by Liaoning People's Press, Chinese Enlightenment Series, 1994. 郭嵩焘. (1994) 伦敦与巴黎日记《使西記程:郭嵩燾集》第三卷, 陸玉林選注;連寧人民出版社, 中國啟蒙思想文庫

Hegel, Georg Wilhelm Friedrich. (1953) *Reason in History*, transl. by Robert S. Hartman, Library of Liberal Arts, p. xvii.

Huntington, Samuel. (2004) *Who Are We? The Challenges to America's National Identity*, Simon & Schuster.

Lake, Marilyn. "Chinese Colonists Assert Their 'Common Human Rights': Cosmopolitanism as Subject and Method of History, *Journal of World Hisotry*, 2010, vol. 21 No.3, University of Hawaii Press

Leung, William. (2008) "So Queer Yet So Straight: Ang Lee's *Wedding Banquet* and *Brokeback Mountain*" in *Journal of Film and Video*, Vol. 60 No.1

Liang, Shuming. (2011). *The Essence of Chinese Civilization*, Shanghai People's Press, 梁漱溟,《中國文化要義》上海人民出版社

Liao, Hongfei. (2012). Nolstagia and Imaginary Time: An Interpretation of "What Time Is It There by Cai Mingliang," Forum of Arts; 廖鴻飛, "哀悼与想象的时间性-蔡明亮《你那边几点》的一种解读"; 藝苑 (Forum of Arts) 影視長廊

Liu, Lydia. (1995) *Translingual Practice, Literature, National Culture, and Translated Modernity*; Stanford University Press

Liu Qing. (2013). *How Unique Is China*, China CITIC; 刘擎,《中国有多特殊》中信出版社

Mann, Thomas. (1987). *Reflections of a Nonpolitical Man*, transl. by Walter D. Morris, Ungar,

Nadeau, Randall. (2002) "Confucianism and the Problem of Human Rights," published in *Intercultural Communication Studies* XI;1

Neal, Stan. "The Chinese Character: Race, Economics, Colonization," a chapter in *Singapore, Chinese Migration and the Making of the British Empire, 1819–67*, p. 154

Olutola, Sarah. (2015). "Liberal Spaces: The Costs and Contradictions of Representing Hegemonic National Subjects in Ang Lee's *The Wedding Banquet* and *Brokeback Mountain*," *Atlantis*, 37.1

Rojas, Carlos. (2016) "Queer Utopias in Wong Kar-wai's Happy Together," in *A Companion to Wong Kar-wai*, First Edition. ed by Martha P. Nochimson. John Wiley & Sons, Inc.

Shi Jie. 石介《中國論》https://devinfitz.com/translations/zhengtong-and-history/shi-jie-on-china-%E4%B8%AD%E5%9C%8B%E8%AB%96/

Tocqueville, Alexis de. (2000) *Democracy in America*, University of Chicago Press.

Tu Weiming. (1994) ed. *The Living Tree, The Changing Meaning of Being Chinese Today*, Stanford UP.

Turner, Frederick Jackson. (1966). *The Significance of the Frontier in American History*, University Microfilms.

Wang, Weiyan. The Seer and Seen in the Gaze: A Study of Body Writing in Film "Happy Together," Radio & TV Journal; 王禕顏. (2017) "凝視中的'看'與'被看'：電影《春光乍洩》中的身體敘事研究" *Radio & TV Journal*.

Wu, Guoguang. *Globlization against Democracy: A Political Economy of Capitalism after its Global Triumph*, Cambridge University Press, 2017

Yan Fu. excerpt from Collections of Yan Fu, quoted in *Bringing the World Home*, Theodore Huters, University of Hawaii Press, 2005.

Yoshimi Takeuchi. quoted by Theodore Huters in "Ideologies of Realism in Modern China." *Politics, Ideology, and Literary Discourse in Modern China*. ed. by Liu Kang and Xiaobing Tang; Duke UP, 1993.

Zhang Xudong. (2015) *Cultural Politics and The Chinese Way*, Shanghai People's Press. 張旭東《文化政治與中國道路》上海人民出版社

AUTHOR'S BIO

Born and raised in Beijing, Professor **RUJIE WANG** has been teaching Chinese language and literature at the College of Wooster for 25 years. He attended Peking Normal University (English), Wabash College (English), and Rutgers University (doctorate in Comparative Literature). His research interests include realist fiction, Chinese cinema, and comparative literature. His work has been published in such journals as *East Asia, Asian Cinema, Journal of Asian Studies, Canadian Review of Comparative Literature,* and *MCLC (Modern Chinese Literature and Culture) Journal*.

10 Self-Rescuing, Self-Healing, and Self-Freeing: The Inner-Oriented Gaze of *Nomadland*

Ying Wang, Mount Holyoke College

ABSTRACT

The Oscar award-winning film *Nomadland*, scripted and directed by Chloé Zhao and starring Frances McDormand, tells the story of the emerging American nomads as the casualty of the housing industry and economic recession. Based on Jessica Bruder's 2017 book of journalistic reporting, it takes an insider's perspective by creating the fictional and composite character of Fern. Contextualized in the 1930s Great Depression that triggered the first surge of American nomads, changes in the economic climate and companies' hiring strategies, and the cultural heritage of Transcendentalism, this review probes the inner-oriented gaze of the movie by analyzing Fern's nomadic journey from three progressive and interwoven developments, namely self-rescuing, self-healing, and self-freeing. In these three aspects of Fern's character development, as this review argues, the movie scrutinizes and combs the nomads' inner struggle: their embattlement with calamity and trauma, their tenacity and resilience to bounce back, their strong belief in self-reliance and freedom, and their spiritual elevation by returning to nature and finding love again. In serving the thematic subject, the movie casts both Hollywood stars and real nomads. The film's artistic strategies are well designed, most fitting, and quite prominent, providing the movie with a lyrical and poetic style that is both beautiful and haunting.

KEYWORDS

Inner-oriented gaze, self-rescuing, self-healing, self-freeing, self-reliance, nature, lyrical, poetic

At the 93rd Academy Awards ceremony on April 26, 2021, *Nomadland* was a star, winning best picture, best director for Chloé Zhao, and best actress for Frances McDormand. Despite receiving glowing compliments, the movie has been criticized for "an inchoate center, an avoidance of the worst things that could conceivably happen to the central character, a borderline kitsch attachment to landscape shots for their own sake, and a knack for gliding over the harder truth underlying the story" (Koehler 2021, p. 72). Criticism like this questions the inner logic of the movie, and seems to deviate from its thematic and philosophical undertaking, which may be contended by most audiences and critics. However, the implied questions of such criticism remain valid: What, then, is the inner logic of the movie? What messages does the movie try to deliver to its audiences? This article tries to probe these questions and argues that with a poeticized and self-reflective style in both thematic treatment and artistic strategies, *Nomadland* offers an inner-oriented gaze through its presentation, its characters, and particularly through the "nomadic journey" of Fern, the female protagonist of the movie, who undergoes a path from self-rescuing to self-healing and finally, to self-freeing.

The movie is a re-creation based on Jessica Bruder's book *Nomadland: Surviving America in the Twenty-First Century*, a documentary title based on years of investigation and numerous real-person interviews. The book deals with the emerging American labor force who are mainly the casualties of the 2008 Great Recession and who were uprooted from their middle-class status and lifestyle, took to the road in recreational vehicles and modified vans and lived on seasonal jobs from Amazon's CamperForce program, sugar beet companies, national parks, and camping resorts. Katherine Boo comments that:

> Nomadland *[the book] tells a revelatory tale of the dark underbelly of the American economy – one which foreshadows the precarious future that may await many more of us. At the same time, it celebrates the exceptional resilience and creativity of these Americans who have given up ordinary rootedness to survive, but have not given up hope* (Boo 2017, back cover).

To Jessica Bruder, researching this book was a painstaking process, even including living as a "nomad" herself by not only befriending the real nomads but also sleeping in a van and taking a seasonal job in one of the sugar beet companies, a typical temporary job for the nomads. Her effort eventually bore fruit, and the book made *The New York Times* 100 Notable Books list in addition to winning multiple awards in 2017.

The movie *Nomadland* deals with the same subject and portrays the same group of people and even includes some of the same nomads interviewed in Bruder's book as non-professional actors and actresses, but it also tells a somewhat different story. The difference between the journalistic report and the movie mainly lies in the creation of the character Fern and her vision/gaze in the film. Giving Fern the first-person point of view, the movie offers its audience an insider's perspective reflecting on a nomad's personal experience and her observations, reactions, and emotions. More importantly, instead of a reporter mediating between her interviewees and her readers, direct access to Fern's inner-thinking and her psychological well-being is made available in the film. Taking a nomadic journey, Fern experiences changes that are constantly savored and contemplated by her, and, through her, by the audience. Her perception of the outside world – the drastic lifestyle changes, the fellow nomads she meets on the road and in the camp, and the landscapes she sees and appreciates – all, in one way or the other, reflect her psyche and thought. Fern is a character with a strong presence of subjectivity: her gaze is inward-looking and her journey is soul searching.

Chloé Zhao wrote the movie script and is responsible for the creation of Fern's character. However, Frances McDormand seems to play a role in shaping this character in some way, as she says: "When I was in my 40s, I said to my husband [director Joel Coen], 'When I turn 65, I'm going to change my name to Fern. I'm going to start smoking Lucky Strikes and drinking Wild Turkey and hit the road in an RV" (Rebecca Keegan 2020, p. 40). Fern denotes "a kind of green and shade-loving plant" in English and "feather" in Greek. The word has a close connection with nature and floating, a perfect symbol for a nomadic character who is connected with nature and drifting. McDormand's vision of her ideal and carefree later years in life is also significant and interesting. Like a Hollywood movie actress who already acquired stardom with two Oscar awards before *Nomadland*, McDormand's choice of the nomadic lifestyle is not forced or inevitable as it was for Fern and many real American nomads, and hers is the romanticized version that turns out to have cultural roots in American history and society (a point we will return to in the latter part of this essay).

Fern is a composite character of the nomads described in Jessica Bruder's book. She used to have a decent job working in the human resources office at Empire, a factory of three hundred workers that is owned by United States Gypsum. She also had a small but loving family, including her husband, who was similarly an employee at Empire. She lived in a house subsidized by the factory and spent most of her life in the factory village located in the Black Rock Desert in northwestern Nevada. Had it not been for the hit of the 2008 economic recession that contributed to the factory's closing, she would have led a life – although not rich in both material and experiential senses – certainly steady and considered good by many people. However, when the movie's curtain raises, everything in Fern's life has collapsed. Her dear husband of many years dies, she loses her job before retirement, her mortgage is foreclosed on, and her house is taken away. She is now jobless and houseless and has no one she could share her life with. This is where Fern's story starts to unfold, beginning with her nomadic journey.

Fern's journey represents a contemporary phenomenon as the result of current American economic and social problems. This phenomenon, however, has historical precedence, cultural roots, in addition to certain epochal economic developments and drastic changes in business hiring strategies.

The historical precedence in the United States, or what Jessica Bruder called an "escape plan," refers to the surge of dispossessed Americans hitting the road and living in house trailers as the result of economic downsizing after the Great Depression in 1929. These Americans "upheld their end of the social contract, yet the system had let them down." (Bruder 2017, p. 74) They were forced to choose this lifestyle for survival because by moving in a trailer from state to state, they could escape from paying taxes and a house mortgage or rental. This group numbered in the millions, and it would be 30 years before the surge began to ebb. "Social critics were split on the trailersites, depicting them as either liberty-loving pioneers or harbingers of social disintegration." (Bruder 2017, p. 75) The writer David A. Thornburg, whose parents lived for fifteen years in a house trailer, describes this historical phenomenon in the following way:

> And so, right out of the heart of the Great Depression a new dream was born: the dream of escape. Escape from snow and ice, from high taxes and rent, from an economic system that nobody trusted anymore. Escape! For the winter, for the weekend, for the rest of your life. All it took was a little courage and a $600 house trailer. (Bruder 2017, p. 75)

In Thornburg's eyes, the 1930s American nomads were full of a rebellious and romantic spirit, and they were both escapers and dreamers – not only disobeying the tyranny of the capitalist system but also creating freer and more enjoyable lives (by returning to nature and living in the warmer and more scenic parts of the country). Thus, the economic recession and downward social mobilization were viewed not merely as crises but also as opportunities to rethink human values, rebel against the abusive social machinery that enslaved and dehumanized humans, and a readjustment to a lifestyle that overburdened and shackled the industrious and law-abiding citizens of the society. These 1930s American nomads were the forefathers of the contemporary ones, and the "Ferns" evidently were modeled after them when history repeated itself in 2008 by making many middle-class Americans homeless, jobless, and economically insecure in their retirement. The difference between the 1930s American economic refugees and their counterparts in the early 21st century is that unlike the "trailersites of the thirties – most of whom eventually went back to 'stick and brick' housing – the new wave of nomads were girding themselves for a more permanent transition." (Bruder 2017, p. 76) The harsh reality is that more and more American seniors had to keep working to support themselves after retirement given that they either lost their life savings as the result of the recession or they were simply unable to save enough in their prime years.

The economic factor that contributed to the formation of the new American nomads is touched upon in the movie but is more clearly indicated in Jessica Bruder's book. With the disappearance of companies like Empire, a different kind of company has been emerging and thriving in America, represented by Amazon CamperForce. Such a company offers part-time seasonal jobs, pays low hourly wages, and hires hundreds and thousands of temporary workers at several of its warehouses to meet the heavy shipping demands of the peak during the holiday season. (Bruder 2017, p. 44) Usually, these temporary employees are ununionized and are more vulnerable in terms of being overworked and lacking job safety. Employees work in shifts that last ten hours or longer, and the tasks are strenuous. Jessica Bruder describes that during each shift "some walk more than fifteen miles on concrete floors, stooping, squatting, reaching, and climbing stairs as they [the workers] scan, sort, and box merchandise." (Bruder 2017, p. 45) This kind of labor certainly is not ideal for the majority of nomads who are retirees in their sixties and seventies, but since these jobs are periodic and do not require much experience and training, they are easier for the nomads to find and get. Other similar part-time jobs include working for sugar beet companies at harvest and being employed as camp hosts in national parks and recreation resorts. In the movie, Fern has tried all of these temporary jobs after failing to secure steadier and better-paid full-time employment. The irony facing the nomads is that although they suffered under and are victimized by the capitalist system and very much want to disengage from it, they became a new labor force working with even less job security and fewer or impermanent benefits. For the sake of survival, the new American nomads escaped from paying high taxes and a house mortgage/rental, but in terms of working conditions and economic security, their lives have not changed for the better. This is likely the "harder truth" and dark reality to which some movie critics refer. However, this is not an issue the movie *Nomadland* focuses on, and evidently, it is too large and complicated an issue to be dealt with in a two-hour movie.

Romanticizing the lifestyle of the free road is a cultural phenomenon deeply rooted in American society. One can find it in daily life, popular culture, and literary heritage. The popular sentiment is clearly indicated in both Mcdormend's and Thornburg's quotes above, in Amazon CamperForce's recruiting websites and posters that package the work with camping experiences, and in Hollywood Western movies that glorify heroes and heroines who are free-spirited, constantly drifting, and unbound to a locality, authority, and the status quo. The literary and philosophical heritage of this sentiment, as many critics have indicated, is the Transcendentalism the appeared in the 19th century in America. Transcendentalism is an idealistic philosophical and cultural movement that emerged from English and German Romanticism to protest against the general state of intellectualism and spirituality at the time. It developed in New England around 1836, and Ralph Waldo Emerson and Henry David Thoreau were central figures. Online surfing of its definition yields the following description about the school of thought and literature:

> A core belief [of Transcendentalism] is in the inherent goodness of people and nature and while society and its institutions have corrupted the purity of the individual, people are at their best when truly "self-reliant" and independent. Transcendentalists saw divine experience inherent in the everyday, rather than believing in a distant heaven. Transcendentalists saw physical and spiritual phenomena as part of dynamic processes rather than discrete entities.[1]

In fact, Transcendentalism is also referred to as the American Renaissance, and most of what the Transcendentalists wrote falls into the category of nonfiction literature, including Ralph Waldo Emerson's *The American Scholar*, *Nature*, and *Self-Reliance*, and Henry David Thoreau's *Civil Disobedience*, *Walking*, and *Walden*, as well as others. According to Lawrence Buell, author of *Literary Transcendentalism: Style and Vision in the American Renaissance*, the three most significant intellectual and literary concerns of the Transcendentalist movement were spirit, nature, and man, (Buell 1973, p. 19) their approach of the issues was poetic rather than analytical, and the leading characteristics of their writings were "inchoate structure, prodigal imagery, wit, paradox, symbolism, aphoristic statement, paratactic syntax, and a manifesto-like tone" (Buell 1973, p. 18). In both subject matter and artistic style, the film *Nomadland* evokes Transcendentalist concepts and aesthetics.

After providing the historical, economic, and cultural factors that contextualize the emergence of the new American nomads, we now return to a closer look at the composite nomad character of Fern. My analysis of Fern proceeds in three stages of her inner self-development, namely self-rescuing, self-healing, and self-freeing. In the movie, these three developments do not progress entirely linearly, and they are sometimes interwoven and interplay with each other. However, for the convenience of analysis and from the lineament of Fern's storyline, such an arrangement makes sense.

The film starts with the scene in which Fern stores her belongings in storage units before hitting the road, and it ends with Fern returning to the same scene in which she gives away all of her old belongings and gradually drives out of view. In appearance, Fern's nomadic journey has come full circle, but psychologically, she certainly has not returned to the same point where she started. When she leaves the location of her old home for the second time at the end of the movie, Fern is renewed as a person and is capable of economic and spiritual self-reliance.

Fern is forced into a nomadic lifestyle before she knows what she is doing: she takes to the road and lives in her van because her house was taken away, and she works for Amazon CamperForce because she is unable to find a full-time job. Before she travels to Quartzsite, Arizona, and attends the Rubber Tramp Rendezvous (RTR) hosted by Bob Wells (a self-made leader of the real nomads), most of Fern's actions are more incidental to the situation she finds herself in. Survival motivates all her actions, but she always believes in self-reliance and her self-rescuing mission is entirely based on this spirit.

Living in a van is tough both physically and psychologically. Throughout the movie, the unpleasant side of the living conditions is touched – when Fern is shivering in her van during the Christmas holidays, when a man is knocking on the door of the van and forbidding her to park overnight, and even at the RTR's workshops in which strategies for stealth parking and dealing with excrement are offered. Furthermore, living in a van can be labeled as "homelessness," a rather derogatory and humiliating tag. When Fern meets Brandy and her two daughters at a sports store and is questioned by one of the girls whether she is "homeless" now, Fern quickly replies to her: "No, I am not homeless. I am just houseless. Not the same thing, right?" Such a question and the concerned expressions of both the mother and daughter obviously hurt Fern's pride and self-esteem. In her way of self-rescuing, Fern not only needs to adapt herself to the hard condition of living in a van but she also must fend off peoples' disapproving glances and prejudice. Fern's experience and emotional reactions best reflect what many real nomads went through in life and what was on their minds. This is why when Steven Patrick Morrissey's song lyric lines that "Home, is it just a word? Or is it something you carry within you?" are shared among the Amazon camp workers in the movie, they all enthusiastically resonated with them. To the nomads, they are not family/ home quitters or irresponsible parasites of society. On the contrary, they are paying their share to society and they make a living through self-reliance. They take pride in what they are doing – taking issue with the housing industry and capitalist economy. Fern named her van "Vanguard," a symbol that she and many of her fellow nomads want to be associated with spiritually.

"I need work. I like work." These are the words a desperate Fern says to Annette Webb, the woman who interviewed her when she applied for a full-time job. Working is another basic self-rescuing strategy that Fern takes in addition to downsizing her living spending. If it is impossible to be a full-timer, Fern will take any part-time work she can get to support herself. No matter whether it's working in the Amazon CamperForce warehouse, at the camping park, at plants processing sugar beets, for a restaurant, or with a rock dealer, and no matter if it's taking an early morning shift or staying late when it gets dark, Fern consistently and continuously industriously performs and gives it her best effort. "The money is good" – she is content as it is made honestly and by herself; she finds joy when she works, particularly in camping parks where she can breathe fresh air, be bathed in the sun, and can appreciate the beauty of nature. Work is hard, but it is what Fern needs and desires to be someone who truly believes in self-reliance. Through Fern and her observations of and association with her fellow nomads in the movie, the audience can see that most of the nomads are honest and hard-working American citizens who have done and are doing the best they can to be independent and contributing members of society. Despite already passing their prime years and falling on hard times, they still firmly hold the conviction of self-reliance.

If making a living by working is economic self-reliance, then challenging the unfairness of society and the tyranny of the capitalist economy can be considered self-reliance in thinking. The nomads certainly can find spiritual enlightenment and philosophical inspiration from the famous Transcendentalist Ralph Waldo Emerson's essay "Self-Reliance." As he says:

> *No law can be sacred to me but that of my nature. Good and bad are but names very readily transferable to that or this; the only right is what is after my constitution; the only wrong what is against it. A man is to carry himself in the presence of all opposition as if everything were titular and ephemeral but he. I am ashamed to think how easily we capitulate to badges and names, to large societies and dead institutions. What I must do is all that concerns me, not what the people think. This rule, equally arduous in actual and in intellectual life, may serve for the whole distinction between greatness and meanness* (Emerson 2020, p. 193).

This spirit of self-reliance and civil disobedience is echoed by the contemporary American nomads and in Bob Wells's speech at RTR in the film in which he describes the capitalist system and economy as "the tyranny of the dollar" and "the tyranny of the marketplace" and the nomads as "workhorses" yoked, used, then thrown out to "pasture" by the system. "The Titanic is sinking and economic times are changing," Wells continues, "we, workhorses, had to gather together and take care of each other. And that is what this is all about." If to Fern and many American nomads, self-reliance and self-rescuing are their subconscious and instinctive reactions to the disaster that brings them down because such a belief is part of their cultural tradition and upbringing, to Bob Wells, it is a more conscious and deliberate decision and undertaking. Indeed, in his speech, one seems to find the reincarnation of Transcendentalism.

In addition to the economic hardship and social prejudice that the Ferns of the country need to face, what is also shared by them is trauma. In the movie, Fern is unable to deal with her loss until the very end, and her healing is postponed and progresses gradually after hearing many heart-wrenching stories and intimate and moving words from her fellow nomads.

The first person to open her heart to Fern is Linda May, a real nomad who tells Fern and the audience her true personal story in the film. Linda, who started to work at 12 years old, brought up two daughters, and worked hard her entire life, was rocked in 2008 when, at 62, she lost her job and her house and had to live on her Social Security worth only $550 monthly. She thought of taking her own life by turning on the propane stove in her car. Eventually finding Bob Wells's online message about cheap living in recreational vehicles (RVs) saved her. She has found new courage and solidarity by working and bonding with the nomads.

At the RTR gathering around a bonfire, more real nomads share their personal stories and traumatic experiences, from a Vietnam veteran who suffers from PTSD (post-traumatic stress disorder) to a woman who lost both parents to cancer, and a former employee of corporate America whose friend died of liver failure before reaching retirement and enjoying his sailboat. Although Fern is not ready to share her story at the time, she is comforted with Bob Wells's advice of "connecting to nature and to a real true community and tribe." Indeed, nature, kindred hearts, and true caring are therapeutic to Fern. However, for her healing, Fern needs to be able to find love again, both as a loving subject and as a love object, as well as in the natural and human world. The most illuminating point is made by Bob Wells to Fern at the end of the film when he tells her about his son's suicide and the pain he, as a father, endured the past five years since his son's death. How could he move on and continue to live after losing his son? In his words: "The question was . . . how can I be alive on this Earth when he is not? And I did not have an answer. And those were some hard, hard days. But I realized I could honor him by helping people and saving people. It gives me a reason to go through the day. Some days that is all I've got." Wells's question and answer are both philosophical and soul-searching: pain and loss may spur one to ponder the meaning of life and love. A more encompassing, embracing, elevated love for nature and humanity is a more enduring and meaningful existence, as Bob Wells and the movie try to suggest to its audience. When Fern is able to find love again in nature, in a relationship, and the people around her and says goodbye to her past, she is setting out on a journey of self-freeing, a completely new journey at the end of the film.

In his prose *Nature*, Ralph Waldo Emerson says the following about nature and its amazing remedial power for humans' exhaustion and pain:

> *To the body and mind which have been cramped by noxious work or company, nature is medicinal and restores their tone. The tradesman, the attorney comes out of the din and craft of the street, and sees the sky and the woods, and is a man again. In their eternal calm, he finds himself. The health of the eye seems to demand a horizon. We are never tired, so long as we can see far enough* (Emerson 2020, p. 211).

The nomads in the movie, including Fern, offer testimonies to this belief, and there are many well-made cinematographic scenes to display the beauty of nature in the eyes of Fern and her fellow nomads. In fact, unlike one critic's accusation that the movie's landscape shots are done "for their own sake," these scenes are carefully and purposefully designed and serve to strengthen the theme and characterization of the story. When Fern is depressed in front of the Empire storage lockers, the sky is gray and the earth is covered with snow, and this is the scenery that reflects how cold and desolate she feels. At the RTR when the nomads gather and share their heartfelt love and consideration for each other, the bonfire in the night rekindles their hope and warms their hearts. And to demonstrate the tenacity of Fern, Linda, and Swarnkie and their resilience to life's harsh realities, the sunset glows and close-up shots of cactus appear on the scene. Without a doubt, the cinematography is used metaphorically and poetically to the credit of Chloé Zhao and her cinematographer.

However, the two best scenes about the healing power of nature in the movie are when a group of nomads views the stars at night and when Charlene Swankie tells about her Alaska kayaking trip. If the former reminds us of Emerson's words that watching stars would make people feel "the perpetual presence of the sublime," (Emerson 2020, p. 208) the latter evokes Henry David Thoreau's story of life on Walden Pond. Swankie delivers the most beautiful and poetic description of nature in the movie, which deserves to be quoted here in its entirety:

> *I'm gonna be 75 this year and I think I've lived a pretty good life. I've seen some really neat things, kayaking all those places. And, you know, moose in the wild. A moose family on a river in Idaho. And, big, white pelicans landing just six feet over my kayak on a lake in Colorado. When I come around a bend, there is a cliff, and I find hundreds and hundreds of swallow nests on the wall of the cliff. And the swallows flying all around, and reflecting in the water. So, it looks like I'm flying with the swallows and they are under me, and over me, and all around me. And the little babies are hatching out and eggshells are falling out of the nests, landing on the water and floating on the water. These little white shells, it's like, well, it's just so awesome. I felt like I'd done enough. My life was complete if I died right then, that moment, it'll be perfectly fine!*

Swankie was a real nomad "who moved into a van at age sixty-four when she was too broke to rent a decent apartment and was struggling with bad knees and asthma. The lifestyle suited her; she dropped sixty-five pounds and embarked on a quest to paddle all fifty states in a yellow kayak that she transported atop her van." (Bruder 2017, p. 77) Swankie's experience is also desired and envisioned by Fern and her nomad friends when they take trips between seasonal work from state to state, go to RV shows, and sing songs in bars. The natural world that is free of the human world's competition, exploitation, and abusive power is romanticized as a utopia where the wounded nomads can be healed and reenergized to find peace and harmony.

For Fern, if embracing nature makes her feel peaceful, calm, and serene, then finding love again allows her to say goodbye to the past and regain happiness. The love that Fern finds comes from her sister Holly and a male fellow nomad named Dave. Her van breakdown brings Fern to her sister Holly's home, and the purpose of her trip is to borrow $5,000 from Holly to repair her van. At the family barbecue dinner, Fern has had an unpleasant conversation with Holly's husband, George, a real estate agent who regrets lacking the money to purchase more low-price houses in 2008 so that he could turn them into a high profit now that housing prices are going up. Being a victim of the housing market herself and knowing so many fellow nomads who suffered from the market, Fern's reaction to George's words is understandable and expected. However, the audience may easily miss the other important plot point – a chance to allow a pair of seemingly estranged sisters to have a heart-to-heart conversation, reach a mutual understanding, and demonstrate their affection for each other. Holly confesses to Fern that although Fern is "eccentric" and "weird" in others' eyes, she is always "braver" and "more honest" than anyone else to Holly. Fern has always been the one who truly understands her; living without Fern created a big hole in her life. These words touch Fern and make her feel loved.

Fern meets Dave at RTR in Quartzsite, Arizona. Dave is obviously attracted to Fern, and several times he awkwardly attempts to show his affection to her. At the Quartzsite Yacht Club after Fern accepts Dave's invitation to a dance, the singer at the club sings: "We will hold each other close, / And fall in love again." However, Fern is not sure if she wants to move a step further in the relationship because she is still unable to forget her former relationship even though her husband had already been dead for several years. Dave's sickness, his repeated invitations to her to visit his son's home, and his family's warm reception of her at Thanksgiving make Fern realize her true feelings for Dave. She has already developed an attachment to Dave and his family, which is demonstrated when it is time for her to leave and she can hardly move away from the piano that Dave and his son played together and the dining table where the whole family had dinner the previous night. She decides to leave Dave and his family without saying goodbye as it might be a difficult moment for her.

A question remains: Fern is invited to stay with Holly and Dave, respectively, and she feels loved by both, but why does she turn down both of their offers to stay in their home and chooses instead to continue living as a nomad? In addition to her firm belief in self-reliance and newly gained attachment to nature, she seems to acquire a new understanding of love: the person being loved by you and loving you can part from you or pass away, but the love shared between you and your loved ones remains and becomes part of you. There is no better evidence of Fern's understanding of this than her recitation of William Shakespeare's Sonnet 18 at the end of the movie. The poem reads:

> *Shall I compare thee to a summer's day?*
> *Thou art more lovely and more temperate.*
> *Rough winds do shake the darling buds of May,*
> *And summer's lease hath all too short a date.*
> *Sometime too hot the eye of heaven shines,*
> *And often is his gold complexion dimmed;*
> *And every fair from fair sometime declines,*
> *By chance, or nature's changing course untrimmed;*
> *But thy eternal summer shall not fade,*
> *Nor lose possession of that fair thou ow'st,*
> *Nor shall death brag thou wand'rest in his shade,*
> *When in eternal lines to Time thou grow'st.*
> *So long as men can breathe, or eyes can see,*
> *So long lives this, and this gives life to thee.* (Shakespeare 2007, p. 27)

As indicated in the poem, beauty, youth, and any form of physical existence are fleeting and short-lived, but the beloved beauty and beloved ones, in the mind of the lover, will never fade, die, or perish, "as long as men can breathe or eyes can see." Indeed, love has the power of transcending life and death or any social bias and bondage, and knowing love in this way gives one complete freedom. At the end of the movie, Fern sets herself free – free from social and personal disasters, free from traumatized emotion, and free from the physical attachment of love and relationships.

In conclusion, I want to directly respond to the critical comment quoted at the beginning of this article. If the movie appears to be inchoately structured or centered, it is not so after closer and more careful examination, as my analysis shows it possesses a clear and tight inner logic. Instead of brushing away the harsh reality and avoiding the harder truth underlying the story, the movie provides an insider's viewpoint of and an inner-oriented gaze at the American nomads and their life through the fictional character Fern. In addition, a two-hour-long film can't deal with all of the social problems raised and addressed in Jessica Bruder's book that is over two hundred pages long. All of the artistic devices of the movie, music, cinematography, cast that blends real nomads and professional actors and actresses, and the mixture of documentary and feature film nicely serve the movie's theme and story, leaving the audience with a beautiful, poetic, moving, and yet provocative and haunting motion picture to watch, ponder, and enjoy.

ENDNOTES

1   https://en.wikipedia.org/wiki/Transcendentalism

REFERENCES

Boo, Katherine (2017). Nomadland: Surviving America in the Twenty-First Century. New York and London: W. W. Norton & Company. Back cover.

Bruder, Jessica (2017). Nomadland: Surviving America in the Twenty-First Century. New York and London: W. W. Norton & Company.

Buell, Lawrence (1973). Introduction. Literary Transcendentalism: Style and Vision in the American Renaissance. Ithaca, New York: Cornell University Press, pp. 1–20.

Emerson, Ralph Waldo (2020). Self-Reliance. Transcendentalism Collection. Independently published, pp. 191–207.

Emerson, Ralph Waldo (2020). Nature. Transcendentalism Collection. Independently Published, pp. 207–233.

Keegan, Rebecca. "Director Chloe Zhao Arrives with Early Oscar Contender 'Nomadland' and Next Year's 'Eternals': It's a Bit Surreal," The Hollywood Reporter, September 2, 2020. https://www.hollywoodreporter.com/movies/movie-features/director-chloe-zhao-arrives-withhot-oscar-contender-nomadland-and-next-years-eternals-4053382/. [Accessed 19 June 2021.]

Koehler, Robert Koehler. Nomadland (Chloe Zhao, US). Cinema Scope. https://cinema-scope.com/currency/nomadland-chloe-zhao-us/. [Accessed 18 June 2021.]

Transcendentalism. https://en.wikipedia.org/wiki/Transcenden-talism. [Accessed 20 June 2021.]

Shakespeare, William (2007). Shakespeare's Sonnets. Ed. Deborah West. Oxford: Oxford University Press, p. 27.

AUTHOR'S BIO

YING WANG is Felicia Gressitt Bock Professor of Asian Studies, Mount Holyoke College. She specialized in pre-modern Chinese fiction (seventeenth to nineteenth-century), traditional Chinese drama, and women in Chinese literature. Her scholarship includes the nineteenth-century imitation and adaptation of *Honglou meng* in fiction and the performing arts (such as ballad and theater art), and Li Yu's (1611–1680) seventeenth-century *chuanqi* plays. Her recent publications include *The Fragrant Companions: A Play About Love Between Women by Li Yu* (1611–1680). New York: Columbia University Press (forthcoming); "Chapter 7: Rewriting *Honglou meng* in the Oral Performing Arts: The Case of *Zidishu* (or The Manchu Bannermen Tale)." In Kirk A. Denton, ed., *Crossing Between Tradition and Modernity: Essays in Commemoration of Milena Doleželová-Velingerová* (1932–2012), Charles University Press, 2016.

11 The Dissemination and Influence of American Musicals in China

Zhitong Chen, Sichuan University

ABSTRACT

An important part of American culture, musicals have been influential in China since they were first introduced in 1987. With a focus on Broadway musicals, this paper discusses the dissemination and influence of American musicals in China in the following five aspects: the characteristics of American musicals represented by Broadway; the 30-year spread of American musicals in China; the influence of American musicals on Chinese musicals; the impact and integration of American musicals with Chinese culture; and the challenges facing Chinese musicals and the possible solutions. This study will be helpful in promoting intercultural communication between China and the United States by exploring the collision and integration of Sino-US culture through the study of a unique cultural carrier – musicals.

KEYWORDS

American musicals, Chinese musicals, dissemination, influence

1. AN INTRODUCTION TO AMERICAN MUSICALS

The musical is a form of theatrical performance that combines songs, spoken dialogue, acting, and dance. American musicals "share with their European operatic counterparts the ideal of a musical drama," integrating various parts but also forming "an interdependent and homogeneous whole" (Block 1993, p. 526). The story and emotional content of a musical – humor, pathos, love, anger – are communicated through the words, music, movement, and technical aspects of the entertainment as an integrated whole. The most famous musical venues in the world are the big-budget Broadway in New York and West End in London.

Inheriting European operatic traditions while being rooted in American culture, musicals have become a cultural symbol of the USA, and were one of the three most widely influential art forms in the first half of the 20th century. Like jazz and films, American musicals have continued to evolve into the present, shaped by other aspects of American culture. For example, the music in musicals is greatly influenced by black music, jazz and rock music. American musicals are interwoven with the formation of the social, cultural, and political aspects of national identity. They are inextricably tied to America's sense of itself as a New World, a land of opportunity, and above all, "the emblem of modernity" (Ju Qihong

1996, p. 14). Examples such as *Anything Goes*, *West Side Story*, and *Rent* delve deeply into the social and political identity of America.

Broadway is a byword for American musicals. It represents the highest level of commercial theater in the English-speaking world, and has acquired a worldwide reputation. American historian Martin Shefter argues that "'Broadway musicals', culminating in the productions of Richard Rodgers and Oscar Hammerstein, became enormously influential forms of American popular culture" (Shefter 1993, p.10). The first theater piece that conforms to the modern conception of a musical is considered to be *The Black Crook*, which tells its story through dance and original music. Premiering in New York in 1866, it was regarded as the symbol of the birth of American musicals. The premiere of *Show Boat* on Broadway in 1927 was also an important event in the history of American musical theater. It was "a radical departure in musical storytelling, marrying spectacle with seriousness" (Lahr 1993, p.123), and carrying local culture that gives American musicals their unique identity. After the lean years of the Great Depression, Broadway theater entered a golden age with the blockbuster hit *Oklahoma!* in 1943, which ran for 2,212 performances. Showcasing American patriotism and individualism, this musical threw off the influence of British musicals and set a new example for America. From 1980 to 2004, Broadway entered a new phase, becoming a truly global phenomenon with new innovations responding to economic challenges. In 1982, Tommy Tune confirmed his reputation with *Nine*, based on a Fellini film and starring Raul Julia; it won the Tony Award for Best Musical. Producer Cameron Mackintosh brought *Cats*, *Les Misérables*, and *The Phantom of the Opera* to Broadway – a series of unprecedented successes. In 1994, Walt Disney Co. made its first foray onto Broadway with its stage adaptation of the animated film *Beauty and the Beast*, which was the longest-running American musical since *A Chorus Line*. In 1996, the rock musical *Rent* won a Tony and a Pulitzer Prize. The same year, a concert version of *Chicago*, revived by City Center's *Encores!* series, proved to be so successful that it was transferred to Broadway. In 1997, *The Lion King* was shown at the renovated New Amsterdam Theatre, and was a phenomenal hit for Disney. Off-Broadway and Off-Off-Broadway shows often provide a more experimental, challenging, and intimate performance than is possible in the larger Broadway theaters. Some Broadway musicals, such as *Hair*, *Little Shop of Horrors*, *Spring Awakening*, *Next to Normal*, *Rent*, *Avenue Q*, *In the Heights*, *Fun Home*, *Dear Evan Hansen*, and *Hamilton*, began their runs Off-Broadway and later transferred to Broadway, seeking to replicate the intimate experience in a larger theater (Bloom & Vlastnik 2010).

2. THE 30-YEAR SPREAD OF AMERICAN MUSICALS IN CHINA

The introduction of Western musicals into China cannot be separated from the efforts of the older generation of Chinese artists. In the early 1980s, writers and artists who had the opportunity to visit or study abroad came into contact with musicals, and introduced them to China. One of the pioneers of Chinese musicals, Shen Chengzhou, visited the United States in 1980 and spent a year investigating American musicals. In 1981, the first national opera conference was held, where Shen Chengzhou presented an investigative report on Western musicals, arousing a warm response from the participants. Its significance lies not only in introducing Western musicals to China, but also in initiating the single mode of Chinese musicals and diversifying it.

1987 was a special and memorable year in the history of Chinese musicals. For the first time, two famous Broadway musicals – *The Music Man* and *The Fantasticks* – were introduced to China. The Chinese versions were produced by the China National Opera House and guided by American artists from the Eugene O'Neill Theater Center (Liu 1987, p. 61). After its premiere in Beijing, *The Fantasticks* went to Hangzhou, Shanghai, and Nanjing on a tour – the first such tour in China. For China, the dissemination of these two American musicals represents the introduction of the Broadway marketing model.

The early dissemination of the original American musicals in China was mainly for the purpose of cultural exchange, so both the number and the scope of the musicals were limited. It was not until 2002, when the Shanghai Grand Theatre hosted the original musical *Les Misérables*, that original musicals began to be introduced to China, including Broadway hits *The Sound of Music*, *Lion King*, and *Rent*. From then on, American musicals became a familiar sight in big Chinese cities. The spread of American musicals in China not only enriches Chinese audiences' cultural life, but also helps to cultivate a Chinese musical market. In recent years, many Western musicals have been performed in China, some of them covering a large number audiences and hit accruing high box office revenue. In 2015, according to the data from Dao Lue (2016), 2,088 musical performances took place nationwide – 570 more than in 2014, which was an increase of 37.5%. The audience for national musical performances numbered 1.24 million – an increase of 41.5%, with box office growth of 44%, representing a yearly increase of 230 million yuan. In 2015, the box office revenue of original musicals increased by 110% to 145 million yuan. Most foreign musicals that succeed in China are market-tested, so become exceedingly popular. However, the box office growth of original domestic musicals is relatively small, representing negative growth. This means that the growth of the musical box office in China mainly relies on the introduction of original musicals.

Between 2004 and 2019, more than 30 original American musicals were introduced to China, some of which are shown in the table below:

Table 1: Some of the original American musicals introduced to China (2004–2019)

Year	Some of the original American musicals introduced to China
2004	Chicago
	The Sound of Music
2006	Rent
	The Lion King
	West Side Story
2007	The King and I
	42nd Street
2008	Aida
	Hairspray
	Cinderella
2009	High School Musical
2011	Kiss me, Kate
2012	Shrek the Musical
	Man of La Mancha
2013	The Little Mermaid
2014	Robinson Crusoe
	Chicago
2015	Sister Act
	I Do! I Do!

(Continued)

Year	Some of the original American musicals introduced to China
2016	*Ghost – The Musical*
	My Fair Lady
2017	*Ghost – The Musical*
	West Side Story
	Wicked
	The Bodyguard
	The Producers
	Jersey Boys
	Sister Act
	Legally Blonde: The Musical
2018	*Rent*
	Chicago
	Kinky Boots
	The Producers
2019	*The Wizard of Oz*
	An American in Paris
	PAW Patrol
	Chicago

Rent was performed in China on more than one occasion. It has been performed in more than 150 cities in nearly 50 countries and has been translated into 25 languages, receiving more than $1 billion in box office revenue worldwide. *Rent* is a typical American musical, reflecting the lives of the ordinary Americans who persist in their dreams despite adversity. The composer Jonathan Larson suggested setting the play "amid poverty, homelessness, spunky gay life, drag queens and punk" (Tommasini 1996, p. 7) in the East Village neighborhood of Manhattan, which happened to be down the street from his Greenwich Village apartment. *Rent* brings social sensitive topics such as poverty and disease to the stage, while showing an irrepressible passion for life. The belief in being brave and not bowing to fate shaped the spirit of a generation of Americans. The thematic concerns of AIDS, homosexuality, and impoverishment were relatively new for Chinese audiences. Nevertheless, *Rent* aroused a sympathetic response by depicting the struggles and triumphs of young people who experience love, hope, and a thirst for life. The music style of *Rent* proved novel and interesting for Chinese audiences, and it has expanded the limits of the sub-genre known as rock opera. Its small orchestra, comprising keyboards, synthesizers, drums, a bass guitar, and two electric guitars, fulfills all of the necessary requirements of rock music set for the stage. It also attempts to mix other genres of music, ranging from soul in "I'll Cover You" to techno in "Today 4 U" to Latin rhythms in "Tango Maureen" to funk and gospel. *Newsweek* enthusiastically claimed it was "the breakthrough musical of the '90s" (Kroll 1996), while *The New York Times* praised it as "a landmark rock opera" (Brantley 1996). In other words, *Rent* symbolizes the spirit of innovation of the United States. It was performed in China for the first time in 2006, only in three or four first-tier cities, and received a warm response. In 2018, the *Rent* 20th Anniversary Tour expanded visited seven Chinese cities: Shanghai, Nanjing, Hangzhou, Guangzhou, Shenzhen, Beijing and Chengdu.

The drive of economic interests is one of the most important reasons for the spread of American musicals in China. In recent years, the successful dissemination of many original and adapted Chinese-version musicals in China has made the musical market very attractive to foreign production companies. By establishing musical companies in China and cooperating with Chinese groups, even more original musicals will be performed and disseminated in China.

3. THE INFLUENCE OF AMERICAN MUSICALS ON CHINESE MUSICALS

Musicals originated in the United Kingdom and developed in the United States. Meanwhile, Chinese musicals follow a three-stage development pattern: the first stage is the introduction of original Western musicals; the second stage is the localization of Western musicals, and the third stage is creating original Chinese musicals. Attempts at localizing Western musicals began in 2008 when *Fame* was produced in Mandarin with a full Chinese cast at the Central Academy of Drama. Since then, other Western musicals have been staged in China in Mandarin with a Chinese cast. The first original Chinese musical in the style of American musicals was *Golden Sand* in 2005, followed by *Butterflies* in 2007, and *In Love with Teresa Teng* in 2011.

American musicals opened the Chinese musical market and introduced the Broadway marketing system to China. According to the latest data released by the Beijing Trade Association for Performances, in Beijing alone, the number of musical performances in major small and medium-sized theaters in 2018 was 775 (an increase of 16.9% over the previous year), and 429,000 people watched musicals – an increase of 26.7% year-on-year (Li 2019). However, the negative impact of American musicals is that it impairs the growth of original Chinese musicals in the long term, because Broadway musicals take the lion's share of the musical market, leaving little room for Chinese musicals to develop.

To remedy this, national and local governments, cultural companies and groups, and television programs have promoted the development of Chinese musicals. With strong support from the National Art Foundation policy, nearly 20 original Chinese musicals of various styles were created in 2018. That same year, musicals entered the public domain through *Super Vocal* – a television talent contest for opera singers and musical performers. After launching on November 2, 2018, it was ranked as the fifth most-watched reality TV show in China, according to iQiyi. As of May 2019, *Super Vocal* ranks first among variety shows on Douban (a review aggregation platform for Chinese TV shows and movies), scoring 9.1 points out of 10, and has been watched by millions online. These popular new televised singing contests in China showcases the vocal prowess of classically trained singers, and fuel interest in both Chinese and Western operas and musicals. "Compared with the mature Western market, Chinese musicals are in their infancy. One of the major problems is a lack of marketing. With limited budgets, you can't afford to promote a production properly," says Zheng Yunlong – a rising musical star who was honored at the 2018 Musical Academy Awards in China. "However, I think *Super Vocal* is a way to communicate with a broader audience, and this is what I need to do as a Chinese musical actor for the development of musicals at this point in time" (Wei 2019).

As television programs increase the popularity of Chinese musicals, governments have also made great efforts to promote them. Since the original musical *Les Misérables* was first performed there in 2002, Shanghai has become the city with the biggest musical market in China, leading the national musical industry with the ambition of becoming the Chinese Broadway. The membership of the SAIC · Shanghai Cultural Square grew to 30,000 in the first quarter of 2019; six sets of original Chinese musicals sold out in an hour; and the sales revenue of environmental protection bags designed with the image of a musical star amounted to 400,000 yuan. The growing enthusiasm of its audience for cultural consumption has contributed to Shanghai's efforts in promoting high-quality musicals for several years. In December 2018, the Shanghai International Musical Festival was the first professional and systematic musical festival in China, gaining significance all over the world. In 2019, six original Chinese musicals were performed in the exhibition season, setting a new record in terms of the quality and quantity of performances. The Festival's 2019 Musical Singing Contest and the Original Chinese Musical Cultivation Project attracted more than 150,000 viewers both online and offline (Wang 2019). In February 2019, the Original Chinese Musical Cultivation Project was launched to provide an incubation platform for large numbers of musical writers and producers, actively supporting and cultivating original Chinese musicals. The project has received 77 original musical works from 72 contributors, five of which will join the market in the next eight months. The 2019 Musical Singing Contest received contributions from nearly 400 applicants from all over China, and related videos have accumulated 100,000 viewings on the network platform, significantly expanding the talent reservoir of Chinese musicals (Wang 2019). The contestants came from a variety of backgrounds in terms of age and occupation. Among them were students from art colleges, ordinary high schools, and colleges, and workers such as dessert makers, environmental supervisors, and business managers. At the finals, some of the contestants sang songs from classical Broadway musicals like *A Chorus Line, The Phantom of the Opera,* and *Dear Evan Hansen,* as well as pieces from original Chinese musicals.

In 2019, the 36th Musical Development Forum at the Shanghai Spring International Music Festival invited industry elites from countries such as Britain, the United States, South Korea, and Singapore to discuss and explore the future development of Chinese musicals from an international perspective. The Musical Development Forum at the Shanghai Spring International Music Festival has been held seven times since 2012. Over the past seven years, this professional forum – which focuses on the development of original Chinese musicals and the operation of professional musicals theaters – has become a platform for communication between musicals practitioners in China and around the world. Thus, Shanghai has gained significance for musical producers both at home and abroad. In other Chinese cities, many parties also support the development of original Chinese musicals. For instance, in Chengdu, the original Chinese musical *Golden Sand* was supported by the Chengdu Municipal Bureau of Culture, Chengdu Radio and Television Administration, and Chengdu Daily Press Group (Zhang 2008, p. 24). The musical exhibits idiosyncratic Chengdu culture, and the local government expects it to become one of the cultural symbols of the city.

Other cultural companies and groups have also made great efforts to promote the development of musicals in China, such as Yang Jiamin of Sevenages – a graduate of the Foreign Language Department at Peking University, who sees great potential in the Chinese musical market. Yang introduced the English version of *Man of La Mancha* to China, and won a critical acclaim, which paved the way for her subsequent dissemination of the Chinese-version of *Avenue Q,* which was hugely popular when it was staged in Beijing and Shanghai. It then expanded into second-tier cities such as Nanjing, Wuhan, and Hangzhou.

4. THE INTEGRATION OF CHINESE AND AMERICAN CULTURE IN MUSICALS

American culture is primarily of Western (European) cultural origin, but is influenced by a multicultural ethos that include African, Native American, Asian, Polynesian, and Latin American people and their cultures. Modern Western musicals emerged during the 19th century as a product of urban entertainment in capitalist society, so its contents and themes are closely linked with the characteristics of Western industrial society. Social problems caused by the development of the capitalist economy, science, and technology, as well as artists' thoughts about life and society, have provided rich sources for Western musicals. Throughout American history, certain subcultures (often based on ethnicity) have only partially melded with mainstream culture. The complex social environment of the United States can partially explain why American musicals are often concerned with the situation of immigrants, African-Americans, and minorities. For instance, *Show Boat* – regarded as a typical successful American musical – deals with the Black community, while *Rent* involves vulnerable groups. American music includes styles such as rock and roll, jazz, rock, techno, soul, country, hip-hop, and blues, reflecting the diversity of the nation's culture (Lubette 2000, p. 35).

Conversely, Chinese culture is more implicit and conservative in emotional expression. In its understanding of beauty, traditional Chinese aesthetics focuses on the spiritual world, stressing "artistic conception" – the extrapolated appearance of something for which the actual appearance is not known or cannot be seen. In theatrical art, Chinese opera pursues "artistic conception," while Western opera strives for "reality." In terms of cultural values, Chinese traditional culture is deeply influenced by Confucianism, Buddhism, and Daoism, focusing on human relations, transcendence in nature, perfection, harmony, and reincarnation. Accordingly, traditional Chinese operas are often about myths, folklore, historical figures, talented scholars, and beautiful women. The themes usually follow traditional Chinese morals and values such as loyalty, filial piety, benevolence, righteousness, chastity, karma, and hierarchy.

The different cultures of the East and the West have created their own aesthetics and moral values, meaning that the creation and expression of literary and artistic works are hugely dissimilar. Since Chinese culture has influenced the style and the theme of Chinese opera, it also affects Chinese audience's acceptance of Western musicals. For American stories to be accepted in China, they must conform to Chinese values. Generally speaking, musicals that promote universal values and arouse common emotional resonance are often widely accepted in China. Examples include *The Sound of Music, Lion King*, and *Ghost*. However, the theme of *The Producers* and the racial problems in *Hairspray* are unfamiliar to most Chinese audiences, so their box office revenues have not been as high as expected.

5. THE CHALLENGES FACING CHINESE MUSICALS, AND THE SOLUTIONS

The greatest challenge facing the dissemination of American musicals in China is cultural hegemony. Western capitalist civilization represented by American culture relies on its strong economic and technological strength to export a continuous stream of industrial and cultural products to the other parts of the world, including movies, soap operas, and musicals. In addition to earning huge profits, these cultural products also cause American cultural values to infiltrate other nations. Without a doubt, US musicals are permeated with an American outlook, which influence unwitting audiences with the diverting effects of beautiful songs and dancing. Therefore, Chinese viewers of Western musicals critically accept foreign cultural values while experiencing their artistic appeal. The introduction of high-quality American musicals has stolen market share from a lot of original Chinese productions. In 2017, nine Western musicals were performed – a record high, among which seven were American. Among the top 10 musicals in terms of box office revenue, 50% were original foreign versions; there was only one original Chinese musical on the list (CAPA & Da Mai 2018). If American musicals monopolize the China market, it will be extremely difficult for Chinese musicals to survive. Thus, a dilemma has emerged. The introduction of Broadway musicals to China guarantees box office thanks to the appearance of famous actors, but this affects the growth and reputation of domestic artists. While it is comparatively easy to introduce American musicals to China, it is difficult to send original Chinese musicals out into the world. Chris Grady, the art director of the musical section of the Edinburgh Festival, said in an interview that due to the major differences in language and culture between the East and the West, eastern countries like China and South Korea usually have to bring musicals involving circuses and acrobatics when they attend the Festival (JieMian 2018).

The second problem is Chinese audiences' acceptance of musicals. Over the past 30 years, with the introduction of many well-known original musicals to China, a market has opened up, and the genre has gained in popularity. However, compared with other stage arts such as opera, drama, and dance, Chinese audiences are not very familiar with musicals. In terms of the number of musicals, the number of performances, the scope of dissemination, and box office revenue, musicals have not yet reached the common people in China. According to data from the National Bureau of Statistics, in 2016, government subsidies accounted for more than 52% of the total revenue of theaters and troupes in China, and accounted for 86% of the total revenue of state-owned theaters and troupes, with even less box office revenue (CAPA 2017).

The relatively high price of musical tickets can be a major obstacle to development. Statistics show that the average fee for a musical at a theater is 160 yuan per ticket, which is much higher than for films (39.5 yuan). According to the Annual Report on the China Performance Market in 2017, Chinese musical viewers had a relatively high level of education. Among them, 93% had a bachelor degree and above (CAPA & Da Mai 2018). In other words, audiences for musicals are comparatively small. Unlike people in the United Kingdom or the United States, the Chinese are not used to going to the theater and watching a musical. In the Internet era, modes of entertainment are multifarious. Watching a movie on the Internet is common for most Chinese, while going to the theater is still a luxury. Even if Chinese people today have the financial capacity to consume musicals, there is a lack of choice. With the exception of classic Western musicals such as *Cats, The Phantom of the Opera* and *Mamma Mia!*, many popular Broadway musical producers are hesitant to attempt entry into Chinese market. As original musicals need enough performances to guarantee profit, it is too risky to introduce musicals to China due to its immature market, shaky revenue, and harsh censorship. Apart from a few famous original musicals that are introduced to China every year, there are just a few musical performances in China. According to the Annual Report on the China Performance Market in 2018, 78% of venues hosted Chinese musicals no more than 10 times a year, and most musicals were only performed in big cities such as Beijing and Shanghai (Daolue 2019).

The third problem is the poor quality of original Chinese musicals. Large-scale capital injections, the short creation cycle, and an eagerness to recoup costs have turned original domestic musicals into a high-fare, short-period, and high-risk "fast-food" genre. According to data released by Dao Lue (2016), 40 original Chinese musicals were performed in China in the first half of 2015, of which 22 had fewer than 10 performances, and only two were performed more than 50 times. In terms of market box office revenue, in 2018, foreign musicals took 268 million yuan in China (63%); Chinese versions of foreign musicals took 103 million yuan (24%), while original Chinese musicals only took 55 million yuan (13%). The data shows that, although the quantity and quality of original Chinese musicals have increased in recent years, most of them have not had a long-term and wide-ranging impact. Although some good examples have emerged, there is a lack of long-term influence, which is harmful for the development of the Chinese musical industry. There is a lack of good scripts, good composers, and genuinely talented musicals producers.

"In the next three years, China's musicals will explode, and the nation will take center stage on Asia's musical scene. The era of musicals in China has come," says Li Dun, a Chinese musical producer (Melvin 2019). However, *Xishi* – Li Dun's first Chinese musical – could not be staged due to a lack of performers and singers. Since then, Li has directed such works as *Butterflies, In Love with Teresa Teng, Mama*, and *Love Me Once Again* (Ju Hong 2017, pp. 19–20). The musical *Butterflies* is based on the traditional Chinese love story of Liang Shanbo and Zhu Yingtai. The Chinese production team tried to stage it by gathering the best scriptwriter, musicians, actors, and set designer. Many world-class experts also participated in its production, such as general director Gilles Maheu, and director Wayne Fowkes. However, like many other Chinese musicals, it failed due to problems with the plot, costumes, performances, and singing. Sanbao and Guansan's *Winter of Three Hairs* and *The Piano in a Factory*, Wang Er's *Long March*, and Nie Xiaoqian and Ning Chechen's musicals are relatively mature. They have changed the concept of musicals from the usual story-telling style to conceptual performances, but fall short in terms of audience approval because the music and the story are not impressive enough.

Therefore, improving the quality and quantity of original Chinese musicals is the basis of the development of the industry. Improving original Chinese musicals can help enhance the status of China's culture within the international discourse system. In 2014, Chinese president Xi Jinping announced, "We should increase China's soft power, present a positive Chinese narrative, and communicate China's message to the world for successfully" (Biswas & Tortajada 2018). Chinese musical artists should absorb the artistic forms of classic Western versions and create new works that embody traditional Chinese culture. Throughout the history of Western musicals, a large number have been adapted from canonical literary works such as *Romeo and Juliet, Les Misérables, Notre-Dame de Paris*, the Legend of King Arthur, and the story of Princess Elisabeth (Sisi). These source stories are easy for people to accept and understand, and allow audiences to pay more attention to the music itself. In order to create musicals with their own cultural characteristics, Chinese artists must work hard on cultural transplantation and transformation. As Broadway producer Randall L. Wreghitt said, American musicals have integrated genres such as jazz and rap, and Chinese musicals could also combine local artistic styles on their unique development path (Zhou 2019, pp. 144–145). After all, a culture that is national is also international, and the art of a nation is great only when it reflects the unique characteristics of its people.

CONCLUSION

Broadway is the best representative of American musicals as well as a symbol of US culture. Since the introduction of American musicals to China in 1987, they have been performed there in increasing numbers. Between 2004 and 2019, about 30 original American musicals were performed in China. In general, American musicals that promote universal values and arouse the emotional resonance of common people are the most widely accepted in China. The positive influence of American musicals on China include opening the Chinese musical market and introducing the Broadway marketing system, while the negative influence is that it impairs the long-term development of original Chinese musicals.

The major challenge facing the dissemination of American musicals in China is cultural hegemony. The second challenge is Chinese audience's unfamiliarity with musicals, and the third is the poor quality of original Chinese musicals. Improving the quality and quantity of original Chinese musicals is the key to meeting these challenges. Chinese artists must work hard to create more original musicals with Chinese characteristics and and strong national narratives.

REFERENCES

Biswas, Asit K. & Cecilia Tortajada. "China's Soft Power is on the Rise." *China Daily*. 23 February 2018. https://www.chinadaily.com. cn/a/201802/23/WS5a8f59a9a3106e7dcc13d7b8.html. Accessed 5 May 2019.

Block, Geoffrey. "The Broadway Canon from *Show Boat* to *West Side Story* and the European Operatic Ideal." *The Journal of Musicology*. Vol. 11, No. 4. Autumn 1993, pp. 525–544. *JSTOR*, https://doi.org/10.2307/764025.

Bloom, Ken & Frank Vlastnik. *Broadway Musicals: The 101 Greatest Shows of All Time*. New York: Black Dog & Leventhal Publishers, 2010.

Brantley, Ben. "THEATER REVIEW; Rock Opera A la 'Boheme' And 'Hair.'" *The New York Times*. 14 February 1996. https://www.nytimes. com/1996/02/14/theater/theater-review-rock-opera-a-la-boheme-and-hair.html. Accessed 4 April 2019.

Kroll, Jack. "A Downtown 'La Boheme': 'Rent' is the Breakthrough Musical for the '90s." *Newsweek*. 26 February 1996. https://www.angelfire. com/in2/everythingisrent/articles/newsweek4.html. Accessed 4 April 2019.

Lahr, John. "Mississippi Mud." The New Yorker. 27 October 1993, pp. 123–126. https://www.newyorker.com/magazine/1993/10/25/mississippi-mud. Accessed 3 April 2019.

Melvin, Sheila. "So Far Off Broadway It's in China." 22 December 2001. https://www.nytimes.com/2011/12/23/arts/23iht-chinatheater23.html. Accessed 3 April 2019.

Shefter, Martin. *Capital of the American Century: The National and International Influence of New York City*. New York: Russell Sage Foundation, 1993.

Tommasini, Anthony. "Theater; The Seven-Year Odyssey That Led to 'Rent.'" *The New York Times*. 17 March 1996, p. 7. https://www.nytimes. com/1996/03/17/theater/theather-the-seven-year-odyssey-that-led-to-rent.html. Accessed 3 April 2019.

Wei Jinnie. "'Super Vocal', Chinese TV Talent Contest for Opera Singers and Musical Performers, Scores Top Ratings." *The Theatre Times*. 17 February 2019. https://thetheatretimes.com/super-vocal-chinese-tv-talent-contest-for-opera-singers-and-musical-performers-scores-top-ratings/. Accessed 3 April 2019.

CAPA (China Association of Performing Arts). "2016中国演出市场年度报告." 2 June 2017. http://www.capa.com.cn/news/showDetail/92018. Accessed 5 May 2019.

CAPA & Da Mai. "2017中国演出市场年度报告." September 2018. https://max.book118.com/html/2019/0506/8042105053002022.shtm. Accessed 5 May 2019.

道略演艺产业研究院 (Dao Lue). "音乐剧年报：票房增至2.3亿, 原版引进音乐剧是主要驱动因素." 3 March 2016. http://www.idaolue.com/News/Detail.aspx?id=971. Accessed 5 May 2019.

道略演艺产业研究院 (Dao Lue). "音乐剧年报：票房下降23%至1.74亿, 原创与引进双双"跳水." 4 March 2017. http://www.sohu.com/a/127893945_273545. Accessed 5 May 2019.

道略演艺产业研究院 (Dao Lue). "音乐剧年报：票房剧增93%, 市场"大年"真正来临?" 23 August 2019. http://www.idaolue.com/Data/Detail.aspx?id=1645. Accessed 12 March 2020.

界面新闻 (JieMian). "破局与生存：音乐剧的水土不服." 23 September 2018. https://baijiahao.baidu.com/s?id=1617885128870211857&wfr=spider&for=pc. Accessed 5 May 2019.

鞠虹 (Ju Hong). 音乐剧在中国的传播研究 [D]. 东南大学, 2017.

居其宏 (Ju Qihong). 音乐剧：摩登艺术与中国市场 [J]. 上海艺术家,1996 (04): 11–15.

李泓 (Li Hong). "2018年北京演出市场再创新高, 音乐剧观众增长26.7%." 中国文化报. 9 January 2019. https://www.sohu.com/a/287840803_109401. Accessed 5 May 2019.

刘爱华 (Liu Aihua). 美国音乐剧将搬上我国舞台 [J]. 戏剧报, 1987(04):63.

艾列克斯·路别特 (Lubette, Alex). 顾春芳,刘颖译.对美国音乐剧音乐制作的思考 [J]. 戏剧艺术, 2000(02):33–39.

王笈 (Wang Ji). "2019上海国际音乐剧节落下帷幕." http://www.sh.chinanews.com/wenhua/2019-04-27/55797.shtml. Accessed 5 May 2019.

张庆娜 (Zhang Qingna). 全球化语境下音乐剧在中国的本土化探析 [D]. 复旦大学, 2008.

周映辰 (Zhou Yingchen). 用音乐剧讲述中国故事——兼论中国原创音乐剧的主体性建立 [J]. 艺术评论, 2019(12):143–148.

AUTHOR'S BIO

ZHITONG CHEN is currently studying contemporary English literature at the College of Foreign Languages & Cultures, Sichuan University, and gained her master degree in June 2021. Her research interests include contemporary English literature and American culture. Her paper "From Nationalism to Cosmopolitanism: Conflicts and Reconciliation in *Villette*" was published in December 2020 in the *Journal of Hefei University* (Comprehensive Edition).

12 The Belt and Road Initiative through American Eyes[1]

Zhou Li, Yixin Zhang, Yao Chen, Siyi Liu
Southwest Jiaotong University

ABSTRACT

Considered as a centerpiece of China's foreign policy, the Belt and Road Initiative (BRI) has been promoted by the Chinese government to capture the world's attention. Yet regardless of China's publicity, the BRI has been subject to the construction of the Western media, especially the US media, since its launch. Under the guidance of Stuart Hall's (1980/2006) encoding/decoding theory, and focusing on the encoding of the US elite media's construction of the BRI, his paper attempts to reveal the social/cultural/political structures behind the media through analyzing the 39 collected reports from both the *New York Times* and the *Washington Post*.

KEYWORDS

encoding/decoding, the Belt and Road Initiative, the US media

In 2013, China commenced a major global effort, the Belt and Road Initiative [hereafter the BRI], aiming to help close the world's infrastructure gap constraining trade, openness, and future prosperity. Since its first introduction by Chinese President Xi Jinping, the BRI has been set up to "promote the connectivity of Asian, European and African continents and their adjacent seas, establish and strengthen partnerships among the countries along the Belt and Road, set up all-dimensional, multi-tiered and composite connectivity networks and realize diversified, independent, balanced, and sustainable development in these countries" (National Development and Reform Commission 2015). Following that, the BRI has been considered a centerpiece of China's foreign policy, and has been promoted by the Chinese government to capture the world's attention.

Regardless of China's publicity, the BRI has unavoidably been subject to the construction of the Western media, especially the US media. Given its long-time occupation of a dominant discursive position, the US media has emerged as another lynchpin, besides the Chinese discourses, for the public to conceptualize the BRI. Though the current scholarship has paid attention to the discourses of the US newspapers, like the *New York Times*, the *Washington Post*, the *Los Angeles Times*, and the *Chicago Tribune*, emphasis has been placed on the mere descriptions of how the BRI has been constructed by the US and/or on exploring its corresponding attitudes to discuss the media's influence on the American public. (Wang 2018; Yang 2018) While researchers like Zhu and Huang (2016) attempted to reveal the ideologies behind the media's construction by utilizing the critical discourse analysis, their examination failed to examine the media institution itself, thus was also constrained when discussing the hidden ideologies. Therefore, focusing on the encoding moment of the US media's construction of China's BRI, this paper attempts to reveal the social/cultural/political structures behind the media through analyzing 39 collected reports from the *New York Times* (*NYT*) and the *Washington Post* (*WP*).

Criticizing the linearity of the traditional mass-communication model as sender-message-receiver, Hall came up with his encoding/decoding theory, arguing that the communication process is a "'complex structure in dominance,' sustained through the articulation of connected practices, each of which, however, retains its distinctiveness and has its own specific modality, its own forms and conditions of existence." (1980/2006, p. 163) That said, instead of taking the process of mass-communication as mere message-exchange, Hall's theory emphasized the specificity of the forms in which the meaning/ message product appears in moments like encoding, distribution, and decoding through the operation of codes within the syntactic chain of discourse in a media context. In other words, only in this discursive form can the circulation of the message take place. Whereas even though each of the moments is necessary to the circuit as a whole, Hall argued that the moments of "encoding" and "decoding" must be "determinate" since one can never communicate a raw historical event as it was. (p. 164) Consequently, to be communicable, a historical event has to subject itself to the rules of language and be dressed up in the "message form." Thus, the "message form" is a determinate moment since it is the necessary "form of appearance" of the event in the passage from the source to the receiver. Yet, at another level, the "message form" only comprises the surface of the communication system and should be incorporated into the entire communication process as its part. That said, Hall's encoding/decoding theory provided an alternative approach to combining the discursive product and the media apparatuses in such an organic way that a better understanding of the message can be produced by tapping into the underlying logic and social power structures of a certain communication modality.

It is in this spirit, we have come up with two research questions as the guidance for our study of the 39 reports from the *NYT* and the *WP*. They are:

RQ 1: What and how have identities been constructed in the 39 reports?

RQ 2: How has analysis of the constructed identities helped to yield a better understanding of the ideologies behind the two media?

We will first flesh out our conceptual framework and then discuss the two themes we identified in the collected reports. After that, we will further our discussion around the second research question to reveal the underlying logic of the *NYT* and the *WP* to shed light on its corresponding wider socio-cultural and political aspects.

CONCEPTUAL FRAMEWORK

Claiming the encoding and decoding moments to be "determinant," Hall emphasizes how sender and receiver process messages based on their respective positions and knowledge structures. Generally speaking, while messages are organized through codes within the rules of language, processed by "discursive" aspects like "historically defined technical skills, professional ideologies, institutional knowledge, definitions, and assumptions ... about the audience," (Hall 1980/2006, p. 164) they may be decoded by receivers through even broader social, cultural, and political structures. That said, the production and reception of the mediated message are not identical; whereas "formed by the social relations of the communicative process as a whole," they are highly related. (p. 165)

Yet since each community has its system of codes, and some codes appear "not to be constructed" but "profoundly naturalized" in a given society for a period of historical time, (Hall 1980/2006, p. 167) distortion/misunderstanding may arise when communicating messages across cultures and societies. To further elucidate this, Hall came up with "dominant/

preferred meanings," (p. 169) the discursive social, cultural, and political orders of different areas of social life imposed by any society and/or culture. That said, when new events contradictory to our taken-for-granted knowledge of social structures come to us, they will be assigned to their corresponding discursive domain and judged by our society/culture imprinted institutional/political/ideological order in that domain before we can make sense of them. Therefore, we, unconsciously, demonstrate a pattern of "preferred readings" which has long ago been institutionalized and became a part of us. That said, treating issues like misunderstanding and/or preferred reading merely as personal problems only shifts us away from delving deeper into the hidden institutional/ideological/structural ones.

Though Hall developed his theory in the early 1970s within the context of television discourse, researchers adopting his model proved its productivity in broad-sense media (Newhagen 2012; Radway 1984) and high relevance in today's world (Aligwe et al. 2018). While scholars who applied Hall's model to their studies tended to have an emphasis on encoding and decoding as two determinant moments, their analysis was still based on the traditional conceptual metaphor of communication: circuit/loop. (Worthington 2008) That said, when examining a communication event, researchers tended to cover the entire communication loop while overlooking the value to dip into one particular moment. Consequently, focusing on the encoding of the *NYT* and the *WP*, we choose to focus our study on the two newspapers' 39 reports on China's BRI, a reflection of both their decoding (messages from China) and encoding (messages to domestic as well as international audiences) moments. We give heed to the *NYT* and the *WP* for two reasons: 1) they have been among the leading newspapers in the US so long that their social influence cannot be underestimated and 2) they are indeed the typical elite media in the US (Lee 2002). That said, the two newspapers' interpretation of China's BRI was not merely their own but a reflection of US elites' attitude. In other words, with the help of the two newspapers, US elites had their "preferred reading" of China's BRI heard by the public. Thus, analyzing the 39 reports together with the apparatuses of the two newspapers, we attempt to reveal both the underlying logic of this communication modality and the hidden power relations in American society today. The organic combination of the journal discourses and the apparatuses of the media institution, as suggested in Hall's theory, is appropriate here for us to investigate the media influence, especially with the elite power behind, on the American public and how the American culture and society have served as the background for the mediated ideas to be spread out.

METHOD

Because President Xi Jinping's speeches about the BRI from September 7, 2013 (the first time the BRI was mentioned) to May 14, 2017 (the first Belt and Road Forum held in Beijing) are the most representative descriptions, we decided to analyze the US elite media reports on Xi's speeches to unravel their attitudes towards China's BRI instead of some random texts. Then after labeling the 25 speeches that Xi has delivered during the identified period of time (see appendix 1), we used the stratified sampling to collect the data. Specifically, having the release time of every Xi speech as the reference, we collected the reports from both the *NYT* and the *WP* on Xi and the BRI within the following week (seven days) to ensure the comprehensiveness of the sample data. For instance, given that the time of Xi's first speech on the BRI was September 7, 2013, our sample selection should be conducted between September 7 and 21 (US Eastern time). Following this, we gathered 53 reports from the *NYT* and 63 from *WP*. Then we went through the sample data again to make sure that every report had directly responded to the BRI in Xi's words and finally arrived at 19 reports from the *NYT* and 20 from *WP*.

Our analysis began with authors reading the sample reports repeatedly, labeling and categorizing key codes regarding China and the BRI, and noting patterns of identity representation. Then, group discussions were arranged with authors posing questions to one another to group the codes and outline the general patterns. After the group work, the authors reached a consensus on two overlapping emergent themes: 1) the aggressive, hypocritical, and problematic China, and 2) the victimized yet responsible US. We present our analysis in the following paragraphs.

"THE AGGRESSIVE, HYPOCRITICAL, AND PROBLEMATIC CHINA"

As a major cultural and ideological force, media stands in such a dominant position defining both social relations and political problems as well as the production and transformation of popular ideologies. (Hall 1980, p. 104) That said, media plays a big part in constituting the cultural other in relation to the dominant group. Decoding the BRI in Xi's 25 speeches, the *NYT* and the *WP* encoded a rising China in their reports, but because of its aggressiveness and hypocrisy, China is incapable of replacing the US to lead the world. For example, Denyer (2016) used the previous president Obama's words to accuse China used to being a "free rider" on the world stage, yet indicated that it attempted to take a more forceful global role under Xi's lead through "launching the Asian Infrastructure Investment Bank in 2014 and a 'Belt and Road' regional development plan." More specifically, three subthemes have been identified in this section demonstrating China's "incapability" in replacing the US to lead the world. Respectively, these themes represented concerns over China's aggressiveness, hypocrisy, and territorial ambition.

"China's Benefits-Driven Project"

One of the most noticeable portrayals of the BRI in the US elite media is that it reflects China's aggressiveness and because China has been so benefits-driven, it can hardly play the role of a world leader. For instance, ever since the launch of the BRI, it has been defined as the Chinese government's ambitious taking to more energy suppliers. Referring to the purpose of the BRI, Perlez (2013a) noted that China "wants to diversify … so that more oil and gas providers are closer to home" regardless of its current dependence on the Middle East to feed its oil needs. Describing China's development plans as linking the port of Gwadar with Xinjiang Province in western China through a network of Chinese rail and road projects to be "ambitious," Masood and Walsh (2015) contended that this economic corridor can certainly "offer China easier sea access to Africa, South Asia, and the Persian Gulf."

Specifically, the depiction of China's aggressiveness has been shown in the reports on Xi's 2017 Davos speech. Coincidently, both the *NYT* and the *WP* interpreted Xi's defense for "globalization" as his action towards the global economic leadership since the president-elect at that time, Donald J. Trump, was obviously not interested and then created a vacuum for the leadership. For example, contextualizing Xi's speech as being delivered three days before Trump's inauguration and Britain's announcement of departure from the European Union, Goodman (2017) argued that Xi's message "appeared meticulously timed" which "underscores China's attempt to improve its international standing just as much of the world appears in turmoil."

In fact, reports on Xi's Davos speech were not the first time that the US media had blamed China for being so benefits-focused that it failed to assume the responsibility of a great power. Perlez (2014) commented on China's proposal for a new regional free-trade area at the C.E.O. Summit of the Asia-Pacific Economic Cooperation meeting, and said that in the name of creating "an Asian-Pacific dream for our people," China would care much less than the US's Trans-Pacific Partnership (hereafter TPP) about items like intellectual property. Given the importance of the protection of intellectual property in the world today, the subtext of Perlez's report was quite obvious that focusing only on benefits, China is incapable of leading the overall prosperity of the entire world. Of course, Perlez's report also reflected a long-time political-strategic accusation that both China and the US got used to making towards each other: hypocrisy (Hartnett 2011). In this sense, how can China help Asia-Pacific people achieve their dreams if no rigorous ethical standard are being held?

"China's Hypocrisy"

The *NYT* and the *WP* have been of great help to American politicians in constructing an image of China as hypocritical. As hooks (1992) noted, within commodity culture, the other becomes a spice that can liven up dull mainstream white culture. In this case, the development of China's BRI has been demonstrated as a showcase for China's hypocrisy in areas like free trade, environmental protection, and internet safety.

Both the *NYT* and the *WP* have attacked Xi's championing for economic globalization and the BRI's characteristics of economic globalization, deriding China for the discrepancy between its words and deeds. For example, commenting on Xi's defense for globalization at the World Economic Forum in Davos, Denyer (2017) noted that the American companies became increasingly unhappy with the way China was treating them since Xi's government has turned "more toward protectionism as its economic growth" slowed down. Furthermore, Goodman (2017) focused on Xi's discursive choice of the phrase "economic globalization" and contended that this reflected "China's spurning of an open internet, universal human rights, and free election."

In fact, as we have seen from the collected data, internet safety has stayed as a consistent issue concerning the US elite media reporters. Frankel (2015) noted that while Xi was pledging to fight against cyberattacks, the Chinese government refused to admit a cyberattack it conducted during the summer. Moreover, Rauhala (2017) reminded the audience to stay skeptical since "China has tightened control over the internet, strengthening the Great Firewall in the name of 'internet sovereignty'" which "keeps China's internet users in a 'room' of their own." The subtext here is quite clear: how ironic and hypocritical China was as it cut off its internet connections with the world on one hand yet championed for the "connectivity" on the other.

Besides international trade and internet safety, environmental protection has emerged to be the third concern in the coverage of elite media. Facing Xi's envision of the BRI to be innovative, open, green, and cooperative, Pomfret (2017) ridiculed, "In his speech, Xi positioned himself as the defender of the Paris climate accord. But China remains the world's largest user of coal and has plans to use more." Moreover, comparing China's usage of clean energy like wind generation to that of the US. Pomfret noted that "wind generation as a proportion of all power generation is about 50 percent higher in the US than in China" to further support the penetrated belief: the impossibility for China to replace the US as the world superpower. Since constructing the "other" is fundamental to the constitution of the self, (Hall 1996, p. 237) identifying China, the cultural other, as hypocrisy indeed helps the US to consolidate its definition of the national "self" as non-hypocrisy.

"China's Problems Concerning Other Countries"

Besides the coverage on China's aggressiveness and hypocrisy, the US elite media also have favored in reporting how China's BRI bothered other countries, especially the neighboring ones over the territorial issues, to buttress its argument that China is the "new evil empire." (Halimi, 2019) In fact, as early as Xi's first proposal of the 21st Century Maritime Silk Road at the People's Representative Council of Indonesia, China's BRI has been portrayed by the US media as a territorial threat to Asian countries. As Perlez (2013b) noted, "Many Asian countries remain wary of China's territorial ambitions and had welcomed the [American] 'pivot' as protection against extensive Chinese claims in the South China and East China Seas." Likewise, Feng (2014) cited words both from Prime Minister Nguyen Tan Dung of Vietnam and President Benigno S. Aquino III of the Philippines and condemned that China has taken too many actions in the South China Sea which created an "extremely dangerous situation."

Picturing China as aggressive and hypocritical and the BRI as problematic has helped the US elite media to restore the US image for both, domestic and international audiences. In particular, our second theme focuses on revealing the US elite media's construction of the national image by responding to China's BRI.

The Victimized Yet Responsible US

Though China has long been identified to play the victim card in diplomacy (Hartnett 2011), through analyzing the data, we argue that the US elite media have been performing the victim's role as well, a victim of China's forceful rising. Yet, the reports still attempted to establish the US's great power demeanor by indicating that as long as China's rising is beneficial to the region and the world, the US can be tolerant of China's aggressiveness. For example, covering China's investment in Pakistan to build up the new "Silk Road," the Editorial Board of the *NYT* (2015) stated,

> *Some suggest the project will further enhance China's standing in Asia at America's expense. But that is perhaps too narrow a view. Both the United States and China share an interest in a stable Pakistan. If China can advance that goal through development programs, the whole region would benefit.*

Being generous and kind as the media depicted, the US can only choose to counter China because China's development plans put others "at danger." Specifically, three subthemes have been located in this section: 1) China's rising at America's expense, 2) the US's responsibility for the global development, and 3) the US: the only country others rely on.

"China's Rising at America's Expense"

Emerging within the play of specific modalities of power, identity, as Hall (1996) argued, is "more the product of the marking of difference and exclusion" instead of being the "sign of an identical, naturally-constituted unity." (p. 4) This is what we have seen in the data and mainly demonstrated in our first theme above. While in this one, by constructing China, not as a competitive rival, but as an evil/bad cultural other who has attempted to rise into another superpower by grasping every opportunity, the *NYT* and the *WP* restored the image of the US as victimized yet responsible.

In fact, the US has blamed the BRI at the very beginning of China's launch as a kind of copycat project. As Perlez (2013a) noted, "the strategy [the BRI] also has the advantage of countering . . . American plans for a 'new Silk Road' announced by Secretary of State Hillary Rodham Clinton in 2011." Yet to reinforce the image of China as a reckless rule-breaker, Perlez cited a piece of Wang Jisi's (an architect of China's "march westwards" policy) words indicating China's determination to act instead of waiting for the US to initiate despite the fact that a similar proposal was brought up by the US before. Whereas although the media acknowledged that some domestic issues have hindered America from leading the world to further develop, it insisted on portraying China's rising-up as unabashed opportunism. Rather than blaming the Republicans for their induced government shutdown undermining American leadership in Asia, the Editorial Board of the *NYT* (2013) focused on discussing how in Obama's absence, China could be able to grab the spotlight and then urged president Obama to reschedule another trip as soon as possible. Similarly, realizing that America's vision and influence have shrunk under the lead of President Trump, the media nevertheless preferred to frame China's active performance on the global stage as plotted. As Goodman (2017) stated, "that Mr. Xi chose this year to make his debut underscores China's attempt to improve its international standing just as much of the world appears in turmoil." Whereas the "turmoil" in Goodman's report referred to Trump's questioning of the institutions like NATO and the World Trade Organization, Britain's divorce from the European Union, as well as the growing electoral strength of populist, anti-European Union parties in France, the Netherlands, Italy, and Germany.

Besides, the US media also connected China's growth to the challenge of the world order safeguarded by the US. As the Editorial Board of the *NYT* (2017) commented, "China clearly aims to dominate the international system. If it succeeds – shaping how vast sums are spent and where, and which laws are followed or not – it could upend a system established by Washington and its allies after World War II." To justify the existing "system," the media continued by recalling "military concerns" like Burma-China territorial issues, saying "China could use the Kyaukphyu ports (a project under the BRI framework) for military purposes." Meanwhile, Harris and Bradsher (2016) highlighted the geopolitical undertones of China's BRI and emphasized how that could be a threat to the established balance in the Asian region. In other words, instead of being a beneficial project to the world, the BRI, as Harris and Bradsher interpreted, has forced China's neighboring countries into a dilemma: either they agree to China's territorial demands or they lose access to China's vast market. Yet as a responsible superpower, the US had attempted to counter China's vicious plan by coming up with its TPP since 2013 even though it was finally abandoned by Trump.

The US's Responsibility for The Global Development

From the chosen nation to America's attachment to its position atop the world, those widespread beliefs have largely shaped the American attitudes towards other countries (Edwards 2008). In particular, the "city upon a hill" mythology granted the US its self-proclaimed moral legitimacy and religious justification to lead the world (Lu 2011). Besides, in the mainstream of American life, as Hughes noted, most had the rooted conviction of "the ultimate meaning of their nation: America stood for good against evil, right against wrong, democracy against tyranny, and virtue against vice." (2004, p. 153) It was under this situation that the US has justified its fight against China's BRI by bringing up the TPP, a trade bloc led by the US yet excluding China. Correspondingly, compared with China's BRI, the TPP has been constructed by the elite media as a more feasible and countable alternative, the project that the US has strived to achieve to lead the world to prosperity.

Responding to Obama's absence at the Asia-Pacific Economic Cooperation, which gave Xi the chance to be the dominant leader at the gathering, Perlez and Cochrane (2013) mentioned that Obama was trying to use "personal persuasion to push forward negotiations for the Trans-Pacific Partnership," "the complex negotiations that cover all economic sectors from intellectual property to agriculture to automobiles and aim to bring regional economic integration through trade and investment liberalization." To highlight the possibility of succeeding in this project, they quoted Michael Froman, the US trade representative, indicating the TPP was "ambitious but doable." Similarly, countering Xi's expansion of his "China Dream" onto a broader stage, Denyer (2014) acknowledged the contribution made by the Obama government saying that Obama came to the APEC summit with his proposal, the TPP, "a putative free-trade area stretching from Chile to Japan that could encompass 800 million people and 40 percent of the global economy." Though the TPP was not developed as well as China's BRI, Denyer commented that probably Obama has done too little to win over Democrats. Even during the Obama-Trump presidential transition and when Trump declared zero interest in furthering the TPP, the media still chose to emphasize the TPP's geopolitical importance and its potential benefits to countries and regions included. In fact, the media not only portrayed the positivity of the TPP directly, it also attempted to buttress its argument by quoting other countries.

The US: The Only Country Others Rely on

In addition to demonstrating how China's rise is based on the expense of the US's interests and what a contribution the US attempted to make to the world's prosperity, the media has employed words from other countries' leadership to prove

America's unshakable stance in both Asia and the world. Especially, quotations were selected to cover two intertwined areas 1) America's lead is desirable and urgent and 2) joining China's BRI is always a second choice.

In its early response to China's investment in the Asia region through the building of the BRI, the US media has adopted the words from the leaders of other Asian countries to prove the incomparable stance that the US has in Asia. For example, according to the prime minister of Singapore, Lee Hsien Loong (as cited in Perlez and Cochrane 2013), "No other country can replace the American engagement in Asia ... Not China, not Japan, not any other power. This is something which we continue and encourage at every opportunity." To demonstrate how the TPP has been welcomed by Asian countries, Perlez (2014) used Japan as an example and noted that even Japan's most protected agricultural sector would be opened up under terms of the TTP as Prime Minister Shinzo Abe promised the Obama administration. The reality that the media attempted to create was that regardless of China's huge investment into its neighboring countries, these nations would "still be keeping a careful eye on China, and many will continue to look to the United States as an important counterweight and ally," (Denyer 2014)

Yet about other Asia-Pacific countries finally considering joining the Chinese-led trade pact, the US media explained: they were out of choice. Peru's foreign minister, Eduardo Ferreyros (as cited in Harris and Bradsher 2016), said that Peru still hoped the TPP to become a reality someday. But since Trump was not interested in pushing the pack forward, Peru would open talks with China to consider the China-led Regional Comprehensive Economic Partnership (hereafter RCEP). Similarly, Prime Minister Shinzo Abe (as cited in Harris and Bradsher 2016) contended, "If TPP doesn't move forward, there is no doubt that the focus will shift." Though in Denyer's (2016) report that countries like Vietnam, Malaysia, and even Chile all expressed their interest in joining China's RCEP, their consideration was because TPP could not be realized.

Consequently, through establishing the image of the US as victimized yet accountable, the reports from the *NYT* and the *WP* echoed their portrayal of China as hypocritical and aggressive and the BRI as only being concerned about benefits. In particular, constructing China as the bad/evil other, the media restored and reemphasized the cultural scripts of the US's national image as good/right/democracy/virtue for both domestic and international audiences even when the reality went the other way around. Moreover, focusing on the encoding moment of the US elite media, the next section reveals the hidden social/cultural/political structures of the two media's construction of China's BRI.

Discussion and Conclusion

As we have demonstrated above, the two elite media's construction of the "other," China, helped to anchor the US's national "self." To further understand how/why the images of "other" and "self" have been constructed like this, we follow Hall's (1980/2006, p. 165) "encoding and decoding of broadcast structures" and expand our analysis especially around two aspects: frameworks of knowledge and relations of production. Referring to frameworks of knowledge, we argue that by employing codes with a strong sense of America's universal value to depict China and its BRI, the two elite media discursively revealed/reconstructed the aggressive, hypocritical, and problematic China and once again fulfilled the America's responsibility as rightfully fighting against wrong, and a good democracy against an evil empire. Though individual Americans may hold on to their various political ideologies, the vast majority still subscribe to fundamental values like individualism, liberty, equality, and democracy.

For example, of all the values to the American nation, individualism has acquired a mythical status equal to none in prestige and influence. (McElroy 1987) What that means, if using Hall's (1980/2006) argument on encoding/decoding, is that since the code of individualism had been so widely distributed in American culture, processing the code was already naturalized. That said, when processing the code of individualism becomes habitualized for individual Americans, equivalence is easy to achieve in the communicative exchange. As shown in the previous section, when responding to the question – "Can China overtake the United States to lead the world?" – posted by the *Global Times*, Denyer (2016) argued that though China has taken a series of actions, it is still not comparable to the US. The point worth our attention here is that by presenting the actions taken by the Chinese government like "launching the Asian Infrastructure Investment Bank" and advancing "the BRI regional development plan," Denyer nevertheless initiated the sentence with an accusation from the previous president Obama in 2014 saying that China has been a "free rider" on the global stage. Regardless of the accusation's relevance to China's plan for development, an ideological phrase like "free rider" positioned China opposite to America's universal value, individualism, as one is expected to be independent, autonomous, and self-reliant. That said, one gets what one pays for if one exploits others' contributions. Yet since the code of individualism has been so rooted in the minds of the American majority, the idea of China being an exploiter was communicated effectively from the media to the public without causing misunderstandings. Besides, adding the accusation of being a "free rider" right before China's approach to global governance, this report made China's ability to lead questionable and the motives dubious. Whereas reminding the public of Obama's comment on China in the interview with Thomas Friedman indicating that China has been doing nothing for the world for the past 30 years strengthened the image of the "responsible" US. Once again as Obama put, "It's for that same reason that people look to America in ways they don't look to China." (*The New York Times* 2014)

Moreover, attacking China under the name of liberty and democracy has been the common strategy adopted by the US and it was no exception this time for China's BRI. Depicting China as turning "more toward protectionism," (Denyer 2017) being "far less liberal," (Editorial Board 2017, as well as spurning "an open internet, universal human rights, and free election," (Goodman 2017) the US elite media indeed created China to be the "new evil empire" (Halimi 2019) with ulterior motives unable even to protect the world's status quo not to mention leading the development. This kind of representation not only awakened America's long-time "yellow peril and red menace memory frames" of China (Yang 2017), but also reconfirmed American exceptionalism together with the notion of manifest destiny, the wildly held cultural belief that it is America's mission to spread and defend American virtues (e.g. democracy and liberty) throughout the rest of the world. Thus, framing the US ambition of seeking political, economic, and cultural influence into those ideological phrases like "Many Asian countries … had welcomed the [American] 'pivot,'" "rebalance" of Asia, the elite media communicated to the public that it is the "exceptional" rather than imperial, colonial, or hegemonic US that can maintain the global order and eventually make the world prosperous.

Referring to the relations of production, we argue that the *NYT* and the *WP* are not genuinely liberal, but are dedicated to defend the interests of the state-corporate complex. Though the two elite media have been known nation-wide as liberally biased, they are liberal only on social issues like race, feminism, and LGBTQ. Whereas economically speaking, they are quite conservative. For instance, regardless of the *NYT*'s pro-environmental protection attitudes, it has maintained a close relationship with the Oil & Money conference and even became an official sponsor of the conference in 2013. (Perry 2019) Meanwhile, the WP is indeed run by a "smart" businessman, having been sold to Jeff Bezos, the founder, CEO, and president of the technology company Amazon, in 2013. (Giuliani-Hoffman 2019) The point to note here is that no matter how socially liberal those journalists are, when they are employed by media institutions structured like this, they know well that they have worked for "these enormous conglomerates that are naturally conservative." (Alterman 2002, p. 37)

Therefore, Chomsky (1990, p. 13) derided the *NYT* as an "official press," defining it as creating "illusions" of liberty on one hand and marking off the ideological boundary for the state-corporate complex on the other. In other words, journalists in this kind of institution do not have to be censored by the companies since they know what can or cannot address in their reports. This explained the journalists' choice to blame China for "grasping the spotlight," "playing the adult," "appearing meticulously timed," and "defending globalization" even though they knew that these were, by and large, caused by the US itself. That said, if the republicans didn't induce the government shutdown, and if Trump insisted on advancing the TPP and didn't exit the Paris Climate Accord, China might not have had the chance to play such a significant role in the past few years on the global stage. Yet instead of pointing out the crux, the two elite media shifted the focus by accusing China of being aggressive and playing the role that should have been played by America.

The analysis of the 39 reports from the *NYT* and the *WP* on China and the BRI reveals the US elite media's discursive construction of the two identities: "us" vs. "them." Focusing on the encoding moment of the 39 reports together with the apparatuses of the two elite media, we have argued that establishing the image of an aggressive, hypocritical, and problematic China helped that media to anchor the US's national self as victimized yet responsible. Delving into the frameworks of knowledge and the relations of production, we have revealed both the underlying logic of the US elite media as "seemingly-liberal yet ideologically infiltrated" and the hidden power relations in current American society that only the truth communicated by the elite media is the truth held dear by those enormous conglomerates.

ENDNOTES

[1] This work was supported by The National Social Science Fund of China [Grant Number 19CYY014] and National Student Research Training Program [Grant Number: 202010613087].

REFERENCES

Aligwe, H. N., Nwafor, K. A., & Alegu, J. C. (2018). Stuart Hall's Encoding-decoding Model: a Critique. *World Applied Sciences Journal, 36* (9), 1019–1023.

Alterman, E. (2002). What liberal media? The Truth about Bias and the News. *Sacred Heart University Review, 22* (1), 25–42.

Chomsky, N. (1990). *Necessary illusions*. Boston: South End Press.

Denyer, S. (2014). China Promotes "Asia-Pacific dream" to Counter US "Pivot." *The Washington Post*. https://www.washingtonpost.com/world/chinas-promotes-asia-pacific-dream-to-counter-us-pivot/2014/11/11/1d9e05a4-1e8e-4026-ad5a-5919f8c0de8a_story.html. Accessed 11 Oct 2020.

Denyer, S. (2016). If the US withdraws, China Wonders Whether it is Ready to Lead the World. *The Washington Post*. https://www.washingtonpost.com/news/worldviews/WP/2016/11/21/if-the-u-s-withdraws-china-wonders-if-it-is-ready-to-lead-the-world/. Accessed 11 Oct 2020.

Denyer, S. (2017). No Longer Welcome? American Companies Fear China's Turning its Back on Them. *The Washington Post*. https://www.washingtonpost.com/world/asia_pacific/no-longer-welcome-american-companies-fear-china-is-turning-its-back-on-them/2017/01/17/bd0e16e6-dcc7-11e6-b2cf-b67fe3285cbc_story.html. Accessed 11 Oct 2020.

Edwards, J. A. (2008). *Navigating the Post-Cold War World: President Clinton's Foreign Policy Rhetoric*. Lanham, MD: Lexington Book.

Ehrenfreund, M. (2017). World Leaders Find Hope for Globalization in Davos Amid Populist Revolt. *The Washington Post*. https://www.washingtonpost.com/news/wonk/wp/2017/01/17/chinese-president-warns-against-trade-war-in-davos/. Accessed 11 Oct 2020.

Feng, B. (2014). As Xi Speaks of Conciliation, Neighbors Voice Disquiet. *The New York Times*. https://sinosphere.blogs.nytmes.com/2014/05/22/as-xi-speaks-of-conciliation-neighbors-voice-disquiet/. Accessed 9 Oct 2020.

Frankel, T. C. (2015). China's President Pledges to Fight Cyberattacks. *The Washington Post*. https://www.washingtonpost.com/business/economy/chinas-president-pledges-to-fight-cyber-attacks-stresses-reforms/2015/09/22/2f019aa6-6c35-4c7f-9e15-6df3278c12ed_story.html. Accessed 11 Oct 2020.

Goodman, P. S. (2017). In Era of Trump, China's President Champions Economic Globalization. *The New York Times*. https://www.nytimes.com/2017/01/17/business/dealbook/world-economic-forum-davos-china-xi-globalization.html. Accessed 9 Oct 2020.

Giuliani-Hoffman, F. (2019). How the Washington Post has Changed under Jeff Bezos. *CNN Business*. https://edition.cnn.com/2019/08/16/media/jeff-bezos-donald-graham/index.html. Accessed 14 Oct 2020.

Halimi, S. (2019). The US's New Evil Empire. *Le Monde diplomatique*. https://mondediplo.com/2019/10/01editorial. Accessed 17 Oct 2020.

Hall, S. (1980). Introduction to Media Studies at the Center. In S. Hall, D. Hobson, A. Lowe, & P. Willis (Eds.), *Culture, Media, Language*. Routledge in Association with the Center for Contemporary Cultural Studies, University of Birmingham.

Hall, S. (1996). Who needs identity? In S. Hall & P. D. Gay (Eds.), *Questions of Cultural Identity*. London: Sage.

Harris, G., & Bradsher, K. (2016). China's Influence Grows in Ashes of Trans-Pacific Trade Pact. *The New York Times*. https://www.nytimes.com/2016/11/20/business/international/apec-trade-china-obama-trump-tpp-trans-pacific-partnership.html. Accessed 9 Oct 2020.

Hartnett, S. J. (2011). Google and the "Twisted Cyber Spy" Affair: US-China Communication in an Age of Globalization. *Quarterly Journal of Speech*, 97 (4), 411–434.

hooks, b. (1992). *Black looks: Race and Representation*. Boston: South End Press.

Hughes, R. T. (2004). *Myths America Lives by*. University of Illinois Press.

Lee, C. (2002). Established Pluralism: US Elite Media Discourse about China Policy. *Journalism Studies*, 3 (3), 343–357.

Lu, X. (2011). From "Ideological Enemies" to "Strategic Partners": A Rhetorical Analysis of US-China Relations in Intercultural Contexts. *The Howard Journal of Communications*, 22, 336–357.

Masood, S., & Walsh, D. (2015). Xi Jinping Plans to Fund Pakistan. *The New York Times*. https://www.nytimes.com/2015/04/22/world/asia/xi-jinping-plans-to-fund-pakistan.html. Accessed 9 Oct 2020.

McElroy, J. H. (1987). *Finding Freedom: America's Distinctive Cultural Formation*. Carbondale, IL: Southern Illinois University Press.

National Development and Reform Commission. (2015). Vision and Actions on Jointly Building Silk Road Economic Belt and 21st-Century Maritime Silk Road. https://en.ndrc.gov.cn/newsrelease_8232/201503/t20150330_1193900.html. Accessed 18 Oct 2020.

Newhagen, J. E. (2012). Hypernews, Biological Authenticity, and the Mediation of What's Important. *Politics and the Life Sciences*, 31 (1), 80–86.

Perlez, J. (2013a). China Looks West as it Bolsters Regional Ties. *The New York Times*. https://www.nytimes.com/2013/09/08/world/asia/china-looks-west-as-it-strengthens-regional-ties.html. Accessed 9 Oct 2020.

Perlez, J. (2013b). Cancellation of trip by Obama Plays to Doubts of Asia Allies. *The New York Times*. https://www.NYTimes.com/2013/10/05/world/asia/with-obama-stuck-in-washington-china-leader-has-clear-path-at-asia-conferences.html. Accessed 9 Oct 2020.

Perlez, J. (2014, November 9). No Fears for China Economy, Xi says. *The New York Times*. https://www.NYTimes.com/2014/11/10/business/international/no-fears-for-china-economy-xi-jinping-says.html. Accessed 9 Oct 2020.

Perlez, J., & Cochrane, J. (2013). Obama's Absence Leaves China as Dominant Force at Asia-Pacific Meeting. *The New York Times*. https://www.nytimes.com/2013/10/08/world/asia/asia-pacific-economic-cooperation-summit.html. Accessed 9 Oct 2020.

Perry, C. (2019). New York Times Drops Oil Sponsorship and Sparks Debate: Should News Orgs Back Agenda Specific Event? *Fox Business*. https://www.foxbusiness.com/media/new-york-times-sponsorship-oil-and-money-conference. Accessed 19 Oct 2020.

Pomfret, J. (2017). Chinese President Xi Jinping Introduces Himself as the Anti-Trump. *The Washington Post*. https://www.washingtonpost.com/news/global-opinions/wp/2017/01/18/chinese-president-xi-jinping-introduces-himself-as-the-anti-trump/. Accessed 11 Oct 2020.

Radway, J. (1984). *Reading the Romance: Women, Patriarchy, and Popular Literature*. The University of North Carolina Press.

Rauhala, E. (2017). Forget Xi's "Defense" of Globalization. China Just Fortified the Great Firewall. *The Washington Post*. https://www.washingtonpost.com/news/worldviews/wp/2017/01/23/forget-xis-defense-of-globalization-china-just-fortified-the-great-firewall/. Accessed 11 Oct 2020.

The Editorial Board. (2013). The International Fallout. *The New York Times*. https://www.nytimes.com/2013/10/08/opinion/the-international-fallout.html. Accessed 9 Oct 2020.

The Editorial Board. (2015). China's Big Plunge in Pakistan. *The New York Times*. https://www.nytimes.com/2015/04/23/opinion/chinas-big-plunge-in-pakistan.html. Accessed 9 Oct 2020.

The Editorial Board. (2017). China's Trillion-dollar Foreign Policy. *The New York Times*. https://www.nytimes.com/2017/05/18/opinion/china-xi-jinping-foreign-policy.html. Accessed 19 Oct 2020.

The New York Times. (2014). *Exclusive Obama Interview: China as a Free Rider* [Video file]. Retrieved from https://www.youtube.com/watch/Hg8ntdSbmCk?reload=9. Accessed 19 Oct 2020.

Worthington, N. (2008). Encoding and Decoding Rape News: How Progressive Reporting Inverts Textual Orientations. *Women's Studies in Communication*, 31 (3), 344–367.

Yang, M. M. (2017). *American Political Discourse on China*. New York: Routledge.

APPENDIX 1: LIST OF THE 25 SPEECHES

(1) 2013.09 first speech on the BRI, primary audience Kazakh people (location: Astana, Kazakhstan);

(2) Speech at the 13th meeting of the Council of Heads of Member States of the Shanghai Cooperation Organization in Bishkek, Kyrgyzstan;

(3) 2013.10 first speech on the maritime silk road, primary audience Indonesian people (location: Jakarta, Indonesia). Indonesian Parliament;

(4) 2014.3.27 speech delivered at the UNESCO Headquarters;

(5) 2014.4.1 speech delivered at the College of Europe in Bruges, Belgium;

(6) 2014.5.21 speech delivered at the Fourth Summit of the Conference on Interaction and Confidence-Building Measures in Asia, held in Shanghai;

(7) 2014.6.5 speech delivered at the opening ceremony of the Sixth Ministerial Conference of the China-Arab States Cooperation Forum in Beijing

(8) 2014.9.18 speech delivered at the Indian Council of World Affairs;

(9) 2014.11.8 speech delivered at the Dialogue on Strengthening Connectivity Partnership in Beijing;

(10) 2014.11.11 speech delivered at the 22nd APEC Economic Leaders' Meeting in Beijing;

(11) 2015.03.28 keynote speech delivered at the Boao Forum for Asia Annual Conference;

(12) 2015.04.21 speech delivered at the Parliament of Pakistan;

(13) 2015.09.22 speech delivered at a reception held jointly by the local government and friendly groups in Seattle, Washington US;

(14) 2015.10.15 speech delivered when meeting with foreign representatives attending the Asian Political Parties' Special Conference on the Silk Road in Beijing;

(15) 2015.10.21 speech delivered at the China-UK Business Summit in the city of London;

(16) 2015.12.04 speech delivered at the opening ceremony of the Johannesburg Summit of the Forum on China-Africa Cooperation;

(17) 2015.12.16 speech delivered at the opening ceremony of the Second World Internet Conference in Wuzhen, Zhejiang Province;

(18) 2016.01.16 speech delivered at the inauguration ceremony of the Asian Infrastructure Investment Bank;

(19) 2016.06.20 speech delivered at the opening ceremony of the Silk Road Forum and China-Poland Regional Cooperation and Business Forum in Warsaw;

(20) 2016.06.22 speech delivered at the Legislative Chamber of the Supreme Assembly of Uzbekistan;

(21) 2016.09.03 keynote speech delivered at the opening ceremony of the B20 Summit in Hangzhou, China;

(22) 2016.11.19 speech delivered at the APEC CEO Summit in Lima, Peru;

(23) 2017.01.17 keynote speech delivered at the opening ceremony of the World Economic Forum in Davos, Switzerland;

(24) 2017.01.18 speech delivered at the UN Office in Geneva;

(25) 2017.05.13 speech delivered at the opening ceremony of the Belt and Road Forum for International Cooperation in Beijing.

AUTHOR'S BIO

Zhou Li (PhD, Ohio University) is an associate professor at the School of Foreign Languages, Southwest Jiaotong University (Chengdu, China). Her research examines the multiple networks in identity construction, from micro to macro levels, to unravel the power structures with the goal of a liberatory politics. She has publications in journals like *Critical Discourse Studies*, *Chinese Journal of Communication*, and *Critical Studies in Media Communication*, and hosts a project funded by the National Social Science Fund of China.

Yixin Zhang is a junior student at the Department of Translation and Interpretation, School of Foreign Languages, Southwest Jiaotong University (Chengdu, China).

Yao Chen is a junior student at the Department of Translation and Interpretation, School of Foreign Languages, Southwest Jiaotong University (Chengdu, China).

13 Ecological Traffic Legislation in the United States and Its Enlightenment in China[1]

Rongrong Zhang and Ziling Huang, Southwest Jiaotong University

ABSTRACT

Compared with developed Western countries, China started relatively late in the legislation of ecological traffic. As the first country in the world to establish an eco-traffic legislation system, the United States has not only established the concept of combining the sustainable development of society with strict environmental protection policies but also formed a relatively complete and systematic legal framework, which is methodical, performable, and in line with the trend of the times. This paper examines the origin, contents, and features of urban ecological traffic legislation in the United States, and points out ecological concerns requiring attention in China's traffic legislation, to improve China's legal system in the field of urban ecological traffic by learning from that of the United States.

KEYWORDS

The United States, ecological traffic, legislation

INTRODUCTION

Since the middle of the 18th century, with the rise of the industrial revolution, urbanization has swept rapidly and overwhelmingly across the West. The population gathered fast and became concentrated in large cities, and urban traffic overspread with the geographic expansion of cities, resulting in ecological deterioration such as shortage of land resources, air pollution, noise pollution, and traffic congestion, which have seriously affected human survival and development. The United States was at the forefront of the industrial revolution, and was the first to consider the management and regulation of ecological traffic during its urbanization, when it was facing environmental deterioration and resource shortage. It not only created the concept of ecological traffic but also implemented a series of legislative practices under this concept. According to the data released by China's National Bureau of Statistics in January 2020, the urbanization rate in Mainland China had reached 60.60% by the end of 2019 and would continue to grow steadily. In this process, China is also faced with ecological problems brought about by the rapid development of transportation. This paper analyzes the basic concepts of the ecological traffic legislation in the United States, along with status quo and existing ecological problems of China's traffic legislation. It can then also hopefully use America's ecological traffic legislation as a reference for China's improvement in this respect.

1. FOR REFERENCE: OVERVIEW OF ECO-TRAFFIC LEGISLATION IN THE UNITED STATES

Faced with severe ecological destruction caused by traffic, the United States began to reflect on the traditional traffic development mode and formulated a series of acts, to promote and ensure the development of urban eco-traffic and solve the environmental resource problems that restrict the development of transportation. This allowed America to play a leading role in the field of global eco-traffic protection.

(1) The background of eco-traffic legislation in the United States

I. The need for sustainable development as an internal drive

After the Second World War, with the rapid development of modern industry, urban traffic expanded, and in the meantime, environmental pollution caused by an increase in vehicles has grown in significance. To balance the development of the traffic economy and to protect the ecological environment, federal and state governments issued a series of acts, which demonstrate a combination of sustainable development strategies and strict environmental protection policies. The ecological principle was brought into traffic legislation due to the infiltration of sustainable development as an instructive concept. According to these acts, in urban traffic legislation, not only should human survival and development be prioritized, but also the protection and optimization of nature. Human activities should be limited to the scope of environmental carrying capacity.

II. The guidance of international organizations as external motivation

Climate and the environment have a significant impact on human survival. Faced with worldwide climate deterioration, curbing global warming has become an urgent concern. Since 1972, when the United Nations conference on the human environment passed the *Declaration of the Human Environment* in Stockholm, environmental issues have gradually aroused the extensive concern of governments and the public. Two programmatic documents adopted at the United Nations Conference on Environment and Development in 1992, *The Rio Declaration on Environment and Development* and *Agenda 21*, received the broadest and highest level of governmental support from almost all countries in the world. In December 1997, the third Conference of the Parties (COP3) of the *United Nations Framework Convention on Climate Change* (UNFCCC) adopted the *Kyoto Protocol*, which came into force in 2005, making it the first legal norm in human history to bind the Contracting States to their environmental commitments. As a contracting party of the above conventions, the United States enacted a series of acts, such as the *Clean Energy and Security Act*, as a key component of national eco-traffic legislation, although the legislation fluctuated due to the different emphasis of successive governments.

III. The content of eco-traffic legislation in the United States

The legislation of eco-traffic in the United States mainly focuses on traffic planning, traffic energy conservation, traffic noise, traffic emission, and smooth traffic.

i. Traffic planning legislation

Traffic planning legislation in the United States is comprehensive legislation inextricably intertwined with land use, environmental quality, safety administration, fund allocation, and other planning. The United States has issued a series of acts, such as the *Federal-Aid Highway Act* and the *Intermodal Surface Transportation Efficiency Act*, which all involve reducing traffic congestion and improving the environment. For instance, the latest *Transportation Authorization Act – Safe, Accountable, and Flexible, Efficient Transportation Equity Act: A Legacy for the Users, SAFETEA – LU*, authorizes all states with more autonomy to stipulate the rules of the road toll pricing, aiming to ease traffic congestion. At the same time, the act also encourages the use of real-time traffic management technology both legally and financially to optimize the configuration of traffic. SEFETEA-LU also set up new environment-related projects, which received more funding for environmental protection than ever before. It has systematically integrated the requirements and procedures for environmental assessment of transportation projects into previous acts, made them clearer and more smooth, and increased the responsibility of transportation agencies for environmental assessment (Zhou Jiangping, 2006).

ii. Transportation energy conservation legislation

The United States, as the world's largest energy-consumption country, passed and implemented the *Energy Policy and Conservation Act* to reduce the energy consumption of traffic. The act established the corporate average fuel economy standard for cars and light trucks. The United States guarantees the implementation of fuel economy standards by imposing fines and high fuel consumption taxes on car manufacturers or owners who fail to meet such standards, aiming to improve the fuel efficiency of vehicles.

In addition, the United States also established a range of acts and regulations, such as the *Energy Tax Law*, the *Motor Vehicle Information and Cost Savings Act*, the *Light Vehicle Fuel Consumption Regulations*, and the *Energy Policy Act*, to impose an energy tax on the sales of new means of transportation that fail to meet the legal fuel efficiency, to provide funds to support the research and development of new energy technologies, thus saving energy and improving the efficiency of energy systems. (Paul R. Botney and Robert N. Stevens, 2004, p. 65) At the same time, the United States also promulgated the *Automobile Alternative Fuel Act*, the *Federal Electric Vehicle Tax Reduction Regulations*, the *Energy Independence and Security Act*, the *Emergency Economic Stabilization Act*, among others. Through preferential tax policies, the government has successfully promoted the research and development of new energy vehicles, encouraged the development of alternative fuels, and propeled the combination of new energy with the motor vehicle industry and the energy structure adjustment.

iii. Traffic noise legislation

Traffic noise is the main component of urban environmental noise pollution. The legislation on urban traffic noise in the United States starts from the control of aircraft noise pollution and extends to the fields of highways and railways. The legislative body of urban traffic noise also expanded from the federal to the state governments. With the adoption of the *Noise Control Act*, the *Quiet Communities Act*, and other regulations aiming at the formulation and implementation of noise emission standards, the standard of urban traffic noise pollution has been redefined, and thus, the framework of the noise pollution standard system in the United States is established on the whole.

iv. Motor vehicle emission legislation

With the high-speed growth of the economy, urban motor vehicles have been rapidly increasing in number, while pollution has become more and more serious. The *Urban Traffic Exhaust Control Act* of the US originated from California, the state with the most serious air pollution across the country. The US's legislation in controlling vehicle emissions, and formulating air-quality standards made it the first country to implement emission standards. Afterward, from the early 1950s, the federal government began to enact and amend a series of regulations, for example, the *Atmospheric Pollution Control Act*, the *Clean Air Act*, the *Motor Vehicle Air Pollution Control Act*, and the *Atmospheric Pollution Prevention and Control Law*, to clarify the evaluation criteria for environmental and atmospheric quality, the emission standards for new motor vehicles, and the fuel economy standards for automobiles, to improve the fuel economy of vehicles. The United States now has the world's largest variety of emission control indicators, and the most stringent emission regulations. The State of California has developed even more stringent emission standards than the federal level, meaning that the impact of urban vehicle emissions on the environment has been significantly reduced.

v. Smooth traffic legislation

Though the US government has increased capital investment and expedited infrastructure construction in cities with the rapid development of the automobile industry, it is still hard to catch up with the growth of motor vehicles. To alleviate the current urban traffic congestion, the United States federal and state governments began to prioritize the construction of public transport from the 1960s, regulating the behavior of all urban traffic participants through legislation. The US Congress enacted the *Housing and Urban Development Act,* the *Urban Public Transport, Intermodal Surface Transportation Efficiency Act,* and the *Surface Transportation Assistance Act* in which Principles have been established to encourage the development of public transportation, restrict private cars, and encourage carpool travel. The state governments have also issued corresponding decrees to promote joint car ride plans, redesign the road toll collection system, and safeguard the rights and interests of pedestrians such as bicycle riders. The promulgation and implementation of these decrees have alleviated the pressure of urban traffic congestion to a certain extent. (Yu Junhong, 2013)

(2) Features of eco-traffic legislation in the United States

i. Timeliness

With the mid-20th century as a watershed, the ecological transportation legislation of the United States can be broadly divided into two stages. In the first stage, the United States federal and state governments enacted acts regarding environmental resource protection but emphasized the exploration of environmental resources intending to guarantee economic development, encourage cooperation between states and support their research into pollution control. In general, these measures have no purpose for environmental protection in a modern context. Whereas, in the latter stage, the rapid economic development in the United States after World War II caused serious deterioration to the ecological environment, the development of science and technology awakened people's consciousness towards environmental protection. Under the pressure of national environmental claims, federal and state governments have begun to regard environmental protection as the top priority of the country and society. A series of environmental protection bills have been introduced, and US eco-traffic legislation has gradually become systemic.

Therefore, the legislation of eco-traffic in the United States has been in line with the trend of the times. When the new concept of environmental protection is recognized and accepted by the people, the legislation has to be adjusted and changed. This timeliness reflects the gradual deepening of the national ecological and environmental awareness, and also shows the flexibility and adaptability of the US's eco-traffic legislation.

ii. Systematization

The United States, as a federal common law country, has a legal system composed of case law and statute law. From the content of eco-traffic legislation of the United States, it can be seen that although it is rooted in case law, it is mainly based on statute law. The United States Congress is the nation's highest legislative body. The executive agencies of the US government formulate administrative regulations following the explicit legislative authorization of many federal laws, and the 50 states have complete sovereignty. They can formulate state laws and regulations respectively, and enact, apply and interpret local regulations following the authorization of state legislation. US eco-traffic legislation also presents both vertical and horizontal levels. Vertically, it is divided into federal legislation and state legislation; horizontally, there are legislature and administrative regulations formulated by the executive organs. The legal system is relatively systematic, and would rather take multiple measures at the same time than be embarrassed due to a lack of legal basis.

iii. Executability

In the United States, 'legislation' does not merely refer to the formulation of statute laws. The national budget, taxation, economy, and other important domestic and foreign policy decisions are all within the scope of legislation, which needs to be approved by Congress. Legislation is a form of direct planning and management. The executive department exercises the functions and powers conferred by the law and carries out the laws passed by Congress. Therefore, eco-traffic legislation in the US also shows the features of the statute law, one of which is its executability.

2. THE STATUS QUO OF LEGISLATION: CHINA'S URBAN ECO-TRAFFIC LEGISLATION TODAY

(1) The status quo of legislation

i. Legislation on urban eco-traffic at the national legislative level
Ecological management and regulation of urban traffic involve administrative departments of environmental protection, transportation, public security traffic management, development and reform, planning, housing, and urban and rural construction, among others. As all the relevant departments have corresponding responsibility for the ecological construction of urban traffic, the responsible body is relatively fragmented, failing to achieve an efficient and unified management function. Although a series of laws, regulations, standards, policies, and planning systems has been formed at the national level, led by the *Environmental Protection Law of the People's Republic of China*, involving urban and rural planning, energy conservation and emission reduction, air pollution prevention and congestion mitigation, a relatively systematic and forward-looking ecological urban transportation legislation has not yet been formed.

ii. Practice of legislation on urban eco-traffic at the local legislative level
In provinces and cities with high levels of traffic development or urgent environmental protection tasks, the governments have actively carried out the practice of urban eco-traffic legislation, bringing the spirit of a series of laws, regulations, and policy documents on urban eco-traffic at the national legislative level to local legislation, and integrating the development of urban eco-traffic into the legal track. For example, the third session of the 15th People's Congress of Beijing adopted the *Regulations of Beijing Municipality on the Prevention and Control of Pollution from Motor Vehicles and Non-road Mobile Machinery* , which came into force on May 1, 2020.

iii. The present problems existing in China's urban eco-traffic legislation
i) Lack of a complete legal system
When facing the ecological problems caused by modern urban traffic, the related traffic laws, regulations, and policy documents reflect the 'emergency response' of legislation only to solve the most prominent problems at the moment. The lack of clear internal logical structure and connections in the entire legal system leads to confusion and fragmentation, which brings great trouble to judicature practice and law enforcement.

There is also often a policy-led governance concept in the field of urban eco-traffic regulations. When governing the problems existing in urban traffic, authorities at all levels often issue various official documents and introduce various policies. Although this is more targeted and effective, it often leads to the proliferation of documents, arbitrary changes in regulations, and a lack of seriousness and stability of the system. Revolving around each department's interests, many separate laws lack the leading role of a unified legislative body and guiding ideology in the process of making legislation, which leads to a lack of coordination among the special laws, and even causes conflicts. (Chen Meng, 2015, p. 527) ii). Strong principles with low executability

The *Environmental Protection Law* is the fundamental and comprehensive law in the field of environmental protection in China, mainly stipulating the basic principles and systems of environmental protection used to solve common problems in this field. Although it involves the investigation and evaluation of environmental conditions, the establishment of a joint prevention and control coordination mechanism, and the stipulation of a control system for the total discharge of key pollutants, the implementation rules are not detailed enough, and there is a lack of systematic provisions for the ecological environment degradation caused by urban traffic. This makes it difficult to play the leading role of environmental protection. Thus, it is impossible to solve the contradiction between the many complicated, unilateral laws in China.

In the fourth chapter (Atmospheric Pollution Prevention and Control Measures) of the *Atmospheric Pollution Prevention and Control Law of the People's Republic of China,* Prevention and Control of Pollution from Motor-driven Vehicles and Vessels is specifically listed in the third quarter, but there are no specific measures for the prevention and control of air pollution in urban traffic operations. The prevention and control of pollution by motor vehicles and vessels are only advocated as general provisions. They are strong in principle and publicity, yet implemented only to a low degree.

The basic traffic law in China lays more emphasis on the regulation of safety than pays attention to traffic coordination and land use. The *Urban and Rural Planning Law* lacks attention to the legislation of urban eco-traffic. The *Cleaner Production Promotion Law*, the *Energy Conservation Law*, the *Atmospheric Pollution Prevention and Control Law*, and the *Renewable Resources Law* all regulate transportation energy conservation, but there is a lack of supporting regulations and measuring standards.

iii) Legislation of low hierarchy

According to the relevant provisions of the *Constitution of the People's Republic of China* and the *Legislation Law of the People's Republic of China*, the overall law regulating the country's political, economic, and social life belongs to the basic law and shall be enacted by the National People's Congress. At present, a series of relatively high-ranking laws such as the *Environmental Protection Law*, the *Law on Prevention and Control of Pollution from Environmental Noise*, and the *Atmospheric Pollution Prevention and Control Law* are formulated by the Standing Committee of the National People's Congress. Their effectiveness is too low to have the status of the basic law. It faces insufficient authority and low legislative authority, and cannot solve the main and core contradictions and difficulties in the construction and development of ecology in urban traffic.

Throughout China's urban eco-traffic legislation, because of the practical requirements of the respective operation of various departments, many relevant laws and regulations are departmental rules, local government regulations, and normative documents. Based on the interests of the department or locality, legislation conducive to the interests of the department or the region often appears, which weakens the scientific and holistic nature of relevant regulations and is inconducive to the implementation of traffic regulations to build ecological cities.

iv) Insufficient foresight

The existing urban eco-traffic legislation and policies, the management system, department duties, rights and obligations, relief methods, and legal responsibilities are not unified, and the sectoral differences and regional differences remain significant.

The environmental problems caused by urban traffic are often latent, in other words, harm to the ecological environment will only appear in time, so the legislation of urban ecological traffic should be forward-looking. However, due to the differences in the scope and degree of information and conditions in the urban transportation industry, the current ecological urban traffic legislation lacks scientificity and progressiveness, and it cannot give clear regulations and guidelines for the construction and management of urban eco-traffic in the future. So that at this stage, there is a lack of supporting regulations, and the systems and standards are relatively backward.

3. REFERENCE AND ENLIGHTENMENT: THE OPTIMIZATION OF ECO-TRAFFIC LEGISLATION IN CHINA

(1) Establishing the legislative concept of cohesive development between man and nature

From the establishment and development of the legislative system for eco-traffic in the United States, the legislative concept guides the legislative activities, while the scientific legislative concept helps the legislators to survey the overall situation and correctly understand the nature and law of legislation, and eventually provide positive guidance for the legislative activities. The nature of law, the state, and the social environment of China have a far-reaching influence on the urban eco-traffic legislation. General Secretary Xi Jinping regards adherence to the symbiosis between man and nature as the first principle that must be adhered to in promoting the ecological awareness in the new era. This shows that China has already passed the stage of development as the absolute principle and economic, social and environmental requiring sustainable development to a new stage of creating a new era for ecological socialism with Chinese characteristics. We should interpret the relationship between humans and nature from the perspective of human society and historical development. Nature exists in the course of social history, and there is a two-way interaction between nature and human beings. Although urban transportation embodies the social responsibility of human beings, both human beings and nature should be taken as the ethical frame of reference in the legislation of urban eco-traffic, to create norms in line with the long-term interests of human beings and nature. (Chi Xuefang, Ye Ping, 2015)

We should establish correct environmental ethics, and abandon the two extremes of Anthropocentrism and Ecocentrism to avoid overemphasizing the power, role, and position of the human in nature, but we must pay attention to the favorable relationship of mutual respect between humans and ecological systems and adhere to the concept of their cohesive development. Therefore, such development should also become the fundamental idea behind urban eco-traffic legislation. Under the legislative concept of the cohesive development of man and nature, China's urban eco-transport legislation should promote development according to the balance of the urban population, economy, resources, and environment. The population scale, industrial structure, and growth speed cannot exceed the carrying capacity of local water and soil resources and environmental capacity if we are to build ecological awareness in society following the law of social development.

(2) Strengthening legislative coordination and planning, and establishing a framework system of laws and regulations on eco-traffic

China implements a unified legislative system with multiple levels, and delimits the local and national legislative authority according to the history and reality of the country. Due to geographical and economic differences, there are only general provisions in the field of urban eco-traffic legislation, which are difficult to adapt to the actual situation in different regions. Therefore, we should learn from the horizontal and vertical framework of eco-traffic legislation in the US, and follow the principle of allowing local initiative play a major role under the unified leadership of the central government.

At the level of national legislation, we should not only amend, but improve the *Constitution*, the *Environmental Protection Law*, the *Urban and Rural Planning Law*, the *Energy Law*, T*axation Law*. On the premise of a full investigation, we should also gradually formulate the *Basic Traffic Law*, as well as the *Urban Traffic Law*, the *Public Transport Law*, and other special laws and administrative regulations, specifying the construction of the design, department's authority, implementation steps, legal responsibility and other contents of the urban eco-traffic support system, and gradually form a legislative model that attaches equal importance to the basic law with the special law and administrative regulations.

At the level of local legislation, due to the strong pertinence and flexibility of local legislation, each city should also maintain its characteristics in terms of legislation for the various ecological traffic issues. Therefore, China's urban eco-traffic legislation should focus on strengthening the local people's congress and local government legislation for ecological traffic.

(3) Implementing scientific legislation and enhancing the operability of eco-traffic legislation

Implementing the general and broad eco-traffic policy into all aspects of social life needs scientific legislative technology. The eco-traffic legislation in the United States is a combination of general law and special law. These legislations are supplemented by the actual needs in various fields and are therefore very operable. China has a vast territory, diverse traffic environments, and complex ecological environment issues. In formulating eco-traffic legislation, we can also draw on the practice of "one state, one law" in the United States and formulate regulations and other documents that conform to the regional characteristics of each province and city, to enhance the effectiveness and operability of eco-traffic legislation.

Urban traffic legislation plans should be carried out, and local regulations or local government rules should be issued in line with local traffic characteristics. These legislations are the details, interpretation, and supplements of national legislation, and the copying of the upper law should be avoided. Urban eco-traffic legislation needs to focus on local realities, and comply with the natural conditions and human requirements. For local characteristics, legislatures at all levels can hold demonstration meetings, hearings, forums, and other channels that reflect the current status to legalize effective local practical experience. Without violating the supreme power of the state, China should first make scientific and reasonable predictions, carry out necessity and feasibility demonstration of the acts, so that local legislation is forward-looking without conflict with higher laws. Local governments can formulate local ordinance or normative documents to accurately arrange systems and norms, and eventually transform local legislation from extensiveness to accuracy.

CONCLUSION

The ecological transportation legislation in the United States is a complete system that is trending towards continuous strengthening and detailing, and can be effectively implemented. In the process of ecological environmental protection over the past 20+ years, China has also established a set of legal and policy systems, which have played a certain role in preventing and controlling the deterioration of the ecological environment in the field of transportation. However, China's eco-traffic legislation system requires improvement in terms of system completeness, operability, and executability. Therefore, it is necessary and feasible to draw lessons from the experience of the United States in the legislation of eco-traffic, strengthen legislation, and formulate eco-traffic legislation that is suitable for China.

ENDNOTES

[1]   This research was supported by Center for American Studies (NO. ARC2019006)

REFERENCES

Zhou Jiangping. "The US Transportation Legislation and Up-to-Date Transportation Authorization Act." *Urban Transport of China* Jan. 2006, Vol.4 No.1

Paul R. Botney and Robert N. Stevens: *Public Policy for Environmental Protection" (Second Edition)*, translated by Mu Xianqing and Fang Zhiwei, Shanghai Sanlian Bookstore, Shanghai People's Publishing House, March 2004. p. 65.

Michael H Gurchin, Michael A Leon, Robert B. Parks: *Proposals for Improving Transportation and Environmental Planning at the State and Local Level*, Trans. and Envt'l Planning, HeinOnline-2Harv. Envtl.L.Rev.1977, p. 542–561.

Yu Junhong, "Research on the Legal Countermeasures of PM2.5 Pollution Control in Beijing." *Master's thesis of Capital University of Economics and Business*, 2013

Chen Meng, "China's Environmental Legislation Should Still Follow the Path of Codification." *National Symposium on Environmental Resources Law (Annual Meeting) Essay Collection*, 2015, p. 527.

Chi Xuefang, Ye Ping, "Eco-Ethical Issues in New Environmental Protection Law: Era Characteristics, System Correlations and Ethical Consciousness Limits." *Journal of Nanjing Forestry University (Humanities and Social Sciences Edition)*, No. 4 of 2015

US Department of Transportation. GROW AMER-ICA ACT of 2014: US2014

US Department of Transportation. Safe, Accountable, Flexible, Efficient Transportation Equity Act: A Legacy for Uses Act of 2005 (SAFETEA-LU): US2005

US Department of Transportation. Transportation Equity Act for the 21st Century Act of 1998 (TEA-21): US1998

US Department of Transportation. Intermodal Surface Transportation Efficiency Act of 1991 (ISTEA): US1991

"US Environmental Protection Agency Office of Noise Abate ment and Control: toward A National Strategy For Noise Control. April 1977." http://www.nonoise,org/epa/Roll/rolldoc28.pdf. Accessed 1 August 2016

"A coevolutionary interpretation of ecological civilization." http://www.centerforneweconomics.org/webfm_send/23, Accessed 5 June 2017

"Towards the Green Environment.Comparison of Environmental Impacts of Urban Public Transport and Automobiles." http://ideas,repec,org/p/fem/femwpa/1999.6.html. Accessed 2 October 2017

AUTHOR'S BIO

RONGRONG ZHANG teaches at the School of Public Administration, Southwest Jiaotong University, and works in the Moot Court, with a research field in judicial reform and law teaching methods.

14

A Historical Alternative: Stilwell, the "Dixie mission," and China-US Relations during WWII

Lei Qin, University of California, Los Angeles

ABSTRACT

The paper explores a historical moment of in-depth engagement between the Chinese Communists and the Americans in WWII. This is perhaps the only moment in recent history when American military personnel and politicians were in such heightened interaction with the CPC in collaboration against Japanese aggression in the far east. The paper explores the brief historical period of 1944–45 when American military personnel lived with and carried out in-depth observation of the Communists in Yan'an, leaving behind a significant number of earnest proposals to urge Washington for a "historical alternative" of switching to back the Communists, whom the American diplomats in China saw as more "popular" than the corrupt Nationalists. The paper uses historical documents from both sides to explore how the short window of opportunity arose, developed, and ended. The archival documents that were finally declassified after a delay of two decades testify how excessive politics in heightened war time could come in the way of advancing mutual political and military goals and how it could threaten the careers of the most patriotic, genuine, and intelligent individual diplomats. In diving into archival documents, the paper intends to ask a similar question as Barbara Tuchman, who implied a potential reversal of American foreign policy in the very title of her essay *If Mao Had Come to Washington*. The value of the "what if" question lies in an objective probing into the historical alternative that is impossible to enter mainstream discussion even, or especially, today.

KEYWORDS

Stilwell, Dixie mission, China-US relations, Communists, historical alternative.

At the time of writing this paper, China-US relations have dropped to a historical low since Nixon's ice-breaking moments in the early 70s. On-going trade-wars, espionage accusations, technology sanctions, and other measures are fueled by mutual distrust and hostilities. President Biden's top Asia man Kurt Campbell recently declared that "the period that was broadly described as engagement has come to an end" (*Bloomberg News*, 2021). Keywords of "confrontation," "strategic competition," and "containment," "adversary" flooded media in coverage of China-US relations, spreading to all realms including politics, economy, technology, and even research collaborations. While growing tension cast bilateral relations in a primarily negative tone, this paper will explore a historical moment of in-depth engagement between the Chinese Communists and the Americans in WWII. This is perhaps the only moment in recent history when American military personnel and politicians were in such heightened interaction with the CPC in collaborating against Japanese aggression in the far east. The archival documents declassified after two decades of delay testify how excessive politics in heightened war time could come in the way of achieving desirable political and military results and how it could snap the career of the most patriotic, genuine, and intelligent individual diplomats.

The abortive results of such contact only led to what the twice Pulitzer Prize winner Barbara Tuchman called an "emergence of an anti-American Communist regime in China" (2001) who would in four years defeat the Nationalists, whom the Americans wrongly backed. What happened soon afterward on the American side was known to all, McCarthy's witch hunt forced all Americans in close contact with the CPC into one form of exile or another.

History since sealed the narratives about American views of the Communists until Nixon's reversal of bilateral relations in 1972. Even when the Nixon administration set the general tone of engagement with China, in-depth contact was lacking, with only Dr. Henry Kissinger's "Mars-landing"-like trip to the then enclosed Beijing before the presidential visit. Out of the shortfall of such experiences, *Foreign Affairs*, the prestigious house organ of the international affairs establishment, used Tuchman's book to go back to the 1940s to carefully re-open the idea of the historical alternative to justify Nixon's "somersault" with China. (Tuchman, 1972)

This paper explores this brief historical period of 1944–45 when the American military personnel lived with and carried out in-depth interaction with the Communists in Yan'an, resulting in a significant number of earnest proposals back to Washington to urge for the "historical alternative" of backing the Communists, whom they saw as more "popular" than the corrupt Nationalists. The paper uses historical documents from both sides to explore how the short window of opportunity arose, developed, and ended. In doing so, the paper intends to ask a similar question as Mrs. Tuchman, who implied a reversal of American foreign policy in the very title of her essay *If Mao Had Come to Washington* (1972). The value of the "what if" question lies in an objective probing into the historical alternative, which is impossible to enter the mainstream discussion, especially today.

WAR INITIATES NEW OPPORTUNITY

US contact with the Communists preceded the general outbreak of WWII. In the high days of international left-wing cultural politics in the 1930s, President Roosevelt dispatched his secret observer, a captain in the US Marines, Evans Carlson, to the newly developed red capital of Yan'an. Upon arrival in Hankou on May 5th, 1938, Carlson was greeted by Edgar Snow, who had already earned his fame as the author of *Red Star over China*, as well as Agnes Smedley, a key member of Comintern's far-eastern spy ring, and once the assistant to the influential and well-respected Mme. Sun, and men who were to play significant roles in war-time China such as Joseph Stilwell and John Davies. (MacFarquhar, 2013) Carlson was later to write *The Chinese Army* based on his experiences alongside Communist guerrillas that provided the US substantial information on Communist military activity.

Around the same time, thanks to coordination between Song Qingling (Mme. Sun) and Smedley, the then Colonel Stilwell first met Zhou Enlai (周恩来), Communist G-3. This early connection and the fact that Stilwell helped transport medical aid to the Communists (Stilwell Papers, 17–24 April, 4 October. and 5 December. 1938) were to sow profound discord between this yet-to-be commander of the China-Burma-India theater and the Chinese war-time commander Generalissimo Chiang Kai-shek. In the telegraph from US Embassy in Hankou, then the temporary capital of China, the

Communists were already seen as rising in power and the Nationalists waning in control. This was seen as "the young generation has come to look to communism or some offshoot thereof as the only means of saving China from the Japanese, that the coming into influence of the young generation will be coincident with the widespread growth of a Communistic or quasi-Communistic movement, which will be directed irrevocably to the freeing of China from the Japanese yoke and will ultimately be successful." (US Diplomatic papers, 19 July 1938)

Doubts about whether American aid to Nationalist China could be put to efficient use were raised at least since December 1941. The "American Mission to China," commonly referred to as "AMMISCA," was established on August 27, 1941, to facilitate lend-lease aid to China. Brig. Gen. John Magruder, head of the mission, frankly gave his impression that "the Chinese [Nationalist government] would shun offensive action, wait until their allies had won the war, and then use their jealously husbanded supplies for the solution of the Communist problem." (Romanus et al. 1987, p. 53)

A similar conclusion was made on July 22, 1942 by John Carter Vincent, Counselor of Embassy, in his long analysis of the GMD leadership as well as its attitude and actions in the present and future based on his contacts with officials in Chongqing in the past year. Vincent elaborated on Chiang Kai-shek's persistent action to first drive out and marginalize, then oppress the Communist force from 1938 until 1942, to have led to the contemporary stage of the GMD-Communists relation, i.e. hostile and oppositional, with popular general support for the latter outside of the Nationalist Party and "numerous and intelligent" young liberals from within. He predicted the future of the Party coming down to two options – either the carrying out of "long overdue measures for social and economic reform" to win "liberal elements in and out of the Party and cut the ground from under the Communists," or to adopt "oppressive and suppressive measures to kill all opposition and to maintain itself in power." He concluded, "Under the present leadership the latter alternative seems to be the more likely of the two" based on the Party's Nazi lines in place – the "C-C" clique, Gestapo under Tai Li, military power and organization under Ho Ying-chin. (US Diplomatic Papers)

In contrast to the corrupted, conservative, and militarily inactive Nationalists, the Communists' rising popularity had been reported several times to the State Department. John Davies started to show interest in the Communists from July 14, 1942. In his memorandum to Stilwell, Commander of the CBI theater, Davies reported how "the Communist strength in North China has spread to a greater extent than is generally realized" so much so that there was "only one district in Shantung which remains under Central Government control." Davies also reported that the Communists had put active fights against the Japanese, while the central government deliberately avoided such conflict. (Ibid)

US' main purpose of showing some interest in the Communists at the time was to force Chiang to give up the fight against Communists and focus on fighting the Japanese. The State Department's statement on October 3, 1942 stated that "the American Government has at no time entertained a policy of 'war against the Communist' in China." (Ibid) At the Washington Conference of May 1943, Commander General Stilwell went further to warn against the bad reputation of the Nationalists as corrupt and unwilling to reform to the then Army Chief of Staff, General Marshall and described the Chinese Communist as a man who wanted taxes cut to a bearable level, and he wanted to restore the United Front of Chinese Nationalists and Communists. (Romanus et al. 1987, p. xiii)

On September 6, 1943, Stilwell made his first proposal for the Nationalist and Communist divisions to both attack the Japanese. According to the plan, Stilwell requested that the 18th Group Army [Communist], the 22nd Army, and the 35th Army occupy a deep position on the flank of the Japanese forces in the north, both to create a threat to the Ping-Han Railroad and Zhangjiakou area and to counteract any Japanese plan to push up the Yangtze River. (The Stilwell Papers) He justified the plan in his memorandum to Chiang as a way to test the Communists' sincerity in fighting the Japanese under Chiang Kai-shek's order, and ended the memorandum with a sense of urgency of the move that "if we do not move, the Japs will."

The memorandum infuriated the Generalissimo, who in his diary entry on the same day decried Stilwell as the "most despicable and stupid villain (最卑劣、最糊涂之小人)," and his plan as "instigated by the Communists, and daring to use a coercive tone . . . ." (Chiang's diary on 6 September 1943, *Working Manuscripts)* The reason Stilwell's plan caused Chiang's affront was its intention to withdraw Hu Zongnan (胡宗南) and Deng Baoshan's (邓宝珊) armies from fighting the Communists in Yan'an and to be moved over eastward to fight the Japanese. Chiang's study of the CPC organ *Yan'an Liberation Daily* (延安解放日报) earlier of the year in July must have led him to the conclusion that Stilwell's plan to halt the attack on the Communists was instigated by them. He called the CPC's increasing victimization propaganda against the Nationalists to attack an "evil plan 毒计" with the purpose not just to alleviate the anti-Communist military campaign but also to raise international attention (referring particularly to Stilwell) as an oppositional force against the central government and thus gave it some legitimate footing. (Ibid, 23 July 1943)

The (in)famous Chiang-Stilwell conflict that appeared on the surface to be a fight for commandership boils down to the two commanders' oppositional attitudes towards the Communists. After failing multiple times to secure an American infantry division to India and being constantly frustrated by Chiang's reluctance to move troops to Burma, Stilwell remarked in casual conversation with his staff that he wished he had some Chinese Communist troops in Burma and later conversed with Marshall in 1942 that the Communists were willing to take his order but had been refused of permission by Chiang. (Romanus et al. 1987, p. 121)

Besides the growing positive impression of CPC on the American side, proactive outreach from the Communists must also have played a key role in facilitating the US-CPC contact. Though based in the enclosed hinterland of China since the Long March in the mid-30s, the Communists had been proactive in making their voice heard by the international audience. With the help of innumerable left-wing intellectuals and influential sympathizers like Song Qingling, the Chinese revolution in Yan'an became a source of inspiration for the left-wing political movements in Europe. (Qin, 2021) Similar out-reach was used in the 1940s, especially through the semi-underground Chongqing office for the Eighth Route Army. The Southern Bureau (南方局) within the office was the secret CPC foreign policy organization headed directly by Zhou Enlai. The main job of the bureau was to have Mao's and other CPC leaders' talks translated into English and distributed among British and American friends in the war-time capital of Chongqing, including Stilwell. (Wang, 1985, pp. 36–7) The bureau served as a nodal point for establishing the network of friends and sympathizers of the Chinese Communists, including the later Counselor of the Embassy Philip D. Sprouse and journalist Joseph Alsop, a remote relative of President Roosevelt. Stilwell was an old friend of Song Qingling and was invited several times to Soong's house in Chongqing where the latter regarded him as a "true friend of the Chinese people."

This goal of the CPC's high-level foreign diplomacy was to win over international support through their sincerity in seeking a united front with the Nationalists, to apply pressure on Chiang to halt his encirclement campaigns, and to get its share of American military aid.

On May 14, 1942, the then US ambassador Gauss met Zhou Enlai where the latter reportedly complained that the Nationalist government had multiple times denied Communists' requests for military aid, pushing the Communists to the choice of accepting aid from Russia. (US Diplomatic Papers) On 13 August, Gauss telegrammed Washington with an unreleased/censored statement by the CPC Central Committee. Upon describing the inter-party antagonism, the document promised to "incorporate its [the Communist] army into the Nationalist armed forces and dissolve its Soviet government," as well as to abandon all its attempts to overthrow the central government by seeking joint efforts against Japanese aggression. (Ibid) A similar statement was published on the CPC organ *Xinhua Daily*, declaring that the Communist party was in "complete agreement with the Guomindang in terms of external and internal policies of the Government." But it also stressed that "despite lack of food and arms," the Communists had "ever since the beginning of our war obeyed commands of the Generalissimo, maintained their lives [lines?] and never retreated" and had actively "organized guerrilla and other mobile bands to attack the enemy." This news article was also included in Gauss' report to Washington.

On another occasion, Zhou Enlai, lying on his sickbed after surgery, said half-jokingly half-seriously that he would put the Communist armies under Stilwell to join the battles in Burma. (Davies, 1972) It was based on this information that Stilwell believed the Communists would be willing to accept his order and reported to Marshall later in 1944 amidst his irreversible conflict with Chiang, whom he complained to have never truly subordinated his army commandership for the battle in Burma.

Zhou Enlai also sent "several messages" to Laughlin Currie, Administrative Assistant to President Roosevelt, who was sent to China by the President to ameliorate the antagonism between Nationalists and Communists, during his time in Chongqing. In his August 6, 1942 telegram to Washington, Currie summarized Zhou's two main points were as follows: first, Zhou urged the American government to keep a watchful eye for its lend-lease supplies to China. "The fear was expressed that unless the American Government maintained a firm and constantly watchful attitude on this score lend-lease supplies would be hoarded for use after the war in maintaining the position of the ruling faction." Second, Zhou extended the invitation for one or several representatives of the American Government to visit the Communist-controlled areas. (US Diplomatic Papers, 1942) Soon on January 20, 1943, Zhou reached out again to the American Embassy in Chongqing, complaining about lack of improvement and that the Communist forces had received no military or financial support from the Chinese National Government for the past three and a half years. He also reported how the Chongqing government's attitude remained unchanged, with generals like Wei li-huang (卫立煌) removed from their posts for being "too friendly with the Chinese Communists and too active against the Japanese forces to suit the wishes of the Chinese high command at Chungking [Chongqing]." (Ibid, 1943)

With will from the American side and the proactive efforts of the Communists, American diplomats in China finally took a substantial move in clearly urging Washington to change track. On January 23, 1943, during his temporary visit back in Washington, Service, the third secretary of the Embassy in China, submitted a historical diagnosis of the GMD-CPC rift and the first-ever proposal to request Washington dispatch a small group to Yan'an and provide the Communists with enough supplies. The report stressed the importance of US assistance of the Chinese Communists for both immediate military and post-war long-term political purposes. Service wrote that the Communist-controlled area with access to Inner Mongolia, Manchuria, and Japanese North China bases were of strategic importance. The upgraded Japanese "mopping up" campaign was named as proof for the effective resistant force of the Communists, which contrasted with inactivity on most of the other Guomindang-Japanese fronts. Service also hinted at the likely Communist victory after the war, naming it as proof the sizeable support from intellectuals, liberals, and youth, the powerful Communist underground activities, and the impossibility of Nationalists to eradicate the extra-orbital mobile struggles. He also warned of "the possibility that economic difficulties may make the war-weary, over-conscripted and over-taxed farmers fertile ground for Communist propaganda and thus bring about a revolution going beyond the moderate democracy which the Chinese Communists now claim to be seeking." (Ibid, 23 Jan.)

Service made three suggestions upon the diagnose of the situation, that the US government should urge GMD to reform to ensure democracy in China, to push the Communists to join the fight, and most relevantly, that the US should send representatives to Yan'an, as Zhou Enlai had proposed, as a way to collect "comprehensive and reliable information regarding the Communist side of the situation." (Ibid)

A couple of days later, Service submitted a follow-up report on "the uncompromising attitude of Chungking military leaders" and recent clashes between the Central Government and the New Fourth Army. (Ibid, 26 Jan. 1943) In the following months, the second secretary of the Embassy in China John Paton Davies joined his colleague. He informed the state department from Chongqing on March 16 that he had received a positive response from Zhou Enlai concerning the American request to "draw on Communist intelligence regarding enemy activities." (Ibid, 16 Mar.) On May 6, Davies forwarded Zhou Enlai's complaint that Chiang's act "to liquidate the Communists continues to be a sure barrier to cooperation." (Ibid) The Nationalist government's hostility was again confirmed in a report from George Atcheson, the Chargé in China, where he quoted CPC military leader Lin Biao on June 24 in his pessimism of expecting any change in the intra-party relation. (Ibid, 24 June)

On the same day, Davies filed his long-awaited report to the President to echo his colleague Service during his temporary visit in Washington. He proposed the setup of a consulate in Yan'an and the dispatch of several observers. He again hinted at the likelihood of the Communists turning to Russia if the situation continued, and that the Communist popularity had grown to a level that posed a fundamental threat to the central government. (Ibid, 24 June) The result, as Davies analyzed, would be the United States finding itself "wrongly backing the Central Government and so setting against Russia." From historical hindsight, one could not help but marvel at Davies' accurate prediction of the post-war order at this high time of war.

Having received no response from FDR, Davies sent another report requesting immediate dispatch of observers to the Communist area to reverse the dangerous potential of driving the Communists to Russia. Davies also emphasized the need for the US President to directly request the dispatch of observers as Chiang would naturally oppose the idea. (US Diplomatic papers, 15 Jan. 1944)

THE ENGAGEMENT

In 1944, earlier reports had raised concerns in Washington with more frequent reports sympathetic towards the Communists. On January 18, Gauss reported on Chiang's men's order of cessation of Communist radio communication with Yan'an, "5,000 tons of military supplies" and additional troops at the Communist border, and the central government's roundup of several hundred Communist suspects in Xi'an. (Ibid, 18 Jan.) This was followed by another report on the upgraded military preparations surrounding the Communist-controlled area. (Ibid, 1 Feb.)

Top GMD military leader General Hu Tsung-nan's chief of staff General Li Kun-kang was asked to testify to the US Embassy on the Nationalists' view towards the Communists, where he said many inner-party military leaders thought the central government's measures were too "weak and soft" on the Communists and believed "China's Communist problem might, in the final analysis, be solved by a collapse from within." (Ibid, 7 Feb.) The GMD view was only to be contrasted as self-assertive with another report from Gauss noting "nine groups of military leaders in free China" who "do not support the Guomindang in its desire to liquidate the Communists." (Ibid, 15 Feb.)

The report was sent along simultaneously with the central government's documents obtained by the Embassy about its anti-Communist campaign and it instructed on distributing posters on the Communist Party's "crimes" in obstructing "war of resistance," and "plots . . . to overthrow of the National Government . . . to establish a 'dictatorship of the proletariat.'" (Ibid, 16 Feb.) The report was soon followed by the letter from the Director of United China Relief at Chongqing Mr. Dwight W. Edwards, who reported a large number of refugees flooding into the Communist control northern China "as a result of military operations, flood and famine, maladministration and difficult living conditions" whereas the central government's troops blocked the shipment of medical supplies into these "blockaded" areas, and confiscated "medical supplies destined for this region." (Ibid, 18 Feb.)

The report aroused strong enough attention from Washington that the Secretary of State dispatched a letter to Gauss requesting more information on whether and how the Nationalists used lend-lease supplies against the Communists and the likelihood of the outbreak of civil war in China. (Ibid, 16 Feb.) Finally, on February 9, President Roosevelt sent a long overdue memorandum to Chiang, requesting that an "'American observers' mission be immediately dispatched to North Shensi and Shansi Provinces and such other parts of North China." (Ibid, 9 Feb.) Chiang Kai-shek replied a highly diplomatic message inviting the American Observers' Mission to gain more accurate information on Japanese troops concentrated in North China and Manchuria, while emphatically excluded visits to the Communist area. (Ibid, 9 Mar.)

Communists and their sympathizers such as Mme. Sun (Song Qingling) and General Stilwell had long waited for the opportunity. On February 23, the Communist representative at Chongqing – Dong Biwu (Tung Pi-wu 董必武) reiterated the CPC's willingness to negotiate with the Nationalist Government on the conditions that the Communists receive an equal level of military supplies and that the latter lift the blockade. He also seized the opportunity to invite foreign correspondents and observers to visit the Communist area to see for themselves about the blockade that the central government consistently denied. (Ibid, 23 Feb.)

The reason the Communists survived the blockade of military and medical supplies was through the help of Soong and Stilwell through the "Protect China Alliance (保卫中国同盟)." With Stilwell's help in greenlighting for foreign aid shipments via "Yunnan-Burma road (滇缅公路)," the only road connecting war-time China with the outside," the Protect China Alliance was able to transport basic medical needs, including the only X-Ray machine, into the Communist area. (Epstein, 1994, pp. 507–8) Soong reached out to Service and held a conversation on February 14 to inform him of the dire situation in Yan'an under blockade, and revealed how she was prohibited to leave the country by the central government and censored by top Nationalist Generals He Yingqin and Zhang Zhizhong from criticizing the authorities in front of Americans. (Ibid, p. 510)

The efforts and pressure both within and without – especially central armies' massive defeat in the battle of Henan-Hunan-Guangxi, left Chiang no choice but to accept the American request in June 1944 concerning sending an observer group to Yan'an. FDR's took a gradual strategy first by sending vice president Wallace to China first, who reported back that "Chiang showed himself so prejudiced against the Communists that there seemed little prospect of satisfactory or enduring settlement as a result of the negotiations now underway in Chungking." (US Diplomatic Papers, 10 July) With this last straw on the camel's back, the "Dixie Mission" group was finally founded under CBI theater, which chief commander Stilwell had long awaited. Two groups of political, military, intelligence, communication, and medical personnel arrived at Yan'an on July 22 and August 7 respectively, with declared purposes of collecting information about the Japanese, the Communists, and the war.

Preparations in Yan'an started with the building of a flat enough single runway for the American flights to touch ground safely. (Hu, 1994, p. 342) The Communist leadership placed high values on the mission as it saw it as "the development of our international united front and the start of our diplomatic work (是我们在国际间统一战线的开展, 是我们外交工作的开始)." (*Selected Documents of CCPCC*, 1992, p. 314) In the preparation meeting for the Dixie Mission group, Mao Zedong spoke of this visit as a likely beginning of a lasting relation – one not just to cooperate for the resistance war for the time being, but also the peaceful post-war building of democracy and national unification. He thus instructed the Yan'an leadership to treat the group with sincerity and honesty concerning what the Communists could and could not do. (CPC Central party Literature Research Center, 1993, p. 522) Zhou Enlai held a similar view, calling this new start one with "unlimited potential development (前途更将无限量发展)." (Wang, 1985, pp. 36–7) The sheer number of front-page reports in the CPC organ *Liberation Daily* proved the level of attention from Yan'an. Mao personally edited and added "战友们 (comrades-in-arms)" to a report title "Welcome US Military observer group (欢迎美军观察组)." (15 Aug. 1944) Mao also personally instructed various Party offices to "fully cooperate with the American military personnel with sincerity and welcome (放手与美军合作, 处处表示诚恳欢迎)." (CPC Central party Literature Research Center, 1993, p. 544) Mao's decision was apparently not purely diplomatic courtesy, but a high level of confidence in impressing the American mission group with a unified, democratic resistance force in the hinterlands under the Communist leadership, and how this would lead to a change in American decision on its China policy. (Hu, 1994, pp. 339–40) The CPC documents also demonstrated a prevailing high expectation for long-term and comprehensive cooperation – "the military cooperation foundation could expand to cultural cooperation, which in turn will give rise to political and economic cooperation." (*Selected Documents of CCPCC*, 1992, p. 314)

In his book on the mission in Yan'an, John Service documented activities like observing the Eighth Route Army training, tactical training of the 359th Brigade, military skills performance like bombing and shooting in Yan'an as well as having observation team leader David Barrett lecturing on US Army training methods. Service wrote highly of the open reception from the Chinese Communists during the eight months of unrestricted travel in the Communist territory, "in-depth cooperation with Communist Party leaders and general staff in Yan'an and the front line every day." (Service, 1971, pp. 19–21)

The CPC-US relationship went so well that the Communists proposed to set up an Allied Command at the ideal timing of worsened Stilwell-Chiang relations. Service held an interview with Zhu De (朱德), who proposed for American landings in China to attack the main forces of the Japanese, and for establishing an American Commander in Chief in the China theater as a way to solve complications in deploying and coordinating both the Nationalist and the Communist troops. (US Diplomatic Papers, 25 Sep. 1944) Zhu De also told Günther Stein, correspondent in Yan'an for the Associated Press who was later charged with spying for China in the Red Scare, that it was necessary for a commander-in-chief from the allies to treat all armies in China equally to clear away internal hurdles in its resistance against Japan. Zhu named General Stilwell in particular as the commander-in-chief and expressed that he would be willing to put the Communist Eighth Route Army and the New Fourth Army under Stilwell's command. (Smedley, 1956, pp. 407–8) Mao also told Stein a couple of days later that the Communists would always welcome an American commander-in-chief, though Chiang Kai-shek might very likely disagree. (Stein, 1945, p. 207) Zhou Enlai, in his interview with Service, said the chief commander must be an American and would receive a full welcome from the Communists if approved by the central government. (US Diplomatic Papers, 1944)

That was what prompted Stilwell to pressure Chiang to send out his troops against the Japanese, which Chiang interpreted as a seizure of leadership. On September 13, Stilwell received Lin Boqu (林伯渠) and Wang Bingnan (王炳南), the CPC's top representatives in Chongqing "to bring greetings from Chu Teh & Mao." Stilwell replied to them with his plan to visit Yan'an. (The Stilwell Papers) Stilwell sent a formal proposal to Chiang later to request his recognition of the Communist armies and their equal priority in receiving the US military aides. He also requested to be sent to Yan'an to command the red armies. (Davies, 1972, p. 323)

Stilwell's plan was dismissed by Chiang as "absurd remarks (荒谬言论)" that exposed Stilwell's "wild intentions of ruling China." He turned to his diary, the channel he usually leashed out anger and frustration that he was not able to otherwise in the face of Americans. On the entry on September 15, Chiang cursed Stilwell as part of the sinister complicity with the "rampant Communist bandits" that catalyzed the military and political downturn, and was an utmost "insult and deception (侮辱欺妄)" to him, (Chiang's diary, *Working Manuscripts*) where he determined to "check his ambitions and expose his plot (遏制其野心而暴露其阴谋)." (Ibid, 27 Sep. 1944) Chiang's sensitive character had long convinced him, mostly correctly, that the US "tried to avoid confronting Russia's power in China, and would force the Nationalists to reconcile with the Communists to preserve the latter's power in balancing out (彼避免在华有排挤俄势之嫌, 故其必欲强制我与中共妥协, 以保存中共之势力)." (Ibid, 18 Jul. 1944) Chiang decided that the US strategy was for its interest and not for that of China, and made his determination to "rely on itself and strengthen its power, to overcome its bad tendencies and restore traditional ethics (自立自强, 克己复礼)" to avoid being discouraged by external forces. (Ibid, 6 Aug. 1944) The Generalissimo, with waning control of a country mired deeply in internal and external conflicts, was speaking as much about himself as about his country.

Chiang Kai-shek had all the reasons to be frustrated by the US at the time, as Washington seemed to quickly lean towards the Communists since the arrival of the American observer group in Yan'an. Service reported to the State Department that the CPC was effective in resisting Japan, contrary to what the central government had claimed, and was highly critical of the General Ho Ying-chin's "violent prejudice and utterly unscrupulous disregard of the truth," which was "chiefly of interest for its evidence of the hopelessness of efforts to effect unity in China as long as men of his type exercise important influence." (US Diplomatic Papers, 22 Sep. 1944) The fact that the Japanese "being actively and successfully opposed in Communist-controlled areas," in a follow-up report by Service, "will throw the people into the arms of the Communists." "Democracy will leave the Communists with a great base for political influence. The Communists are certain to play a large, if not dominant, part in China's future." (Ibid, 9 Oct.) Service also wrote to urge Stilwell to adopt "stronger policy . . . toward Chiang Kai-shek and the Central Government." (Ibid, 22 Nov.)

A similar view was shared by other Americans on the team. Davies filed three reports from Yan'an on November 7, stating with a level of certainty and urgency never before, that "the Communists are in China to stay. And China's Destiny is not Chiang's but theirs." (Ibid, 7 Nov.) He continued to clear Washington of the ideological suspicion by differentiating the Chinese Communists from Marxists/Bolsheviks. "Yan'an is no Marxist New Jerusalem," he wrote. (Ibid) He urged Washington to "be realistic," and avoid committing indefinitely . . . to a politically bankrupt regime." The US, Davies understood, should take "determined effort to capture politically the Chinese Communists rather than allow them to go by default wholly to the Russians." (Ibid, 15 Nov.) Following his long talk with Lieutenant Hitch, who spent the past couple of months traveling in the Communist territory, Chief of the Division of Chinese Affairs John Vincent made his proposal that the American supplies should be provided to Communist troops for the more effective defeat of the Japanese. (Ibid, 30 Dec.)

The decision was well-grounded in the substantial military preparations of the Communists. Since August 20, Yan'an had become increasingly assured of an American Army landing on China's east coast. The CPC had since deployed the New Fourth Army to increase information collection "to supply the allied armies," to establish a radio network in eastern Hubei, and to instruct on "coordinating operations with US Navy and Army landing" as the Yan'an leadership believed "the time of landing will not be far according to estimates of Americans in China." (*Selected Documents of CCPCC*) The Yan'an leaders also instructed Chongqing representatives Lin Boqu and Dong Biwu to request aid to assure "the 470 thousand troops behind the enemy lines to prepare for counter-attack with the allies." (Chiang's diary on 23 Aug. 1944, *Working Manuscripts*) Everything looked promising for the long-awaited military collaboration between the Americans and the Chinese Communists until it abruptly ended.

AN ABORTIVE ATTEMPT

At the end of the day, Washington chose politics over reality. FDR's internal contradiction in his China policy, which was first developing some closeness with the Communists as a way to pressure Chiang before quickly allowing it to abrupt in the hands of his envoy Patrick Hurley, must have contributed to the quick liquidation of the American Mission. In the next couple of months, key figures involved in the bundle of pro-Communist proposals were cleared from their posts, ultimately culminating in McCarthy's well-known witch hunt. The end of the mission started with the recall of Stilwell.

Reports by Davies and Service had made their impact on Washington, especially with their careful differentiation of the Chinese Communists from the Marxist hardliners of Russia, so much so that Chiang had to bypass Vincent's China division entirely to lobby directly in Washington. Top Chinese officials Jiang Tingfu (蔣廷黻) and Wei Daoming (魏道明) were instructed to pluck a different chord to Washington that "the Chinese Communists being more Communist than any Communist party." (Ibid, 25 Sep.) At the same time, Chiang had decided to openly expose the conflict with the Communists by whipping up domestic propaganda. On September 24, a top committee within the National Defense Department issued a manual entitled "Documents on the Chinese Communist Party problems," accusing the CPC of plotting to overthrow the government. (US Diplomatic Papers, 13, 20, 27 Oct. 1944) The message to the Americans is that the central government doesn't allow the American ball to bounce between both sides. The strategy turned out to work well – better than all the Yan'an American mission group documents combined. However disappointed Washington felt about Chiang, it followed its gut sense of ideology rather than trust the military and political analyses from Americans on the ground in Yan'an. On October 19, Stilwell was recalled by FDR.

On his last day in Chongqing, Stilwell rejected Chiang's highest decoration with "Vinegar Joe"'s typical sour tone of sarcasm on Chiang, "the peanut." Song Qingling went to bid farewell to Stilwell and cried and wished that situation could improve so that Stilwell could come back "to lead us." (*The Stilwell Papers*, 20 Oct. 1944) That, of course, did not happen. Stilwell left China, without leaving a note for his successor Wedemeyer, and never had another chance to set foot in China again for the rest of his life. In 1946, six months before his death, Stilwell wrote "it makes me itch to throw down my shovel and get over there and shoulder a rifle with Chu Teh," the senior Communist military commander. (Ibid)

Stilwell's recall foreboded Washington's adjustment of strategy for the far east. Though still providing Chiang with aid, the US strategic focus had shifted from an alliance with China to that with Russia. As FDR told Stimson, the US would have to leave the resistance war in China to the Russians. (*Stimson Papers*, 13 Oct. 1944) Service's request for taking Communists seriously did not receive its due attention in Washington, but his shoutout "we need not fear the collapse of the Nationalist government … as any new government will be more capable of mobilizing the country" certainly left its impact on the US foreign policy. (US Diplomatic Papers, 1944) The US moved its hope away from China while still maintaining a basic alliance with Chiang with the purpose of ensuring its post-war interests in the area against the otherwise dominant influence of the UK and Russia. Chiang's dependence on US support made it easy for the US. But Washington, unfortunately, in the words of Elliot Roosevelt, FDR's son, "bet on the wrong horse."

Atcheson's report to Washington on February 28, 1945 indicated how the US decision "greatly increased Chiang's feeling of strength" and "resulted in unrealistic optimism on his part and lack of willingness to make any compromise." It also made the Communists follow the line of action of "actively increasing their forces and aggressively expanding their areas southward" out of self-protection. The conclusion by Atcheson was that if the US continued to assist only the central government "chaos will be inevitable and the probable outbreak of disastrous civil conflict will be accelerated." (Ibid., 1945) So was the blueprint for history to come.

When Patrick Hurley, FDR's representative, was sent to China to "reconcile" the intra-Party conflict, he interpreted his task as forcing the Communists to take Chiang's orders. In his letter to FDR on January 15, he reclaimed his assigned task in China as "to prevent the collapse of the National Government; sustain the leadership of Chiang Kai-shek; unify the military forces of China, and, as far as possible, to assist in the liberalization of the Government and in bringing about conditions that would promote a free, unified, democratic China." (Ibid.) The following month, Hurley reported back twice to urge Washington to reject all requests from the Communists regarding sending personnel or supplying aid – apparently a firm critique of Stilwell's softness. His long report on meetings with representatives from both sides concludes with a verdict: "It is our steadfast position that all armed warlords, armed partisans and the armed forces of the Chinese Communists must without exception submit to the control of the National Government before China can in fact have a unified military force or unified government." (Ibid, 7 Feb.) Roosevelt was said to have made no corrections to Hurley's interpretation of the job, probably not wanting to waste time "contemplating failure." (Bland et al. 1998, pp. 597–616)

There had been several letter communications back and forth between Mao Zedong and Hurley in January alone. Though having pushed both sides to meet and talk, Hurley already set a firm tone to adverse Stilwell and the mission group's strategy and became a sole supporter of Chiang. His view was clearly stated in the report on January 31, "in all my negotiations with the Communists I have insisted that the United States will not supply or otherwise aid the Chinese Communists as an armed political party or as an insurrection against the National Government. Any aid from the United States to the Chinese Communist Party must go to that party through the National Government of China." (US Diplomatic papers, 1945) So not surprisingly, he decided to refuse to grant "Lend-Lease and monetary assistance requested by General Zhu De" to "prevent the collapse of the National Government and to sustain Chiang Kai-shek as President of the Government and Generalissimo of the armies." (Ibid, 17 Feb.) What Hurley rejected was also a chance of Washington leadership's direct engagement with the Communists, a chance that did not surface again until almost 30 years later. On January 9, Major Ray Cromley, Acting Chief of the American Military Observers Mission then in Yan'an, transmitted a report to the state department that Mao and Zhou wanted their request to be sent to the "highest United States officials." (Ibid.) The proposal was sent to Washington bypassing Hurley who was able to convince FDR to reject the meeting request from Mao and Zhou. (Ibid, 14 Jan.)

The tension between Hurley and the entire Embassy in China fully played out in late February. Hurley squeezed David Barrett out of the mission group and successfully kicked Davies out of the Embassy. (Davies, 1972) In his numerous reports back to Washington and his letters to FDR in early 1945, Hurley imbedded explicit or implicit accusations of the entire China Embassy personnel's soft policies towards the Communists. Davies, Service, and Vincent were unaware and continued to file reports from Yan'an to urge more American assistance to the Communists. Tension continued to brew to a point where Hurley requested that all reports from the American diplomats in China be reviewed and signed by him before being sent to Washington. (Schaller, 1972.) Hurley's arbitrary suppression at least annoyed the Embassy in China, so much so that a long telegram "drafted with the assistance and agreement of all the political officers of the staff of the Embassy" was sent to the State Department during Hurley's trip back to Washington. They warned Washington of the "inevitable chaos in China" and "the probable outbreak of disastrous civil conflict" if the current US strategy of denying Communists and assisting only the central government continued. (US Diplomatic Papers, 28 Feb. 1945) Davies, who had already been ejected from China by Hurley, continued to urge Washington in his new position as the second secretary of the Embassy in the Soviet Union. Basing his information on the well-respected overseas Chinese scholar Dr. Chen Hansheng, he restated his point that the Mao-Zhou clique of Communists were not Bolsheviks, where another clique of the CPC under the leadership of Wang Ming was, and therefore US political alignment with Mao-Zhou should be cleared of ideological hurdles. (Ibid) All these reports didn't raise enough attention in Washington, which gave rise to Hurley's emboldened action against those who dared to report against him. Upon his return to China, nearly all old personnel at the Embassy in China were removed, including Service. (Schaller, 1972)

The history that followed the anti-communism wave Hurley successfully set off was predicted precisely in Davies' and Service's reports. The fact that General Marshall, after efforts by Hurley and Wedemeyer, was able to bring Mao and Chiang to sit down for a talk did not change history. After genuine efforts from Mao, Zhou, and Zhu De in working out the relations between Wedemeyer after Stilwell left, the outbreak of civil war and the US decision to support only Chiang's government had driven the Communists to the opposite side of America. After Hurley announced in a press conference in Washington that the US government only supported Chiang Kai-shek's government and would not recognize or assist any other political forces (US Diplomatic Papers, 1945), the CPC quickly responded with a critique on Hurley's devastating policy towards China. *Xinhua Daily* published a commentary three days later, refuting Hurley's remarks as "completely misunderstood and distorted the Communists' sincere efforts to cooperate with the Americans in the resistance against Japan." Mao later published two essays in *Liberation Daily*, criticizing the adversarial strategies of Hurley. (Mao, 10, 12 July 1945) At the same time, Mao gave instructions to limit the Army observer group's activities in Yan'an. After the laborious build-up of trust and good will, the cooperation – with a common goal of containing the Japanese invasion in China and the success of overcoming massive differences – finally came to an end.

In his book *The Great Chinese Revolution 1800–1985* on China's long century of revolution, John Fairbank lamented the end of the benign chapter of history by critiquing Hurley's delusion in believing himself to be able to broker a deal "with his Oklahoma horse sense and lawyerly acumen." (Fairbank, 1987) With his wish failed, Hurley abruptly expressed his intention to resign to Secretary of State James Byrnes on November 26, 1945, blaming the failure on Davies and Service for unfairly criticizing Chiang and coddling the Communists, as well as for being disloyal to him and their nation. (US Diplomatic Papers, 26 Nov. 1945) And this was before Joseph McCarthy became a red-baiting senator and the subsequent 25 years of ideological crusading in America for the "loss of China." The unfair treatment of American diplomats also forced the change of tone in the later writings of Barrett and Davies. In the preface to his monograph in 1969, Colonel Barrett substituted the analytical style he was trained to report to Washington with an apologetic tone and a new purpose – to convince his readers "to try to believe me when I say I have never had but one loyalty, the United States of America." (Barrett, "Preface") Davies also apologized for having referred to the Communist government as "democratic" where he should have said "popular" instead. A similar frustration was felt with the much postponed publications of the documents of 1944, 45, and 46 in 1967, 69, and 72 respectively, (Gittings, 1972) the years leading up to Nixon's ice-breaking visit to Communist Beijing. These documents provided a look into the unfair treatment of the American diplomats in China (and Stilwell too, for that matter), as well as providing an insight into an alternative history to shed some light on today's deadlocked US-China relations.

REFERENCES

Barrett, David. "Preface." In *The Making of an Army "Old China Hand": A Memoir of Colonel David D. Barrett*. By John Hart. Berkeley: University of California Press, 1985.

Bland, Larry I., Roger Jeans and Mark F. Wilkinson edited. *George C. Marshall's Mediation Mission to China, December 1945–January 1947*. Marshall George C Research. 1998.

Bloomberg news. "Biden's Asia Czar Says Era of Engagement With China Is Over." https://webcache.googleusercontent.com/search?q=cache:-Zh5hcIGm3MJ:https://www.bloomberg.com/news/articles/2021-05-26/biden-s-asia-czar-says-era-of-engagement-with-xi-s-china-is-over+&cd=1&hl=en&ct=clnk&gl=us

CPC Central Party Literature Research Center 中共中央文献研究室, *Chronicle of Mao Zedong* 毛泽东年谱 (*1893–1949*), Vol. 2, People's Publishing House, Central Party Literature, 1993.

Chiang Kai-shek. *Working Manuscripts. Documents of President Chiang1943* 事略稿本. 蒋中正总统文件 1943 年卷. Taipei: Academia Historica 国史馆, 2010.

Davies, John Paton. *Dragon by the Tail: American, British, Japanese, and Russian Encounters with China and One Another*. W. W. Norton & Company, 1972.

Epstein, Israel. *Biography of Song Qingling – the Road of Revolution from Sun Yat-sen to Mao Zedong* 宋庆龄传 – 从孙中山到毛泽东的革命之路. Translated by Shen Suru 沈苏儒. Vol. 2 Rizhen Press. 1994.

Fairbank, John. *The Great Chinese Revolution 1800–1985*. Harper Perennial. 1987.

Gittings, John. "A Shameful Tale." Chinafile.com, 1972. https://www.chinafile.com/library/nyrb-china-archive/shameful-tale#fnr17

Henry L. Stimson Papers. Manuscripts and Archives. Yale University Library.

Hu Qiaomu 胡乔木, *Hu Qiaomu Remembering Mao Zedong* 胡乔木回忆毛泽东, People's Publishing House, 1994.

Liberation Daily 解放日报. August 15 1944. China Academic Journals Full-text Database.

MacFarquhar, Roderick. "The 'Breaking of an Honorable Career'" Chinafile.com. 2013. Retrieved at: https://www.chinafile.com/library/nyrb-china-archive/breaking-honorable-career#fn8

Mao Zedong, "Bankrupcy of the Hurley-Chiang Kai-shek collaboration 赫尔利和蒋介石的双簧已经破产" *Xinhua Daily*. July 10. 1945. Retrieved at: https://www.marxists.org/chinese/maozedong/marxist.org-chinese-mao-19450710.htm

"On the Danger of Hurley's Policy 评赫尔利政策的危险" *Xinhua Daily*. July 12.1945. Retrieved at: https://www.marxists.org/chinese/maozedong/marxist.org-chinese-mao-19450712.htm

Qin Lei 秦蕾. "Song Qingling as an Internationalist Fighter 作为国际主义战士的宋庆龄." In *Documents and Research on Sun Yat-Sen and Song Qingling* 孙中山宋庆龄文献与研究. Vol. 6. Shanghai: Shanghai Book Store. June 2021

Romanus, Charles and Riley Sunderland. *China-Burma-India Theater. Stilwell's Mission to China*. Washington D.C., Center of Military History, United States Army, 1987.

Schaller, Michael. *The US Crusade in China. 1938–1945*. Retrieved at: https://archive.org/details/uscrusadeinchina00scha

Selected Documents of the CPC Central Committee 中共中央文件选集: Vol. 14, Beijing: Party School of the Central Committee of CPC Press, 1992. Zhou Enlai "Instructions on Foreign Relations work 关于外交工作指示."

Service, John. *The Amerasia Papers: Some Problems in the History of US-China Relations*. Berkeley: Center for Chinese Studies, University of California, China Research Monographs #7, 1971.

Smedley, Agnes. *The Great Road: The Life and Times of Chu Teh*. Monthly Review Press. January 1956.

Stein, Günther. *Challenge of Red China*. Whittlesey House. 1945.

Stilwell, Joseph. *The Stilwell Papers*. Edited by Theodore H. White. Schocken Books, 1972.

Tuchman, Barbara. *Stilwell and the American Experience in China, 1911–45*. Grove Press, 2001.

"If Mao Had Come to Washington: An Essay in Alternatives." *Foreign Affairs*. Oct. 1972. https://www.foreignaffairs.com/authors/barbara-w-tuchman

United States Diplomatic Papers, the Far East, China. Office of the Historian. Department of State Archive.

1938, the Far East, 19 July. https://history.state.gov/historicaldocuments/frus1938v03/d218

1942, Pacific War, 14 July. https://history.state.gov/historicaldocuments/frus1942China/d175

China, 14 May. https://history.state.gov/historicaldocuments/frus1942China/d170

      30 July. https://history.state.gov/historicaldocuments/frus1942China/d177

      6 Aug. https://history.state.gov/historicaldocuments/frus1942China/d178

      13 Aug. https://history.state.gov/historicaldocuments/frus1942China/d179

      3 Oct. https://history.state.gov/historicaldocuments/frus1942China/d191

1943, China. 20 Jan. https://history.state.gov/historicaldocuments/frus1943China/d152

      23 Jan. https://history.state.gov/historicaldocuments/frus1943China/d153

      26 Jan. https://history.state.gov/historicaldocuments/frus1943China/d155

      16 Mar. https://history.state.gov/historicaldocuments/frus1943China/d168

      6 May. https://history.state.gov/historicaldocuments/frus1943China/d182

      24 Jun. https://history.state.gov/historicaldocuments/frus1943China/d201

      https://history.state.gov/historicaldocuments/frus1943China/d202

1944, China. 15 Jan. https://history.state.gov/historicaldocuments/frus1944v06/d256

      18 Jan. https://history.state.gov/historicaldocuments/frus1944v06/d259

      1 Feb. https://history.state.gov/historicaldocuments/frus1944v06/d265

      7 Feb. https://history.state.gov/historicaldocuments/frus1944v06/d270

      9 Feb. https://history.state.gov/historicaldocuments/frus1944v06/d272

      15 Feb. https://history.state.gov/historicaldocuments/frus1944v06/d276

      16 Feb. https://history.state.gov/historicaldocuments/frus1944v06/d281

      https://history.state.gov/historicaldocuments/frus1944v06/d279

      18 Feb. https://history.state.gov/historicaldocuments/frus1944v06/d283

      19 Feb. https://history.state.gov/historicaldocuments/frus1944v06/d284

      23 Feb. https://history.state.gov/historicaldocuments/frus1944v06/d291

      9 Mar. https://history.state.gov/historicaldocuments/frus1944v06/d303

      10 Jul. https://history.state.gov/historicaldocuments/frus1944v06/d224

      22 Sep. https://history.state.gov/historicaldocuments/frus1944v06/d444

      25 Sep. https://history.state.gov/historicaldocuments/frus1944v06/d447

      9 Oct. https://history.state.gov/historicaldocuments/frus1944v06/d458

      7 Nov. https://history.state.gov/historicaldocuments/frus1944v06/d486

      https://history.state.gov/historicaldocuments/frus1944v06/d485

      15 Nov. https://history.state.gov/historicaldocuments/frus1944v06/d499

      22 Nov. https://history.state.gov/historicaldocuments/frus1944v06/d513

      30 Dec. https://history.state.gov/historicaldocuments/frus1944v06/d546

1945, China. 9 Jan. https://history.state.gov/historicaldocuments/frus1945v07/d131

      15 Jan. https://history.state.gov/historicaldocuments/frus1945v07/d135

      31 Jan. https://history.state.gov/historicaldocuments/frus1945v07/d149

      7 Feb. https://history.state.gov/historicaldocuments/frus1945v07/d155

      17 Feb. https://history.state.gov/historicaldocuments/frus1945v07/d160

      28 Feb. https://history.state.gov/historicaldocuments/frus1945v07/d174

      26 Nov. https://history.state.gov/historicaldocuments/frus1945v07/d530

Wang Bingnan 王炳南. *Memoirs of Nine Years' Sino-US Talks* 中美会谈九年回顾, World Knowledge Press 世界知识出版社, 1985.

AUTHOR'S BIO

Lei Qin was Assistant Adjunct Professor in Modern Chinese Studies at the University of California, Los Angeles from 2018–2020. She received her PhD in Comparative Literature from Washington University in St. Louis in 2017. Her current research interests are early 20th-century cultural politics and political communication with transnational perspectives, in which field she published several articles. She has taught a wide range of topics on modern China, including history, society, politics, culture, and literature, which find interdisciplinary co-existence in her research.

15 A Study of the Differences in the Development of Venture Capital Investment between China and the US

Tongxia Che, Hebei Academy of Social Science[1]

ABSTRACT

Along with the improvement of the capital market over 30 years, venture investment has gained momentum in China. This paper examines the history of Chinese venture investment development in both China and the United States, and the problems encountered in China in the current development of venture investment, and puts forward several suggestions for the improvement of China capital market, intellectual training, and investment laws.

KEYWORDS

Venture investment, exit mechanism, registration system

DEFINITION OF VENTURE CAPITAL INVESTMENT AND BASIC CHARACTERISTICS OF THE VENTURE CAPITAL INVESTMENT IN CHINA AND THE US

For start-up firms, venture capital investment is a lifeline for their development; for venture capital investment, angel investment is an inexhaustible "reservoir" of funds, although government support is also important.

Should be "Venture capital investment, also called "risk investment," is investment in which capital is invested into the R&D area of enterprise aiming at accelerating the commercialization and industrialization of hi-tech products or services and obtaining returns from the investment. The purpose of venture capital investment is not to control a company, but to obtain some equity of the invested company, and in turn to boost enterprise growth and to add value to the start-up enterprises through the infusion of capital and exertion of management. Venture capital investment usually consists of four stages, namely financing, investing, management, and exit. Venture capital is defined as temporary equity investment in young, innovative, non-listed companies that stand out in the market, expecting a promising future. Although the companies don't have liquid current earnings, they do have above-average growth potential, which makes them an attractive investment opportunity.

Venture capital investment has four basic characteristics: firstly, it offers high risk and high return. Venture capital investment targets hi-tech enterprises relating to newly emerged technologies and it invests in sci-tech enterprises in their early stages. Since products and technologies are still in their early R&D stage, the probability of failure is very high with high degree of risk. Yet if the investment proves successful, the rate of return is also very high. Secondly, venture capital investment is usually distributed into several start-ups to lower the risk of investment. Venture capitalists would rather invest in a portfolio of investment projects so that if some of the investment projects fail, they probably can still offset the resulting loss with some successful investment projects and reap some overall benefits. Thirdly, venture capital investment is generally a long-haul investment that spans 3–7 years and may have to increase the amount of investment to the project during the investment period. Finally, venture capital investment is highly professional; investors and managers have different functions and take on different responsibilities for the same purpose of tracking and benefiting from the success of start-up enterprises.

1. BASIC CHARACTERISTICS OF VENTURE CAPITAL INVESTMENT IN CHINA AND THE US

Venture capital investment has a very long history in the US At the very least, it can be dated back to the 19th century when the US started to raise funds to construct railways and build textile factories across the country. In the wake of WWII, venture capital investment in the US grew to a considerable size and gave rise to the venture capital industry. Early venture capital in the US was of a strongly private nature, with private funds being a primary source of the venture capital. For example, there were once more than 2,000 private venture capital investment companies in the US and these companies accounted for 70% or so of the total start-up investment.

Later, the sources of venture capital in the US became all the more diversified. They included not only personal funds of rich individuals but also the funds of institutional investors, which are primarily pension and insurance funds, as well as the funds of some large corporations, fiscal funds of the government, and funds of financial institutions, e.g. banks. However, the fiscal funds of the government accounted for only a very small portion. Business incubators in the US mainly serve start-up enterprises, while business accelerators more often than not serve grown enterprises. The business incubators in the US tend to adopt the model featuring a combination of "incubators + financial support + entrepreneurship mentors + management experience," which is a specialized venture capital investment model. According to statistics of the US National Business Incubation Association, there were roughly 1,500 incubators across the US in 2016 which offer services for start-up enterprises. Limited partnership venture capital institutions are relatively more developed institutional investors in the US at the present. They are private partnerships consisting of limited partners and general partners, such as the well-known Draper Fisher Jurvetson (DFJ), which is focused on investing in start-up internet companies, and Kleiner Perkins Caufield & Byers (KPCB), which is focused on investing in entrepreneurship projects of various famous universities.

At the early stage of the opening-up policy, the majority of the industrial investment funds in China were closely related to public support finance at various levels. Along with the private sector booming, investors of the seed venture capital funds in China included governments, venture investors, and incubators. Venture capital investment has a relatively short history compared with its counterparts in the USA. Business incubators in China adopt a two-dimensional "incubator + financial support" model that provides venues and funding for start-up enterprises. The most prominent government support incubators in China are Zhongguancun in Beijing, Caohejing and Zhangjiang Hi-tech in Shanghai. A proportion of the business incubators are jointly funded by government and enterprises, and a lot of emerging incubators are private-owned. Governments give a lot of preferential policies and funding support to business incubators. Through an introduction from overseas and innovation at home, China has so far developed many incubators, which attract private equity to participate in investment in start-up enterprises.

2. FORMATION OF THE VENTURE CAPITAL INVESTMENT SYSTEM IN THE US

1) The Initiation of Venture Capital Investment in the 1940s and 1950s

The US is the cradle of venture capital investment and therefore a leader in the field. In the mid-1950s, due to the Cold War-induced fear of the scientific and technological advancement on the part of the former Soviet Union, the US conducted a study and found that the shortage of funding was an important barrier to business development in the US. In a bid to improve the situation, the then US President Dwight David Eisenhower signed and the US Congress ratified a Small Business Act in 1958. The law mandated the US Small Business Administration to establish a Small Business Investment Corporation program so that small businesses could obtain loans from the government at lower-than-market-level interest rates. Meanwhile, Congress permitted banks to set up small business investment corporations so that they could engage in other commercial activities as well as banking. During the four years that followed, there were more than 600 small business investment corporations in operation across the US.

2) The Prolonged Plump of the Early 1970s

The American stock market plumped quickly because of tax reform, the rate of investment return in 1969 increased 10% to 35%, and jumped to 49.5% in 1976, which severely burdened venture capital. American Congress issued the "retired income security act," within which the clause concerning prudent investors proscribed that retirement funds were prohibited from being invested in securities and venture funds issued by start-ups.[2]

3) Improved Environment for Venture Capital Investment in the Late 1970s

There were several reasons for this improvement: firstly, US Congress lowered the capital gains tax rate from 49.5% to 28%. Secondly, the listing of some companies that received venture capital investment, including the listing of FedEx in 1978 and the listing of Apple Inc. later, stoked the investment of venture capitalists. Venture capital investment gained unprecedented growth in the 1980s. Venture capitalists raised no more than $600 million in 1980 but managed to raise $4 billion in 1987.[3]

4) Institutions Arising in the 1980s as the Primary Source of Venture Capital

In 1978, rich individuals and families were the largest sources of venture capital, accounting for more than 1/3 of the total. Subsequently, their share gradually reduced to 10%, and public and corporate pension funds became the largest sources, accounting for 1/2 of the then total venture capital in the 1980s.[4] In 1985, Peter Peterson and Stephen Schwarzman co-founded Blackstone. Relying on private equity investment, it rapidly grew into one of the best-known asset management companies in the United States. By 1990, however, the average rate of return on venture capital investment dropped to below 8%, putting it into the doldrums. As a consequence, individual and institutional investors exited one after another from 1980 to 1991.

5) The Steady Rise of Venture Capital in the 1990s

Economic recovery during the period of 1991–1994 enabled venture capital investment to rebound, embarking on an upward-moving path. From 1991 to 1994, economic recovery led to the rise of venture capital, and since then, it has been on the rise. The great development of the second board market beginning in the mid-1990s boosted the flourishing of venture capital. Its prosperity was due to the rise of the information industry, which precipitated the growth of a large number of new high-tech enterprises and led to the rapid development of the NASDAQ market in the United States.

6) The Development of Venture Capital Investment in the 21st Century

In 2001, the US Small Business Administration (SBA) enacted the New Market Venture Capital Program and revised the original Uniform Limited Partnership Act, which succeeded in boosting venture capital investment. In 2003, the US government issued the Jobs and Growth Tax Relief Reconciliation Act, which lowered the capital gains tax rate from 20% to 15%. In the same year, the US government amended the Jobs and Growth Tax Relief Reconciliation Act, which lowered the long-term capital gains tax rate from 20% to 15% and the dividend tax rate from 38.6% to 15%, greatly fueling the enthusiasm of investors.[5] In 2004, the US adopted the American Jobs Creation Act and the Deferred Compensation Act, prohibiting the transfer of SILO-related revenues from taxable items to non-taxable items. In 2005, the US issued venture capital partner law, exempting most of the private stock investors from the newly imposed tax burdens under the foreign account tax compliance act (FATCA) adopted by the US Congress. In 2015, the US issued a Credit Guarantee Act, making the SBA responsible for offering credit guarantees for start-up enterprises. Under the law, loans for less than $155,000 can be 90% secured, while loans of $155,000–250,000 can be 65% secured, by the SBA.

In 2016, the SBA planned to invest $2 billion over a period of five years to support start-up enterprises, with $1 billion being used to set up an impact investment fund and another $1 billion being used to set up an early-stage innovation fund. Moreover, it planned to create two general incubators, and required that young students use 15% of their income to repay their loans and be exempted from their remaining loans 25 years later. In 2017, the US Department of Homeland Securities announced that start-up entrepreneurs of foreign origin could apply for two-year entrepreneurship visas. In the same year, the US government sharply cut its corporate tax rate from 35% to 15%.

Currently, there are nearly 2,000 venture capital investment institutions across the US, and around 10,000 hi-tech projects are funded by venture capital investment every year. Many well-known hi-tech companies start and grow fast with the help of venture capital investment. The following table shows the value of venture capital investment in the United States from 1995 to 2018. In 2018, the value of VC investments in the United States amounted to approximately 99.5 billion US dollars. Nearly $28 billion was invested into early-stage start-ups in 2018, with median deal size increasing 25% to $7 million last quarter. Corporate venture capital activity is heating up. This year, CVCs invested $39.3 billion in US start-ups, more than double the $15.2 billion invested in 2013.[6]

As for developing trend of venture investment in the United States, VC investment has sprinted ahead in the past decade and shows no signs of slowing down, though fewer companies are raising money, and round sizes are swelling. Unicorns, for example, were responsible for about 25% of the capital dispersed in 2018. Those companies, which include Slack, Stripe, and Lyft, have raised $19.2 billion so far this year – a record-breaking amount – up from $17.4 billion in 2017. There were 39 deals for unicorn companies valuing $7.96 billion in the third quarter of 2018 alone. The strong performance of Chinese venture capital deals last year was due to a large amount of financing by Ant Financial Services Group and a series of large deals throughout the year. In June last year, Ant Financial Services Group announced that it had completed a round of the financing of 14 billion US dollars, except for the original shareholders, who continued to invest with each other. Several international strategic investors have been added to the round, including world-renowned sovereign funds such as GIC, Malaysian Treasury Holdings, Warburg Pincus, Canadian Pension Fund Investment Corporation, and Silver Lake Investment in the United States. Temasek, Singapore, Transatlantic Capital Group and other top global capital companies are also on the list.

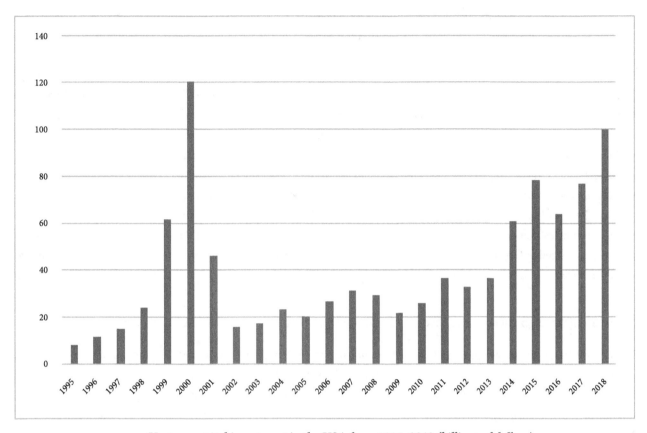

Venture capital investment in the USA from 1995–2018 (billions of dollars)

3. DEVELOPMENT OF VENTURE CAPITAL INVESTMENT IN CHINA

1) Origins of Venture Capital Investment

Venture capital investment originated in China in the mid-1980s. The first venture investment company, China New Technology Venture Investment Company, was founded in 1985. However, venture capital investment boomed in China only after the China National Democratic Construction Association's Central Committee submitted a Proposal on Accelerating the Development of Venture Capital Investment in China at the first session of the 9th CPPCC convened in early 1998. Since then, venture capital companies and venture investment management companies have mushroomed across the country. They invest in a large number of hi-tech enterprises, such as Baidu, Mengniu, and Focus Media.

2) The Development of Government-led Venture Capital and the Construction of Capital Market

From the beginning, most of the venture capital in China was guided by the government, and mainly by the state-owned capital investment, which mainly came from the special allocation of the governmental funds and the loan of the financial institution. Many venture capital funds, high and new technology risk-guarantee funds, and venture capital companies have been established in China.

Since 1999, the Shenzhen Stock Exchange has been preparing for the establishment of the GEM (growth enterprise market) board. After October 2000, it even stopped IPO projects on the mainboard. However, with the collapse of the Nasdaq myth in early 2001, the gem of Hong Kong also dropped from 1200 points to a minimum of more than 100 points. In 2002, Cheng Siwei put forward the proposal of "three steps forward" on the gem, and the small and medium-sized board was the transition of the GEM board. In May 2004, it was approved by the State Council. The Securities Regulatory Commission approved the Shenzhen Stock Exchange to set up small and medium-sized enterprises in the mainboard market. The establishment of the SME Board was an important measure to build a multi-level capital market, and also a prelude to the GEM board. In June 2005, the 50th stock market of the Small and Medium-sized Enterprises Board was listed, after which the Shanghai and Shenzhen stock markets stopped issuing new shares and gave way to the reform. The China GEM board was officially established. One of its functions was that it provided an exit for venture capital funds to alleviate the risk of venture capital, promote the virtuous cycle of high-tech investment, and improve the flow and efficiency of high-tech investment resources. Exit mechanisms are at the core of the GEM board. As an important channel for small and medium-sized enterprises to raise funds, the GEM board is a primary channel for venture investment companies to exit the market.

3) Entry of Foreign Investment Forces to Promote Domestic Market-oriented Investment

In the early 1990s, the knowledge and information industry was prosperous both in the USA and China, venture capital came to Mainland China as an imported concept, including AIG, IDG, Fidelity, Pan Asia, GIC, Goldman Sachs, and Morgan Stanley. Almost all of those most important Internet companies were born in 1998–1999. Some investors with foreign investment banking backgrounds brought foreign investment resources or investment banking experiences to Mainland China, such as Xiong Xiaoge and Sun Qiang, who led IDG and Warburg Pincus into the Chinese market, as well as Xu Xin, Wu Shangzhi, and Wang Chaozhong. The super-giants of related internet enterprises continued to sprout and flourish, and Chinese venture institutions and private equity investors subsequently became very active. In 1999, there were 40 new venture capital institutions, and in 2000, 102 new venture capital institutions were added, and the stock jumped to 201. The growth rate is unprecedented. In the Internet 1.0 era, the early players who entered venture capital enterprises gained substantially, such as IDG and Sequoia Capital, which became the two most important giants in the venture capital circle in China.

Entering the 21st century, local Chinese private equity began to loom large. After 2003, the capital markets in both China and the USA began to recover. In 2004, the Chinese venture capital industry entered a period of comprehensive recovery and accelerated. After only four years of achievement, with venture capital investment, Ctrip completed its listing in December 2003. In 2004, China ushered in the listing "window period." Behind these Internet companies, there is venture capital investing. One notable phenomenon is that in this wave of rising Chinese local investment institutions, there are private equity funds in China to operate as a limited partnership. Ding Hui investing in Mengniu preluded the era of large investment merger and acquisitions. Lenovo set up an investment branch, Hony Capital, and also started its venture capital activities. Today, Hony Capital has become one of the local benchmarking PE institutions, completing state-owned enterprise restructuring projects for China Glass, zoomlion and Shijiazhuang Medicine Group. In 2005, the Chinese stock market ushered in "the full circulation of shares," which ended the historical split of tradable shares and legal person shares, and created a four-year bull market from 2005 to 2008. A local venture capital investment project can withdraw in the secondary market, while the listing of Coship is considered an epoch event in the local venture circle. Dachen Venture and Shenzhen Capital Group recovered with vitality after withdrawing from investing in Coship. After 2004, the listing of Google brought 1,500 times the return, and Sequoia Capital and KPCB of the United States became the stars of the Silicon Valley investment circle. The surge of investment demand in China made it possible for top American VC groups to enter China seeking new investment opportunities.

Domestic venture investment institutions raised 32 new funds in 2006 against the backdrop of favorable venture investment policies, including several trusts and limited partnership funds. These new funds were created following the "new trust policy" and with the newly revised Partnership Enterprises Law. They not only widened the channel for private funds to access the venture capital market but also enriched the management models of venture investment institutions in China.

The total amount of venture capital investment saw explosive growth in 2007, reaching $3.247 billion – a striking growth of 82.7% over 2006. Moreover, the number of venture investment cases also increased from 324 in 2006 to 440 in 2007, representing a growth of 35.8%.[7]

4) The Advent of the Era of Mass Entrepreneurship and Innovation

Chinese Premier Li Keqiang set forth a slogan of mass entrepreneurship and innovation in 2014, initiating a wave of entrepreneurship activities across the country. The Chinese government reiterated the slogan in its work report in 2015. After years of development, venture investment has made great strides in China, so much so that today, it is almost complete in categories and mature in operating methods. Many famous venture investment companies are emerging, boosting the fast growth of angel and venture investment in China.

5) The Arrival of the Registration System and the Current Situation of Venture Capital Investment

The Shanghai Stock Exchange set up a science and technology board and piloted registration system to support the construction of the Shanghai International Financial Center and Science and Technology Innovation Center. In the real economic market, the innovation and entrepreneurship have a clear prospect of capital listing and an exit mechanism, which will drive the capital market to the real economy and serve its development more effectively, especially to support the development of small and medium-sized enterprises.

Chinese venture capital transactions hit a record high of $70.5 billion in 2018, up 52.9 from $46.1 billion in 2017. According to the KPMG report, the volume of venture capital deals in Asia in 2017 was $93.5 billion, compared with $254.7 billion globally, with China accounting for 75% and 27.7%, respectively.[8]

4. PROBLEMS OF VENTURE FINANCING IN CHINA COMPARED WITH THE US

In over more than two decades of development, venture capital investment has seen considerable growth in China, both in terms of size and growth speed. Compared with its counterpart in the US, however, China's venture investment is still in the start-up stage.

1) Incomplete Venture Financing Laws and Regulations

Firstly, the slow development of venture investment, the inability of private savings to enter the venture capital market, the hi-tech venture investment market in particular, and the backwardness of laws and regulations induce the risks of venture investment, leading to its all too high cost. Secondly, due to the lack of laws and regulations, existing venture investment companies are still imbued with irregularities in their operations. For example, some do not operate normally. Instead, they speculate on stocks under the disguise of "venture investment" and even operate private securities investment funds.

The US government classifies seed venture funds into venture capital funds, planning them according to market mechanisms and having investors manage them freely. The US government makes quite a small contribution to the capital of seed venture funds. Apart from setting up seed funds under the venture capital funds category and using them for seed-stage venture investment, the US government supports start-up enterprises mainly by providing various preferential policies, e.g. credit guarantee, government procurement, tax preferences, and intellectual property protection.

2) Shortage of Venture Investment Personnel

Venture capitalists bear responsibility for the entire process of fundraising, project screening, investment management, and supervision. They are therefore the key to venture capital contributors reaping any profit in the end, thus playing an important role in the development of venture investment. In recent years, a group of venture investors has emerged in China, but they are still too few. Consequently, the venture investment funds in China generally lack top-quality management teams and sound institutional arrangements, and are still in the primary, exploratory stage of development.

3) Start-up Enterprises Lacking the Right Financing Concepts

With the successful introduction of venture capital, some venture teams do not focus on improving corporate performance, but concentrate on the distribution of interest, resulting in a lack of specialized knowledge. Some venture investment companies even put some of their money into the real estate or securities market, severely deviating from the original mission of venture investment institutions.

4) Relatively Narrow Sources of Venture Capital in China

Foreign institutions contribute the greatest share of the venture capital in China, followed by non-financial enterprises and individuals, and government. The contribution rate of financial institutions is far lower than that in the US. Moreover, the number of investors is relatively small, as is the amount of venture investment.

5) Relatively Late Creation of the Capital Market

In the 1960s, many regions of the world, such as Europe and North America (represented by the US), began to create their own growth enterprise markets in an effort to resolve the financing problem facing small- and medium-sized enterprises. The HKEX growth enterprise market finally came into being on November 25, 1999 after a decade of preparations. It was positioned to serve small- and medium-sized high-growth start-up enterprises and hi-tech companies in particular. On October 30, 2009, 28 Mainland companies were listed for the first time on Shenzhen Stock Exchange's growth enterprise market board for public trading, putting the growth enterprise market of China into operation and providing a platform for SMEs to thrive.

6) Overdependence on Government Funding at the Seed-stage of Venture Investment

Seed venture capital funds in China are still in their early stage. With quite a small coverage, they are mainly restricted to economically developed tier 1 or 2 cities. With their small size, they tend to provide limited funding support. Other problems include the lack of social contributions, the singularity of operating mechanisms, the shortage of mature investment teams, and the lack of effective policy supports. Seed-stage venture capital funds in China are dominated by various types of start-up venture funds led by the government, whereas those created by social investment groups account for a very small share. Moreover, the Chinese government invests in seed-stage venture funds mainly in the form of creditor's rights, e.g. providing security for loans, making financing subsidies, which is not conducive to shouldering the risks of start-up enterprises. On the contrary, seed venture capital funds in the US are led by enterprises and supplemented by the government, which features a coordination mechanism between enterprises and government. The seed-stage venture capital in the US is, moreover, derived from many sources, including seed funds from angel investors, seed venture funds from venture capitalists, and entrepreneurship guidance funds from the government. In addition, seed venture funds in the US derive their money mainly from equity financing, where investors subscribe to shares of the start-up enterprises and withdraw upon the successful listing on the stock market of the invested companies.

7) The Reasons Why China's Venture Investment Model Lags Behind That of the US

Firstly, the US has a sound risk-shouldering mechanism in that it has developed a venture investment market, where the number of investors is larger, the amount of investment is bigger, and therefore the risk of investment is highly dispersed by a lot of private capital. Secondly, the US has a strong entrepreneurship culture and start-up development environment. For example, many successful alumni will return to their colleges to support the entrepreneurship activities of current university students, providing them with financing channels, and therefore expanding the size of the investment. In China, however, there are few risk-shouldering mechanisms in place, meaning that private investors are not willing to invest in start-up enterprises due to high risks. Secondly, China is still weak in many northern areas (except for Beijing, which has a strong venture investment culture, environment, and platform), resulting in the disconnection between venture investment projects and capital market channels and poor communication between investors and entrepreneurs. As a consequence, governments in these areas have to play a leading role in venture investment in an attempt to get start-up enterprises out of the financing dilemma.

5. CONCLUSION

The introduction of the registration system will reduce the market's speculation on shell resources and fraud. The speculative nature of China's capital market will likely be completely rewritten, and value investors will likely enter the Chinese capital market, the impact of which may be far-reaching.

Still, there is a need for China to draw on the experience of the US to foster the capital market, open up diversified financing channels, and create funding sources for venture investment. In addition, there is a need to accelerate a sound system of laws and regulations for venture investment to play a guiding role through government policies, improving the capital market, introducing high-caliber venture investment personnel, and ultimately promoting the healthy development of the venture investment industry in China.

ENDNOTES

[1] Correspondence: 13111575899@163.com. Che Tongxia, Shijiazhuang , (1972–), Associate Researcher, Sociology department of Hebei Academy of Social Sciences, Majoring in Sociology and Finance, and Specializing in Researching Employment, Start-ups, and Venture Investment. Yuhua West Road, No. 67, Hebei, China, 050051.

2   Xiao Yun, The Study of Venture Investment, 01, Curriculum PPT, https://max.book118.com/html/2018/0407/160478738.shtm, 2018.04.07.

3   Xiao Yun, The Study of Venture Investment, 01, Curriculum PPT, https://max.book118.com/html/2018/0407/160478738.shtm, 2018.04.07.

4   Wang Hui, "A Comparative Study Between China and America on Venture Capital Development," The Monthly Journal of Technology Start-ups, 2012, 25 (02).

5   The Origin and Development of v C (PPT)-DOKBA, https://www.docin.com/p-1011813361.html, 2015.

6   Kate Clark: Venture Capital Investment in US Companies to Hit $100B in 2018, @kateclarktweets , https://techcrunch.com/

7   Zhang Bowei, Fu Hua. The Development and Prospect of Venture Capital Industry, China Technology Investment, 2008.03.05.

8   KPMG: Last year $70.5 Billion Venture Capital Deal in China Soared 52.9% from a Year Earlier, Feb. 11, 2019: 12: 25 TechWe

REFERENCES

Investment website, (2017): *A Brief History of Chinese Venture Capital,* People Post and Telecommunications Press.

The origin and development of v C (PPT)-DOKBA, https://www.docin.com/p-1011813361.html, 2015.

Kate Clark, (2018), *Venture capital investment in US companies to hit $100B in 2018,* @kateclarktweets , https://techcrunch.com/.

KPMG, (2019), *China Venture Capital Transactions Last year hit $70.5 billion, up 52.9%,* Feb. 11, 2019 12: 25 TechWe.

Song Li, (2002). *Research report on Venture Capital Development in China.*

Xiao Yun, The study of venture investment, 01, curriculum PPT, https://max.book118.com/html/2018/0407/160478738.shtm, 2018.04.07.

Wang Hui, "A comparative study between China and America on venture capital development," The monthly journal of technology start-ups, 2012, 25 (02).

Zhang Bowei, Fu Hua, *The development and prospect of venture capital industry,* China Technology Investment, 2008.03.05.

AUTHOR'S BIO

TONGXIA CHE is an associate researcher at the Hebei Academy of Social Sciences. Her major research field covers start-ups and finance. She has published over 40 papers and two two books.